Praise for *How the South Wo*

T0047338

"Heather Cox Richardson, a professor
College, explains Goldwater's crusade and the trajectory of modern
conservatism in her masterful *How the South Won the Civil War:
Oligarchy, Democracy, and the Continuing Fight for the Soul of
America*. A timely book, it sheds light on what was perhaps the most
important political coalition of the 20th century."

The Washington Post

"Good revisionist history jars you, forces you to look at the past in a
new way, and thereby transforms your view of the present. Heather
Cox Richardson is a master of the genre, to the benefit of us all. Even
those who take issue with her will be forced by this powerful book to
come to terms with aspects of our past that we often just sweep under
the rug of memory."

**E.J. Dionne, Jr., author of *Code Red: How Progressives and
Moderates Can Unite to Save Our Country***

"In a tour de force, Richardson exposes the philosophical connective
tissue that runs from John C. Calhoun, to Barry Goldwater, to Donald
Trump. It's not party, it's a complex ideology that has swaddled white
supremacy and its political, legal, economic, and physical violence
in the language of freedom and rugged individualism, and, in doing
so, repeatedly slashed a series of self-inflicted wounds on American
democracy."

**Carol Anderson, Emory University, author of *One Person,
No Vote: How Voter Suppression is Destroying our Democracy***

"The themes are broad and the implications mighty, but this isn't history from on high. Richardson uses a human lens to tell her tale, revealing the passions and power-plays that have sustained this battle for dominance. The end result is something rare and invaluable: a skilled work of history, deeply grounded in the past, that speaks loudly, clearly, and crucially to the present."

Joanne Freeman, Yale University, author of *The Field Of Blood: Violence in Congress and the Road to Civil War*

"What the great books do is retell history in a way that creates a deepened and clarified connection between what was an what is. I love this book. For anyone seeking to understand how we got here, and where we're likely bound, this is a must-read."

Ron Suskind, Pulitzer Prize-winning journalist and author of *The Price of Loyalty* and *A Hope in the Unseen*

"Those interested in American history, politics, and its historical development will find much to enjoy in this well-written, argued work."

***Library Journal,* starred review**

"Heather Cox Richardson's skill with connecting events into a cohesive narrative is on full display in this brilliant study . . . This book speaks to the heart of life in the United States and should be in every private, public, and school library."

Deborah M. Liles, *Southwestern Historical Quarterly*

"If you want to understand this moment in American politics, here's a suggestion for you: It's the must-read book of the year."

Bill Moyers, *Moyers on Democracy*

HOW THE
SOUTH WON
THE CIVIL WAR

Oligarchy, Democracy, and the
Continuing Fight for the
Soul of America

HEATHER COX RICHARDSON

OXFORD
UNIVERSITY PRESS

OXFORD
UNIVERSITY PRESS

Oxford University Press is a department of the University of Oxford. It furthers
the University's objective of excellence in research, scholarship, and education
by publishing worldwide. Oxford is a registered trade mark of Oxford University
Press in the UK and certain other countries.

Published in the United States of America by Oxford University Press
198 Madison Avenue, New York, NY 10016, United States of America.

Library of Congress Cataloging-in-Publication Data
Names: Richardson, Heather Cox, author.
Title: How the South won the Civil War : oligarchy, democracy, and the
continuing fight for the soul of America / Heather Cox Richardson.
Description: New York, NY : Oxford University Press, [2020] |
Includes bibliographical references and index. |
Identifiers: LCCN 2019036155 (print) | LCCN 2019036156 (ebook) |
ISBN 9780190900908 (hardcover) | ISBN 9780190900922 (epub) |
ISBN 9780190900915 | ISBN 9780197581797 (paperback)
Subjects: LCSH: Political culture—West (U.S.)—History. |
Political culture—Southern States—History. | Oligarchy—United States—
History. | Conservatism—United States—History. | Equality—
United States—History. | United States—Territorial expansion—
Political aspects. | United States—History—Civil War, 1861–1865—
Influence. | United States—Politics and government.
Classification: LCC JK1717.R54 2020 (print) | LCC JK1717 (ebook) |
DDC 306.20973—dc23
LC record available at https://lccn.loc.gov/2019036155
LC ebook record available at https://lccn.loc.gov/2019036156

Paperback printed by Sheridan Books, Inc., United States of America

For Buddy Poland

CONTENTS

ACKNOWLEDGMENTS

Every book is a team effort, but this one, which took shape only after four years of grappling with theories of language and power as well as with the research of terrific scholars, required great indulgence from colleagues, friends, and family.

The project was sparked when Richard Young invited me to give a two-day talk on race in the West almost a decade ago. The theme percolated, and two years later I called him to see if my changing ideas were worth pursuing. After asking a lot of very smart questions, he said yes. Those initial thoughts drew strength from Mary Bilder, Jim Cronin, Dennis Dickerson, Kevin Kenny, Jim O'Toole, Alan Rogers, David Shi, Joel Wolfe, and Howard Bloom, who all urged me to throw ideas at the wall and see what stuck. Marquette University let me try out my ideas about power and language; the attendees at the 2016 conference of The Center for Civil War Research at the University of Mississippi conference greeted an early version of this book with enough enthusiasm that I was encouraged to continue. Graduate students Colin Notis-McConarty, Michael McLean, Katherine Carper, Elizabeth Pingree, Mia Michael, Heather Shar, and Laurel Teal read, listened, and argued. Literary agent Lisa Adams's steady conviction that there was an important story emerging from my early musings saw the project through to a proposal.

Once there was a proposal there had to be words on a page. Todd Arrington and Kevin Gannon kept me focused with writing sprints, and my #BookSquad colleagues—Liz Covart, Sara Georgini, Kevin Levin, Seth Jacobs, Megan Kate Nelson, and Nina Silber—provided criticism, encouragement, and mint chip ice cream. Jason Herbert, Peter Josephson, T. J. Stiles, Josh Rothman, Kathryn Cundiff, and Amanda Shaver let me bounce ideas off them, and persuaded me to make some hard decisions about what to include and what to leave out.

Once there were words on the page there had to be readers and critics. Eric Arnesen, Michael Bazemore, Lora Dawn Burnett, Philip Cardella, Michael Miles, and Virginia Scharff were all generous with their time and comments.

And finally, once there was a book there had to be editors. Timothy Bent, Melissa Yanuzzi, Susan Warga, and Mary Anne Shahidi shaped this project and saw it through to completion.

Colleagues become friends over projects like this, and friends become vital to the intellectual work of the project. Nancy Evans and Leonie Glen shared their observations about power and language in the ancient world on walks and over dinner. Carol Nowacki and I hashed out power and politics, while Kristina Dahl read an early version of this manuscript and took me to task for underplaying gender. Lynn Lyerly and Eric Rauchway argued and prodded, and kept an eye out for my health and happiness, too, which was much appreciated.

I owe a profound debt to Michael S. Green, who has been reader, researcher, critic, advisor, and cheerleader to this book, as well as a dear friend to its author. Because the subject matter is in his wheelhouse, he was the first person I called with these ideas, and his faith in the project—and in me—has been unstinting. I am most grateful.

I could not do what I do without the cheerful indulgence of my kids—Rob, Marshall, and Eva Pontrelli—and my family: Kath and Jens, Irv and Katie, Cara and Chris, and all my nieces and nephews. I am also indebted to Jetsy and Joe Reid, who went out of their way to keep me fed and my life on track in the years I spent on this book.

When I first began to talk about this project, Buddy Poland noted that I had not mentioned Kit Carson, and said that no one could write about the image of the American West without talking about the infamous mountain man. He was right, and from then on, he has quietly made comments, corrections, and suggestions while providing me with writing space—both literal and metaphorical—encouragement, support, and raspberry cream cheese coffee cake. He helped to anchor both the project and its author, and this book is dedicated to him with my deepest thanks.

With the help of such wonderful people I should have produced a perfect book. That I did not is my fault alone.

INTRODUCTION

The moment in July 1964 when Arizona Senator Barry Goldwater took the stage at the Cow Palace outside San Francisco and beamed at the cheering Republicans who had just nominated him for president is iconic—but not for the reasons we remember. Goldwater delivered the line that became a rally cry for a rising generation of conservatives in the Republican Party, saying that "Extremism in the defense of liberty is no vice. And . . . moderation in the pursuit of justice is no virtue." But the moment did much more than galvanize activists. It marked the resurrection of an old political movement by a modern political party. In Goldwater's time, people claiming to be embattled holdouts defending American liberty called themselves "Movement Conservatives." A century before, their predecessors had called themselves "Confederates."

While Goldwater's supporters in 1964 talked generally about liberty, their actual complaint was specific: the business regulation and social welfare legislation of FDR's New Deal and Eisenhower's Middle Way had trampled their rights. In the wake of the Great Depression, the U.S. government had focused on creating economic security and equality of opportunity. These widely popular policies became known as the "liberal consensus," because most Americans agreed that government should protect the country's most vulnerable citizens and regulate the economy.

Movement Conservatives, however, maintained that the liberal consensus was destroying America. People should be free to operate however they wished, without interference from government bureaucrats and regulations. They hated that the government had taken on popular projects since the 1930s. Highways, dams, power plants, schools, hospitals, and social welfare legislation cost tax dollars. This, they warned, amounted to a redistribution of wealth from hardworking white men to the poor, often to poor people of color. Such a dangerous trend toward an activist government had to be stopped before it destroyed the liberty on which America was based.

Although Goldwater was a westerner through and through, it was the delegation from South Carolina that put him over the top to win the 1964 Republican presidential nomination. This was no accident. Movement Conservatives embraced the same ideas that, a century before, had led South Carolina slave owners to attack the United States government.

Like elite slaveholders before the Civil War, they believed in a world defined by hierarchies, where most people—dull, uneducated, black, female, weak, or poor—needed the guidance of their betters. In turn, the wealth those lesser people produced as they labored at menial work would funnel upward to the top of society, accumulating in the hands of those who had the knowledge and skills to use it most effectively. Those educated, wealthy, and connected men would create progress. In 1858, a slaveholder put it this way: the upper class should rest on the lower classes the same way a stately edifice rested on "mudsills"— timbers driven into the ground for support.

That mudsill vision of the world stood against a very different set of principles that lay at the heart of American democracy: equality and self-determination. Those who embraced this vision believed that society moved forward because self-reliant individuals produced and innovated far more effectively than a small group of elites, whose wealth insulated them from the need to experiment.

These two ideologies were incompatible, yet they were woven together into the fabric of America from its start.

★

America began with a great paradox: the same men who came up with the radical idea of constructing a nation on the principle of equality also owned slaves, thought Indians were savages, and considered women inferior. This apparent contradiction was not a flaw, though; it was a key feature of the new democratic republic. For the Founders, the concept that "all men are created equal" depended on the idea that the ringing phrase "all men" did not actually include everyone. In 1776, it seemed self-evident to leaders that not every person living in the British colonies was capable—or worthy—of self-determination. In their minds, women, slaves, Indians, and paupers depended on the guidance of men such as themselves. Those unable to make good decisions about their own lives must be walled off from government to keep them from using political power to indulge their irresponsible appetites. So long as these lesser people played no role in the body politic, everyone within it could be equal. In the Founders' minds, then, the principle of equality depended on inequality. That central paradox—that freedom depended on racial, gender, and class inequality—shaped American history as the cultural, religious, and social patterns of the new nation grew around it.[1]

In the last half century, we have begun to pay attention to how the American paradox has kept people of color and women from the full enjoyment of their rights. But we have paid far less attention to the fact that it actually threatens all Americans. It has given a small group of wealthy men the language they need to undermine our democracy, and to replace it with an oligarchy.

As Republican Speaker of the House Newt Gingrich noted in 1995, "language matters." Words drive stories, and stories drive politics by shaping the way voters understand the world. Twice in our history, a small group of extraordinarily wealthy men have taken over our government by using a peculiarly American narrative, a corollary to the paradox: If equality depends on inequality for women and minorities, the opposite should also be true. That is, inclusion of women and minorities as equals in American society would, by definition, destroy equality.

Thus, at times when it seems as if people of color or women will become equal to white men, oligarchs are able to court white male voters by insisting that universal equality will, in fact, reduce white men to subservience. Both slaveholders in the 1850s and Movement Conservatives a century later convinced white American men that equality for people of color and women would destroy their freedom. Rallying their voters behind the idea that they were protecting the country's founding principles, they took over the political system. Once in control of Congress, the White House, and the courts, they used the government to solidify their own control. Eventually class divisions emerged, and the wealthy turned on the poorer white men who had fueled their rise to power. Convinced they alone should rule, this minority set out to destroy democracy.

Their rise depends on the successful divorce of image from reality in political narrative. Oligarchs tap into the extraordinary strength of the ideology of American freedom, the profoundly exciting, innovative, and principled notion that has been encoded in our national DNA since Englishmen first began to imagine a New World in the 1500s. That ideology asserts that individuals must have control of their own destiny, succeeding or failing according to their skills and effort. It speaks directly to the fundamental human condition, and rather than bowing to the dictates of religion or tradition, it endows us all with the ability to control our own fate. This ideology is the genius of America, and we have embodied it in two distinctive archetypes: that of the independent yeoman farmer before the Civil War and that of the western cowboy afterward. In each period, those seeking oligarchic power have insisted they were defending the rights of those quintessential American individuals.

But the reality was that they were undermining individualism. While they promised to protect the status quo, and rallied support for doing so, as they gained control these men used their political influence to consolidate their own power. Their policies hurt ordinary Americans, creating a disaffected population ripe for leaders who promised easy solutions to their problems. They began to solidify their base by dividing society between those hardworking and quintessentially American individualists, on the one hand, and minorities, women, and, eventually, the poor on the other. Either silenced or afraid to be included in one of the demonized groups, Americans adjusted to this new normal. Religion, popular culture, and politics all reflected and got in line with the powerful, even as these leaders' vision became increasingly divorced from reality.[2]

Over the course of a generation, both elite slave owners and Movement Conservative leaders came to believe that they alone knew how to run the country. They saw it as imperative that others be kept from power. They suppressed voting, rigged the mechanics of government, silenced the opposition press, and dehumanized their opponents. At the same time, quite logically, they did not see themselves as bound by the law. As the only ones who truly understood what was good for everyone, they were above it. So long as they continued successfully to project the narrative that they were protecting democracy, their supporters ignored the reality that oligarchs were taking over.

★

They ignored it, that is, until it was too obvious to ignore any longer. The reassertion of democracy against oligarchy created the two greatest crises in American history. The first crisis came in the first half of the nineteenth century. In the early years of the Republic, Americans had rallied around the idea of the yeoman farmer, an independent man who worked in his own fields, supported his wife and children, and promoted good policies when he voted to advance his own interests. In the 1830s, though, westward expansion into rich cotton lands in what we now call the Deep South concentrated a great deal of wealth into the hands of a very small group of slaveholding planters. As those men increasingly controlled politics, culture, and the economy, upward mobility for poorer white men stalled. Planters staved off popular distrust of their growing power by insisting that those who opposed them were trying to make black people free. To secure voters who were increasingly dissatisfied with their own economic opportunities, slave owners steadily dehumanized black Americans and ratcheted up their appeals to white supremacy.

Northerners were outraged at the slaveholders' attack on democracy. By 1856, they had coalesced into the Republican Party and insisted on keeping slavery out of western lands so that slaveholders could not accumulate enough wealth and power to dominate the entire nation. As Abraham Lincoln mused, if slavery depended on skin color, any man could be enslaved to a man with lighter skin than his own. If it was based on intelligence, then any man could be enslaved to a man with a better intellect. Lincoln saw where this argument led: "Say you, it is a question of interest; and, if you can make it your interest, you have the right to enslave another. Very well. And if he can make it his interest, he has the right to enslave you." "I should like to know," he continued, "taking this old Declaration of Independence, which declares that all men are equal upon principle, and making exceptions to it, where will it stop?"[3]

Elite slaveholders insisted that they, not the Republicans, were the ones protecting ordinary citizens. Trying to limit the spread of slavery was, in their telling, an attempt to uproot the democratic system by prohibiting poor white men access to the cheapest labor that would enable them to rise. They insisted that their opponents' ideas could only lead to forced "equality" between blacks and whites and even intermarriage between former slaves and white women. Where would that stop? As full participants in American society, black men would use their newfound power to turn democracy into anarchy. They would butcher white folks and take all their possessions for themselves. Slave owners insisted that their opponents were trying not to prevent oligarchy, but rather to destroy democracy.

Southern oligarchs fueled their rise with overt racism, but they won the political support of poor white men by leveraging the American paradox. Slaveholders tied racism, sexism, and eventually classism to the uplifting ideal that had inspired the Founders: faith in the possibilities of equality. Poor voters who backed the slaveholders were not either vicious racists or fervent democrats; they were both at the same time.

As their policies concentrated the South's lands and money into their own hands, wealthy slaveholders retained popular support by resorting to extraordinary claims that could succeed only if they made sure that voters could not check their propaganda against reality. So they stifled opposition media and invented stories that supported their own version of the world. Southern white men were not capitalists hustling to make money, one southern writer said, but a chivalrous aristocracy charged with overseeing their subordinates: women and slaves. White southerners were "a race of men. . . incapable of servility and selfishness." Wealthy slaveholders demanded utter adherence to orthodoxy on the issue of slavery and bled anti-slavery opponents out of the Democratic Party, which during the course of the 1840s and 1850s became ever more extreme on the issue. Increasingly isolated from reality, a minority of southerners and an even smaller minority of northerners came to believe that any popular move that might in any way limit slavery was, by definition, an attack on their liberty. In 1857, in the *Dred Scott* decision, Chief Justice Roger Taney made their belief the law of the land. He declared that Congress could not regulate slavery because it could not "exercise any more authority over [slaves] than it may constitutionally exercise over property of any other kind."

Numbers finally overwhelmed elite southern planters in 1860, when voters, appalled by the rise of an American oligarchy, split the Democratic Party and elected to the White House the Republican Abraham Lincoln, who promised to keep slavery from spreading into the West. Before Lincoln even took office, southern slaveholders announced that their bonds to the Union were dissolved.

The Confederate States of America was based on the principle that the Founders were wrong. Elite slave owners would resolve the American paradox by shearing off the portion of it that endorsed equality. The idea that all men were created equal was an outdated fallacy that flew in the face of both natural law and God's law. Confederate leaders were proudly leading the way into the future with a government that conformed to the way God had actually made the world, and all other modern nations would someday follow. The "cornerstone" of the Confederacy, as Vice President Alexander Stephens put it, was that "the negro is not equal to the white man; that slavery subordination to the superior race is his natural and normal condition. This, our new government, is the first, in the history of the world, based upon this great physical, philosophical, and moral truth."

The slaveholders' attempt to destroy the nation failed. In the inferno of the Civil War, Americans tried to uproot oligarchy once and for all, and to cement democracy at the nation's heart. It seemed, briefly, as if they had indeed managed to give the nation what Lincoln called "a new birth of freedom."

★

But just as democracy seemed to triumph along with the Union troops, the balance of power shifted. As soon as war broke out in 1861, the Union government pushed west at an astonishing rate. Congress brought into the Union the Territories of Colorado, Nevada, and Dakota (the last of which would be split into North Dakota, South Dakota, and Wyoming after the war), and in 1863 it added Idaho and Arizona Territories. In 1864, it created Montana Territory and admitted Nevada to the Union as a state. By the end of the Civil War, the political boundaries of the West looked much as they do today. Immediately after the Civil War, Americans moved westward, to a land that had its own history, quite different than that of the American East. In the West, Confederate ideology took on a new life, and from there, over the course of the next 150 years, it came to dominate America.

American settlers in the West had written racial hierarchies into their laws before the Civil War—taxing Mexican and Chinese miners more severely than white miners, for example—and while people in the East had been promoting equality during the war, most in the West were reinforcing racial distinctions. In late summer 1862, Dakota Indians, starving because the U.S. government had reneged on its treaty obligations, turned against settlers in Minnesota. This "uprising," coming at a moment when the Union's military fortunes were at their lowest ebb, convinced observers that western Indians were a profound threat to the nation itself. In 1864, the Army forced Navajos on a deadly three-hundred-mile march from Arizona to Bosque Redondo, a camp in New Mexico. Later that year, a militia unit attacked a group of peaceful Cheyennes at Sand Creek in Colorado. They butchered their victims, taking body parts as trophies.

After the war, Indian treaties, military actions, and territorial and state laws limited land ownership, suffrage, and intermarriage by race. Western legislators interpreted the Fourteenth Amendment, adopted in July 1868, to include only African Americans. The amendment itself excluded Indians, and westerners argued that Chinese and other immigrants fell under a law passed in 1802 that established that enslaved immigrants were different from white immigrants. The 1802 law said only "free white" people could be citizens. Banished in the East, the shadow of legal slavery continued to dim the West.

Angry southern Democrats, who hated that racial equality could be enforced by the government, saw the West as the only free place left in America. Republicans who passed laws to protect freed people were not advancing equality; they were destroying liberty. They were stealing money in the form of taxes from hardworking Americans and giving it to those who were too lazy to work. Republicans' vaunted "equality" was nothing more than theft.

Democrats contrasted what they saw as a system of race-based wealth redistribution taking hold in the East with an image of the American West where hardworking men asked nothing of the government but to be left alone. They promoted the image of the western cowboy as a hardy individualist, carving his way in the world on his own. Ignoring the reality that American soldiers and cowboys were often men of color and that the government provided settlers with land, protected them from Indians, and helped develop the western economy, Democrats celebrated cowboys as brave heroes who worked their way to prosperity as they fought for freedom and American civilization against barbaric Indians, Chinese, and Mexicans. Although in reality the West also depended on women, in the male-dominated world of the cowboy myth they were depicted as either submissive wives or prostitutes.

The image of the western individualist changed American politics after 1880, when the West took on new political significance. In that year, the Republican Party lost control of the southern states, which went solidly Democratic in the presidential election and would stay Democratic for a century. Without electoral votes from the South, Republicans could not retain control of the White House, a control they considered vital to the very survival of the nation.

They began to court western voters. To do so, they had to cater to the West's racial hierarchies. In 1882, a Republican Congress bowed to pressure to recognize racial distinctions and inscribed them back into American law with the Chinese Exclusion Act, the first federal law in history that restricted immigration. After Republicans nonetheless lost the 1884 election, at their first opportunity they admitted six new states to the Union to bolster their numbers in the Electoral College and the Senate.

Between 1889 and 1890, North Dakota, South Dakota, Montana, Washington, Idaho, and Wyoming joined the United States. Republicans believed the new states would keep the Northeast in power, but they miscalculated. By 1890, the West had an ideology more in common with that of the South than that of the North. Both the South and the West had extractive economies that consolidated wealth and power in a few hands. Those who controlled mining, oil, cattle, railroads, irrigation, and agribusiness controlled the West. Just as the antebellum cotton industry had done, these industries required huge capital investments—and lots of unskilled workers.

Rather than working with eastern Republicans, western politicians instead often worked with southern Democrats. Together, they pushed back on eastern economic policies and worked to kill federal protection for black voting. Then westerners created their own political organization to promote costly water reclamation projects that would both irrigate the West and stop devastating flooding in the South. Southern Democrats in Congress supported the West's water plans; in turn, western congressmen helped southern Democrats kill anti-lynching legislation.

Just as the image of the yeoman farmer in the East after the Revolution had helped pave the way for the rise of southern planters, the image of the cowboy helped spur a return to a caste system. In 1893, historian Frederick Jackson Turner claimed that American democracy itself was continually reinvented in the West, where ordinary men worked together and stood against the repressive government back in the settled East.

The idea that the government should stand behind western individualism and self-reliance took over American culture, bolstering the position of wealthy white men across the country. In 1892, in both Wyoming's Johnson County War and Idaho's Coeur D'Alene strike, industrialists successfully appealed to the federal government to protect them first from small ranchers and workers, and then from the local elected officials who took the people's side. Similarly, in Wilmington, North Carolina, in 1898, white leaders launched a coup against a biracial government. It did not matter that local officials had won office fairly; white men vowed they would "never again be ruled, by men of African origin," who were joining with unscrupulous white men to "dominate the intelligent and thrifty element in the community." At the turn of the century, the Supreme Court cast racial categories into national law, creating the notion of "noncitizen nationals." Under this doctrine, the United States could acquire Puerto Rico, Guam, and the Philippines as "unincorporated territories" without making their inhabitants American citizens.

So the original American paradox of freedom based on inequality was reestablished. That restoration relegated people of color to inequality, but it also undercut the ability of oligarchs to destroy democracy. Black and brown people were subordinate, so wealthy men could not convincingly argue that they were commandeering government to redistribute wealth and destroy liberty. With that rhetoric defanged, white Americans used the government to curb wealth and power. From the presidency of Theodore Roosevelt in the early 1900s to that of Franklin Delano Roosevelt thirty years later, Progressives regulated the economy, protected social welfare, and promoted national infrastructure. That government activism, though, privileged white men over women and people of color. Even the New Deal programs of the Depression, designed to lift the poor out of desperation while reining in runaway capitalism, carefully maintained distinctions between women and men, black and brown and white.

World War II forced a reckoning. Americans stood together against the rise of fascism, a political theory based in the idea that some people were better than others, and that those natural leaders must keep followers in line by stifling all opposition. Fascists had actually taken some inspiration from America's own racial laws, and during the war FDR felt obliged constantly to hammer home that democracy was the superior system. Americans during the war championed ordinary soldiers—the GIs—who were men and women from all backgrounds and ethnicities. Churches, films, reformers, and government officials insisted that Americans must not discriminate against people of different religions, races, or ethnicities. As Superman—who took the nation by storm when he first appeared in 1938—warned a group of schoolchildren shortly after the war ended: "Remember, boys and girls, your school—like our country—is made up of Americans of *many* different races, religions and national origins. So . . . if you hear anybody talk against a schoolmate or anyone else because of his religion, race or national origin—don't wait: tell him THAT KIND OF TALK IS UN-AMERICAN."

After World War II, veterans who had fought for their country came home to fight their second-class status, and government officials supported their cause. Presidents Truman and Eisenhower desegregated the military and contracting; state courts declared racial housing covenants and then bans on interracial marriage unconstitutional. Then, in 1954, the justices of the Supreme Court unanimously declared school segregation unconstitutional. It appeared that Americans had coalesced around the idea of using the government to achieve equality of opportunity for all.

Instead, the use of the government to promote equality launched democracy's second crisis. The new "liberal consensus," as it became known, challenged the American paradox. Once again, oligarchs rolled out their corollary, that inclusion destroys democracy. And this time they had a new base of support in the West, to which resources and people had streamed during the war.

At first they had had little luck turning voters against the New Deal. Organizing as Movement Conservatives, they declared war on the liberal consensus. They tried to convince voters to reject the laws that protected workers, promoted social welfare, and undertook national improvement projects such as the interstate highways. The New Deal government was tantamount to communism, they insisted. But their argument didn't work.

The Supreme Court's 1954 *Brown v. Board of Education* decision and Eisenhower's enforcement of racial equality at Little Rock Central High three years later enabled Movement Conservatives to enlist racism in their cause. Just as slaveholders had done in the 1850s, they took the stance that no matter how popular an activist government was, it would eventually destroy America by destroying liberty. In an echo of Reconstruction, they warned that expanded voting enabled black people to elect leaders who promised "special interest" legislation. All appearances to the contrary, they said, this was not equality. It was tyranny. Making wealthier men pay for policies that would benefit poorer people undercut democracy because it was an attack on the nation's core principle: liberty. Movement Conservatives took as their standard the American cowboy, the western individualist who, according to legend, wanted nothing from government but to be left alone.

The nomination of Goldwater in 1964 as the Republican candidate for president marked the ideological shift by the larger Republican Party toward the hierarchical ideology of the West. As Democrats centered their power in the East, Republican leaders chose to hold the 1964 nominating convention at the Cow Palace outside San Francisco, in recognition of the central importance of the West to the party's fortunes. At the convention, Goldwater supporters rejected what they called the "Eastern Establishment" and handed him the nomination. When Goldwater, who personified the post–Civil War western cowboy, picked up five states of the Deep South—Louisiana, Mississippi, Alabama, Georgia, and South Carolina—the association of the West and the racial ideology of the southern slaveholders was complete.

★

Between Goldwater and 2016 Republican nominee Donald J. Trump, every Republican presidential nominee except Gerald

Ford (whose elevation did not come through usual channels) has associated himself with the region west of the Mississippi River. As party leaders gradually came to embrace the ideology of Movement Conservatives, they undermined democracy, using the same pattern their southern predecessors did. In 1968, Richard M. Nixon—once a congressman from California—abandoned federal support for desegregation with his "southern strategy," and adopted the practice of building a base by attacking people of color as lazy people who wanted handouts. By 1970, he had also ostracized women who demanded government policies, including reproductive rights, that would guarantee them equality before the law. Movement Conservatives went further, stigmatizing women who advocated equal rights as feminist bra burners, and demonizing them as baby killers.

Former actor and California governor Ronald Reagan deliberately assumed the mantle of the cowboy. Running for the presidency in 1980, he wore boots and a white Stetson, and warned that only the actions of a few good men were holding back a redistribution of wealth. He championed the idea that America was a land of equal opportunity at the same time that he promoted the myth of the welfare queen, a grasping black woman who sucked tax dollars from hardworking Americans. Once in office, Reagan began to shape policy according to the Movement Conservative view, a process that would gradually concentrate wealth at the top of society. In 1979, the top 1 percent of Americans claimed 33.5 percent of the nation's capital income. By 2010, that same cohort claimed 54 percent. Americans of color, workers, and women fell far behind white men economically; they also suffered disproportionately from the structure of criminal laws and policing.[4]

As their policies began to hurt even their own supporters, Movement Conservatives first bled the Republican Party of those who didn't share their ideology—traditional Republicans they called RINOs (Republicans In Name Only)—and then manipulated the political system to stay in power. They insisted that America was in danger of being overawed by the votes of the wrong people. "Voter fraud," while statistically almost nonexistent, became a rallying cry for those who opposed policies embraced by a majority. In 1998, Florida passed legislation that disfranchised tens of thousands of voters, mostly Democrats, and other states followed suit. After 2010, legislatures controlled by the Republican Party gerrymandered districts and restricted voting to guarantee that its leaders would remain in power, even as they lost a majority of voters. Entrepreneur billionaire Peter Thiel summed up the changing political climate when he wrote, "I no longer believe that freedom and democracy are compatible."[5]

To justify their continued control, Republicans used language that sounded remarkably like that of slaveholders. They began to defend a society in which wealthy elites should rule over the masses. Republican spokespeople harped on "makers" (leaders who were "job-creators") and "takers" (people whom 2012 presidential candidate Mitt Romney identified as the 47 percent who "are dependent upon government . . . believe that they are entitled to health care, to food, to housing, to you name it"). By 2016, Republicans had expanded this category to include poor white people. In March 2016, *National Review*'s Kevin Williamson claimed their problems were not a result of policies that concentrated wealth upward but rather came about because they were dependent on welfare, addicted to drugs and alcohol, had no family stability, and "whelp . . . human children with all the respect and wisdom of a stray dog." Anti-government activist Cliven Bundy made the principles of this ideology clear when he speculated that African Americans might be "better off as slaves, picking cotton and having a family life," rather than living "under government subsidy."[6]

In 2016, Trump stripped off whatever genteel veneer remained on Republican ideology, actively cultivating the support of white supremacist groups and declaring of his supporters, "I love the uneducated." A leaked tape in which Trump boasted of sexual assault revealed his conviction that women were objects for the use of wealthy men, and the willingness of Republican leaders to overlook that language as "locker room talk" indicated that they shared Trump's belief. Trump supporters talked openly of secession and perhaps even of revolution if their candidate did not win.

Once in office, President Trump and his allies in Congress reinforced this ideology by slashing taxes for the rich while gutting health care and government regulations. His supporters attacked minorities and women, and after deliberately creating an administration dominated by white men, he tried to preserve that bias in the future through the makeup of the judiciary. Of more than 150 judicial appointments in the first two years of his administration, for example, only three were African American, and he nominated no Latinos or African Americans to federal circuit courts. He nominated no African American women at all. His followers defended Confederate monuments and accepted the support of the Ku Klux Klan. The parallels between the antebellum Democrats and the modern-day Republican Party were clear.[7]

The American paradox has once again enabled oligarchs to threaten democracy. They have gained power by deploying the corollary to that paradox: equality for all will end liberty. This was the narrative an elite group of slaveholders used to take over the government in the 1850s. They were defeated on the battlefields, but their vision of America moved West after the Civil War, where it gathered the strength to regain power.

How the South Won the Civil War tells the story of the second rise of American oligarchy: the larger story behind the South Carolina delegates' putting western Senator Barry Goldwater over the top to win the Republican presidential nomination in 1964 and its logical conclusion in the present moment. It is the story of modern America.

HOW THE SOUTH WON
THE CIVIL WAR

CHAPTER 1

The Roots of Paradox

The wonder and exciting sense of potential that would eventually create the American paradox was on full display at the Globe Theatre outside London's city gates in summer 1612. The people coming to that "wooden O," picking their way past brothels, gambling houses, and bear-baiting and cockfighting shows, were there to leave behind the grimness of life and escape into a glorious new world.[1]

There was plenty to escape from. In the early 1600s, the wool industry that supported the English economy had collapsed. In London, unemployed weavers cast around for work to keep body and soul together, walking narrow cobbled streets where rats nosed through slops tossed from windows and doorways carrying the lice and fleas that always bit and sometimes carried the plague. The disease was at bay in 1612, but Londoners knew that it was only a question of time until someone with a headache would suddenly start to shiver, their swollen lymph nodes blackening, and the city would grind to a halt until the plague passed, leaving carts of dead in its wake.[2]

But for all that early seventeenth-century London was cramped and dirty and dangerous, it was also exciting, awash in innovations unimaginable only a generation before. New seafaring technologies had opened up Atlantic ports, and sailors brought to town new ideas, new money, new goods, and new languages. In the streets, voyagers who had been to a land across the ocean exhibited "savages" clad in animal skins, people the sailors claimed to have caught in virgin forests with trees that dwarfed those that remained in the British Isles. Businessmen accumulated wealth and invested their money in new schemes; scholars marveled at maps and the newly accessible scholarship that moved along with trade goods. Printed books were for sale to those who were familiar with the written word, and in new translations they introduced readers to Plato and Aristotle, geometry and religion, and also told of shipwrecks on islands near a continent Spanish explorers had discovered only a little over a hundred years before.[3]

Theater in Shakespeare's day captured this magic, and in the summer of 1612, audiences at the Globe might have seen Shakespeare's last and most magical of plays, *The Tempest*. Duke Prospero has been thrown out of power by his brother. Cast adrift, he and his daughter, Miranda, are shipwrecked on an island, deserted but for a savage man-beast whose name, Caliban, is an obvious anagram for "cannibal," and by a spirit named Ariel, whom Prospero binds to his service. The story of Prospero is that of an old man cast off by civilization and building in a wilderness something new, something "rich and strange" that enables him to rule both a savage and a good spirit and, eventually, to forgive his brother's usurpation of his position as a European aristocrat.[4]

But it is Miranda who captures the mood for the audience. Reared in isolation from the world, Miranda is a blank slate, seeing everything for the first time. In the midst of a stage full of men, each jockeying to control the rest, some betraying others, she stands to proclaim her innocent joy in the extraordinary world around her: "Oh, wonder! How many goodly creatures are there here! How beauteous mankind is! O brave new world that has such people in't!"[5]

America's roots lie in this particularly opportune moment in world history: a moment when the traditional walls that had bounded Western society since the dawn of memory were crumbling under a tide of new ideas. And some men were innovative enough, and others desperate enough, to take an extraordinary leap: stepping onto leaky wooden vessels to brave two months at sea, beating across an ocean to see what a new world could look like. Unlike Miranda, though, these adventurers were no innocents. They brought with them the world-view that had defined their lives and the lives of their fathers and mothers before them.

The men and women who traveled from England to arrive on the Atlantic shores of the North American continent in the early 1600s came from a land dominated by aristocrats related to each other by family and tradition and overseen by a monarch who, theoretically, at least, had been elevated to that exalted position by God. For as long as anyone could remember, the world had been ruled by a system in which a few wealthy white leaders, almost always men—their era's Elizabeth I was a notable exception—controlled the government and economy of their nations, with the vast majority of people living and dying under their rule. Wealth, family, education, connections, and religion all reinforced the idea that people belonged to the stations into which they were born. Kings and noblemen were born to rule those below them, peasants to labor for and serve those above. Women were in a category all their own: God had made them lesser than men in the very act of creation. So most women worked, gave birth, reared children, created, loved, worshipped, and died without moving the levers of power.[6]

But while that worldview shaped early American colonists, its foundations were beginning to crack under the pressure of religious shifts. In the 1530s, spurred by King Henry VIII's desire to ditch his wife so he could marry a woman who could give him a son, and his determination to be the sole ruler of his people rather than deferring to the Pope, England had broken away from the Catholic church. The establishment of the Anglican church meant years of religious seesawing before Elizabeth took the throne in 1558 and tried to hew to a moderate course for her forty-five-year reign, establishing Protestant religious practices that would not alienate Catholics. Her willingness to honor Catholic traditions in the English church upset strict Protestants. Their quest to purify the church earned them the name Puritans.

Puritans believed that every individual had a direct relationship with God, a relationship that must be discerned by the individual himself, and not be mediated by priests and sacraments. This belief had earth-shattering political implications. If God saw all men as equal in the profound matter of eternal salvation, how could it be possible that he distinguished among them in the less serious matter of human government?[7]

This was a logical leap that few religious leaders made initially, but King James I, who ascended to the throne after Elizabeth I died in 1603, certainly thought that Puritanism raised the specter of political revolution. "No bishop, no king," he warned. When James's son Charles I took the throne in 1625, he vowed to harry the Puritans out of his kingdom. With that, Puritans allied with Parliament to limit the king's power.

The English Civil Wars that followed gave rise to the philosophy that would create the American nation. In response to that crisis of upstarts—a crisis that left King Charles and at least 100,000 of England's 5 million people dead—thinkers speculated about the nature of man and government. Thomas Hobbes crabbed that man was inherently selfish and naturally lawless and must be kept within bounds by the power of a strong state, overseen by an absolute monarch. John Locke, the son of Puritans, took a different lesson from the political chaos.

Locke hailed from Bristol, a maritime town along the River Avon on the southwest coast of England, from which fishermen were already traveling to New England and returning with cod and stories. The Puritans' emphasis on each man's responsibility for discovering his own true relationship with God fit nicely with the flood of new ideas and information coming into England. Puritans valued education and logic, believing that people must use their brains to recognize the workings of God in the world lest they be misled into doing the work of Satan. Since every man bore responsibility for perceiving the path God had foreordained for him, he must constantly seek to absorb and make sense of new information; that is, to learn.

Educated at Oxford, Locke turned his considerable mind to the problem of human society. First, he concluded that humans were not born with ideas about the world but rather learned from their experiences, much like Shakespeare's Miranda. All knowledge came from trying out new facts and ideas. If men figured out their own appointed path in their world, they would also discern the natural rules that God had established. New information could change one's understanding, and this meant traditional patterns of society did not necessarily reflect those natural rules. Government was an agreement—a social compact—put together to enable men to live together in peace. It should rest not on birth or wealth or religion, all of which were arbitrary, but rather on natural law. Government, then, depended on the consent of the governed. In 1690, Locke published *Two Treatises on Government*, developing his ideas about how society worked.

Locke had no children, but he left plenty of intellectual descendants. By the time he died in 1704, others were following his lead, arguing that reason and self-interest, not birth or religion, were the true sources of authority and political legitimacy. In France, Voltaire wrote plays and poems ridiculing a world bounded by superstition and intolerance; in Scotland, political economist Adam Smith argued that men constructed a rational economy as they acted in their own interests. In what has become known as the Age of Enlightenment, men and women interested in the world around them embraced the scientific method and the search for knowledge to discover the natural laws of earth and the heavens, rather than falling back on culture, religion, or aristocratic rule. These thinkers began to focus on fact and reason, instead of old social and religious traditions, to make sense of the world.

In part, the new ideas of Locke and the Enlightenment thinkers who followed him reflected the need of Europeans to make sense of the new information coming from the North American colonies: new peoples, new languages, new religions, new animals, new plants, new constellations and ocean currents. In turn, the ideas traveled back to those colonies. When Benjamin Franklin tied a key to a kite tail in June 1752 during a thunderstorm to learn about electricity, he was not some lone crank with a death wish; he was part of an international movement to use inquiry and reason to learn about the natural world. Enlightenment principles took root in America among society's leaders.[8]

These principles affected every aspect of colonial life, including politics. The thirteen colonies that would eventually become the United States of America were peopled with Indians and those who hailed from Europe, Africa, and the Caribbean, but they were organized politically under the British crown. Colonial governments initially were a hodgepodge: some colonies were governed by companies, some by proprietors, others by royal governors, and one—Georgia—by trustees. Over time, though, distance from England and the need to make rules on the ground meant that colonial governments began to resemble one another. By the 1740s, every colony had a royal governor who answered to the king, but elected colonial assemblies wielded unusual power because they controlled the purse strings of their local governments. The British government extracted resources—timber, furs, and fish—from the colonies but otherwise paid them little attention. From the perspective of Britain, a thriving world power with the bustling ports of London and Bristol and Newcastle, the American colonies seemed a backwater.

The push and pull between royal officials and colonial assemblies, as well as between different colonial interests, began to align colonials with Enlightenment political ideas simply out of practicality. In the colonies, different authorities exercised power at different times and in different ways. Queries to England and orders from royal officials had to travel across the Atlantic, sometimes creating months of uncertainty that local authorities had to navigate. Colonials began naturally to grasp that the exercise of power was not the province of any divinely ordered leader, but something temporal and temporary. Something new grew organically in this chaotic system: the space for different interests to learn to share power.[9]

★

This patchwork system held sway in the colonies until 1763, when American colonials discovered that they did not share the same relationship to their government that Englishmen at home did. The decade-long French and Indian War had pitted colonials and English regulars against French soldiers and their Indian allies across the North American English colonies. In the end, English forces had won. Colonials were proud of their membership in the powerful British Empire and saw themselves as equals to their countrymen across the Atlantic. So they were shocked when British officials abandoned their former position of benign neglect and turned to the colonies to pay for the war, which had been expensive and had been waged—as Parliament argued—in part to protect the colonials. To British officials, it only made sense to steady finances by adjusting the high costs and low tax burdens of the colonies. But to the colonists, the series of measures put into place after 1763 made them feel they were being unfairly targeted.

British regulations governing the American colonies came at rapid-fire pace after the French and Indian War. Shortly after the conflict ended, the king issued the Proclamation of 1763, which laid out a series of policies to prevent further expensive wars. One of these policies prohibited colonials from moving west across the Appalachians, where their incursions invariably created conflict with Indians. Land-hungry colonists, who had fought in part to get access to the West, loathed this new rule. The next year the Revenue Acts began. In 1764, Parliament taxed sugar, imposing regulations that buried shipmasters in paperwork. In 1765, it required colonials to pay the expenses for the room and board of British troops stationed in the colonies, a law known as the Quartering Act. And then, in that same year, it passed the Stamp Act, a law that levied a tax on all paper documents: newspapers, legal documents, almanacs, and so on. When the tax had been paid, the document was "stamped" to show compliance. Knowing that local juries would acquit fellow colonists charged with violating the revenue acts, Parliament provided that suspects would be tried before admiralty courts overseen by British military officers.

Under this onslaught of revenue measures, colonials' enthusiasm for their status as British subjects cooled quickly. But they were not rebels, not yet; they were still Englishmen. So they gravitated toward those in the previous generation who, like them, opposed the king's policies. Opposition leaders, such as Henry St. John, 1st Viscount Bolingbroke, believed that England needed a permanent check to the power of the Court Party, which supported the monarch. More a persuasion than an organized unit, these loosely affiliated opposition men, known collectively as the Country Party, lived outside the circles of power. They shared a number of attitudes about the ruling government, attitudes that resonated with Americans after 1763.[10]

Country Party thinkers castigated the Court Party for twisting government to serve its own interests. They believed that its members were deliberately cementing control by handing out official positions in a "patronage" system, and that the increasing power of the prime minister—who was appointed by the Crown—over Parliament must be checked. Insisting that they represented the entire country rather than the particular interests of a favored few, Country Party men argued that others like them, the landed gentry, rather than urban bankers, merchants, and royal officials, should control Britain. Because they stood against government power, they opposed taxes and a standing army, and called for small government and individual liberty.[11]

In the 1760s, these ideas spoke to Americans, especially those living in the seaports, New York, Philadelphia, Portsmouth, and Boston, where ship masters and merchants felt the new regulations were choking trade with paperwork and fees. Men in the seaports also disliked the idea of a standing army whose soldiers intruded on their towns and ate their food, and who often deserted and competed with colonials for jobs on the docks. To make sense of their situation, colonial leaders turned to the writings of the Country Party. Boston lawyer John Adams had been rooting around in political theory even before the Stamp Act caused a crisis; he claimed to have read Bolingbroke five times.[12]

They applied the discontents of the Country Party to their own circumstances, and worked to sway public opinion with a flood of pamphlets and newspapers. Adams and his older cousin Samuel saw in the Revenue Acts the growing strength of a central government and its oppression of its subjects. Four years into their resistance, they had an established system: on September 3, 1769, John Adams wrote in his diary that the two men and another revolutionary leader, James Otis, had spent the evening with two printers from the *Boston Gazette*, "Cooking up Paragraphs, Articles, Occurrences etc.—working the political Engine!" Their efforts convinced their countrymen that the government's use of admiralty courts to try individuals charged with violating the Revenue Acts meant colonials had lost their right to trial by jury. The Quartering Act meant they had to support an army out of their own pockets, with no control over its activities. And then there were the new taxes. These, they argued, had been imposed without their consent. Recalling the Enlightenment idea that government was a social compact that depended on the consent of the people governed, they insisted that the Crown's power had limits. Colonists began to resist the king's policies, especially the Stamp Act.[13]

Royal officials pushed back, arguing that English representatives acted in the interests of colonists, who bore a disproportionately small tax burden compared to their countrymen in England. Angry at what its members saw as restive ingrates, Parliament declared that it could legislate "in all cases whatsoever," and in 1767, Chancellor of the Exchequer Charles Townshend set out to strengthen royal rule. He designed a series of revenue measures, known as the Townshend duties, both to raise money to pay royal officials in the colonies and to demonstrate that Parliament had the right to tax the colonials.

Spurred by merchants and shipmasters, colonists revolted against the new laws. In the port towns, so-called "committees of correspondence" wrote to town leaders in the hinterlands, making the argument against the power of royal officials. Their ideas spread to the back-country thanks to a religious revival that had swept across the frontier after 1730. The Great Awakening was, in part, a backlash against the Enlightenment emphasis on reason and learning, but its emphasis on a personal relationship with God actually led evangelical adherents to a similar political stance as Enlightenment thinkers. Evangelical ministers rejected the cool intellectualism of such Enlightenment deists as Benjamin Franklin and championed individual grace. Their insistence that everyone was equal in the eyes of God taught followers to question authority, especially that of colonial officials who tended to ignore rural areas.[14]

Colonials' conviction that their new land required a new kind of government, based on popular rights rather than oligarchy, continued to grow. Nervous British lawmakers repealed all of the Townshend duties in March 1770 except the one on tea, which colonials recognized as a demonstration of Parliament's right to tax them without their representation. In December 1773, a group of colonists dressed as Indians turned Boston Harbor into a teapot by throwing a shipload of tea into it. When the king retaliated by closing the port, colonial leaders responded by organizing their own governing body: the First Continental Congress. Meeting in Philadelphia in 1774, it declared that it had the right to legislate without Parliament. When the Royal Governor of Massachusetts, Lieutenant General Thomas Gage, tried to crush the Massachusetts rebellion by dissolving the Massachusetts legislature, its members simply reconvened as the Massachusetts Provincial Congress and took control of the colony. And when Gage tried to stop them by seizing their military supplies in Concord, Massachusetts, in April 1775, on the dark, cold ground of Lexington Green, someone fired the "shot heard round the world." By that evening, more than three hundred colonials and British soldiers lay dead or wounded.

It was only in retrospect that that hail of gunfire was seen as launching a modern democracy. Colonials still hoped to retain their position in the British Empire, though as equals rather than second-class citizens. They wrote to King George III offering peace, so long as they could go back to the terms of 1763, only twelve years earlier. As their Olive Branch Petition traveled to London on a sailing ship, they prepared for the eventuality of war. When King George refused even to receive their petition, the die was cast.

Colonials had always been careful to charge their political complaints to the king's ministers, insisting that they still dutifully offered their allegiance to the monarch. That would change in early 1776. A recent migrant to Philadelphia from England, an artisan who had turned his hand to political journalism, laid out the justification for the British colonies to govern themselves. Thomas Paine wrote a pamphlet that ridiculed the idea of monarchy and hereditary aristocracy. Starting from the premise that men were inherently equal, he declared the distinction between monarchs and subjects completely artificial. It could only lead to misery. In an argument that wedded Enlightenment principles to religion, Paine paved the way for disaffected colonials to embrace a new, popular form of government. *Common Sense* became a runaway bestseller.

In July 1776, leaders of thirteen of the British colonies in America gathered in Philadelphia as the Second Continental Congress, revealing their emerging view of legitimate governance. They tapped the young Virginian Thomas Jefferson, already known for his skill with a pen, to explain to watching nations why they were not illegitimate rebels but rather were acting lawfully. Jefferson began his document with an assertion of the Enlightenment idea of government as a social compact, saying that the laws of nature and of nature's God entitled the colonists to create a separate government equal to that of England.

In the next paragraph, Jefferson turned to the heart of the Declaration of Independence. Cribbing from John Locke, he wrote: "We hold these truths to be self-evident, that all men are created equal, that they are endowed by their Creator with certain unalienable Rights, that among these are Life, Liberty and the pursuit of Happiness." Men created governments to secure these rights, and when any form of government denied them, men had the right to create a new government to reclaim them. To that end, the representatives of the colonies declared they were "Free and Independent States . . . Absolved of all Allegiance to the British Crown."

This was not simply an act of rebellion against a particular king; it was an act of rebellion against all kings, a resounding declaration that all men were created equal and had an equal right to have a say in their government. It was a reworking of the very basis of human governance, a rejection of distinctions among men in the name of equality. It was dangerously radical, and the men who signed the Declaration of Independence knew it. Anyone who put his name to such a document understood that he might well be signing his own death warrant. Yet sign it they did, in hope and fear, relying on the protection of divine providence, pledging "to each other our Lives, our Fortunes, and our sacred Honor."

The world had a new model of government, based not in oligarchy but in equality. As Thomas Paine had said in *Common Sense*: "The cause of America is in great measure the cause of all mankind."

★

But were all men really equal in the newly independent colonies? Jefferson, and many of the others who signed the Declaration of Independence, didn't just treat human beings differently than themselves; they outright *owned* them. They held human beings in hereditary legal slavery. By definition, slaves were neither free nor equal, nor did they enjoy the unalienable right—that is, a right that cannot be given or taken away—to their lives, their liberty, or the pursuit of their own happiness. There was a profound contradiction between Jefferson's declaration that "all men are created equal" and the fact that he and many of the founders enslaved other people.

How did slave owners make sense of that crucial contradiction? They didn't. In their minds, freedom and slavery depended on each other. Freedom did not stand in contrast to slavery; freedom required slavery.[15]

America had begun as a dream of freedom, but if it was shaped by ideas, it was also shaped by the reality of life on the North American continent, a life carved out by men and women deeply steeped in European traditions. The land was rich beyond imagining, but also demanding. Fishermen who hailed from a temperate land of fields and farms worked their boats around the rugged Atlantic coastline, hauling cod into their dories, surrounded by seemingly endless stands of towering white pines. Settlers in the Chesapeake region found heavy forests of beech, cypress, and cedar growing in the damp heat that nurtured mosquitoes and made it hard to breathe in the summer. The settlers who landed further south found rich land at sea level, thick with twisted live oak trees that stayed green all year, and cut through with channels whose dense grasses provided shelter for fish and birds. This was indeed a paradise, but it would take hard work to mine its resources for a global economy.

The land was inhabited by people far more adapted to it than the European newcomers, although those native tribes were themselves going through upheaval. Early fishermen had brought epidemic diseases, which decimated the coastal tribes and unsettled their economies, politics, and social webs, forcing them to trade and ally with the intruders to shore up their teetering systems. Europeans who previously knew Indians only by word of mouth, or from seeing captives exhibited in cities, discovered that these peoples had sophisticated societies. Settlers had to rely on them for supplies and sometimes for protection. Indians were no Calibans, savage and easily controlled by a European patriarch, but it was not immediately clear just who they were and how they fit into a European worldview that did not yet have a concept of "race."[16]

While settlers did not yet have a concept of race, they certainly had one of gender. Women's lives in America were bounded by the expectation that they were unequal to men. They had no right to own property or to control their own lives; they and their children were the property of their husbands. Within those boundaries, they carved out their own lives, working from childhood—cooking, sewing, gardening, milking, preserving food, tending children, attending church, nursing the ill, preparing the dead for burial. Marriage meant childbirth, a terribly dangerous undertaking in an era of disease, malnutrition, and midwifery. Colonials quoted the old proverb: "A man can work from sun to sun, but a woman's work is never done." For all their contribution to the economic and social life of the colonies, though, women were never considered equal to men. Rather, colonists assumed that the orderly functioning of society required that women submit to their fathers or husbands.[17]

European settlers also had a clear understanding of class distinctions, and from the beginning colonial leaders in Jamestown and Massachusetts Bay reinforced class lines. The Virginia Company sent wealthy men and their servants to the Chesapeake, hoping to find vast riches like those the Spanish had uncovered in the gold mines of South America. Instead they found rich land. Bringing forth crops from that wilderness would require backbreaking work—clearing trees and brush to create fields, planting, tending, harvesting, preserving— as well as building homes and sheds and finding and preparing food until the crops were ripe. At first, economic failure plagued the colony and a horrific death rate culled its few workers. As word of the appalling conditions leaked back to England, the company had a hard time finding replacements. By the 1620s, though, the colony had stabilized around tobacco, a valuable export. This native plant was labor-intensive, and planters scrambled to find enough people to plant it, pull the hornworms off, sucker it, cut it, cure it, pack it for shipping, and load it on boats . . . all in the heat of a Chesapeake summer.[18]

So Virginia Company leaders enslaved local Indians and then imported English workers, mostly young men. They had a vast pool from which to draw. England had undergone a population boom in the years after the Great Plague had ripped through the country from 1346 to 1353 in an epidemic that killed 60 percent of Europe's population. As the population rebounded over the centuries, inflation soared, and in the late 1500s, English planters pushed tenant farmers off their land in order to enclose fields for sheep and make their own plantations more efficient. Newly homeless, small farmers and their families had migrated to cities, where they found work in the woolen industry. And then, in the early 1600s, a recession crippled the market for woolens.[19]

Once again, poor folks cast about for work and for any reason to hope that the future might be better. In the cities, they heard rumors about the extraordinary riches of the New World, and maybe saw a captured Indian or two exhibited on the streets as proof that an exotic new continent awaited anyone who dared to take a chance. Some, desperate or hopeful or crazy—or all three—raised the money for passage by promising to work for an employer in the colony for a period of time, usually from four to seven years, to work off the debt. Planters snapped up their contracts. They also declared that Indians could be enslaved permanently so long as they were captured in wars. And when the first cargo of Africans arrived on a pirate ship in 1619, they thought nothing of adding black slaves to the workforce, too, although there were few of them available.[20]

No one in the colony had any expectation that indentured and enslaved workers would be treated as equal to their masters. But the distinction between planters and workers was generally rooted not in race but in class. England had a long history of dividing the rich from the poor, and class markers had only gotten more pronounced in the years since the enclosure movement had created roving bands of homeless people. As folks who had been pushed off the land moved about the country looking for work, the English gentry began to consider them lazy, unprincipled, savage. Reformers warned that the vagrant poor were "vicious, idle, dissolute," habitually prone to "Laziness, Drunkenness, Debauches, and almost every Kind of Vice," and were "Ignorant," "seditiously inclined," and "a Curse to the Kingdom." These were the workers who moved to Virginia, where their masters continued to complain of their laziness and savagery. Conditions in Virginia initially reinforced traditional English class lines, as masters tried to get as much work out of their servants and slaves as possible before they died.[21]

Driven by the men who ran the colony, those at the bottom of society made common cause against their masters. Enslaved people and indentured servants in Virginia suffered and worked and socialized together, and, according to advertisements and court cases, they ran away, committed crimes, and had children together. They also suffered similar punishments when they ran afoul of the law. And those few who lived past the deadly early years of their servitude shared similar access to the benefits of freedom, although slaves could not simply outlive their contracts; they had to buy their way out of bondage with money they earned in their spare time.[22]

At first, so many poor Virginians died in the colonies that the few who survived posed little threat to their former masters. Once free, they managed to buy land and rise into security. But when death rates stabilized, men outliving their indentures began to threaten planter rule. In the 1640s, leaders tried to make it harder for former servants to become free men. They lengthened the time of servitude and increased penalties for those who ran away, stole food, or conceived children.[23]

It didn't work. By the 1660s, there was a large population of poor men who could not afford prime land. They either moved around eastern Virginia, squatting on other men's property, poaching wild hogs, and hunting, or they migrated to the western frontier hoping to become farmers. Even those who found some measure of independence, though, never forgot conditions back east, in Tidewater Virginia, and those who had rigged the legal system to keep them landless and poor.[24]

★

Tidewater leaders struggled to figure out a way to minimize the growing threat from the underclass. After 1670, they passed a series of laws that created a form of slavery based on race and went far beyond the boundaries of the legal system, twisting every aspect of colonial society. Indeed, the imposition of one restriction after another wound racial slavery far more organically into the colonies than any simple policy could have done.

The laws that were to become hereditary racial slavery at first mirrored efforts the English had made back home to bind criminals to hard labor and trap the poor into workhouses, where they could be supervised out of vice and idleness and into supporting themselves. Criminals were marked by their clothing, haircuts, and loss of the tip of an ear, while those who received poor relief were required to wear a red or blue "P" on their right shoulder. Those who designed this system expected that the degradation of penal slavery would remind able men of the virtues of good behavior. They also thought that poverty would be passed down generationally. No one anticipated the possibility that workers could move upward. They believed the poor made up a class whose members would always be subordinate to their betters. The most that could be done was to keep them out of trouble and working for their own subsistence. These ideas came to the colonies. And so, as Virginia workers started living longer, colonial leaders passed laws to tie slaves and servants more and more tightly into a permanent underclass.[25]

In 1676, the Virginia Colony erupted into violence. Those living in the western parts of the settlement took up arms against the easterners they felt were standing between them and their fortunes. Western settlers were generally unhappy with the eastern government and the Tidewater planters who controlled it, for they seemed unconcerned about the dangers of hostile Native Americans on the frontier and unwilling to protect western settlements. Westerners' anger was inchoate until Nathaniel Bacon, a new arrival from England who was well connected and wealthy but frustrated at his lack of authority in the colony, welded them into a powerful coalition. Under him, vagrants and poor farmers, including former slaves and servants, marched on the seat of government at Jamestown and burned it down. Only Bacon's death from dysentery stopped them. Their revolt made clear the dangers of the Virginia Colony's class lines.[26]

In the wake of Bacon's Rebellion, the Tidewater elite set out to preserve their control over the colony's government, and thus over its economy and society. To do that, they began to split the lower classes apart along racial lines. They pushed Indians off their land and enslaved those who fought back. From 1670 to 1715, colonists enslaved between 30,000 and 50,000 Indians. Entire tribes disappeared, and white farmers moved onto their lands.[27]

In 1680, the General Assembly began to drive wedges between black slaves and white servants with a series of regulations establishing greater punishments for black slaves. The assembly pulled all those regulations together in 1705 with the Virginia Slave Codes, laws that gave white servants legal rights they had not had before. They could, for example, sue a master who did not adequately feed or clothe them, or who treated them too harshly. The codes also permitted servants to own property. Most significant, though, the codes established that white servants could not be held to servitude after they turned twenty-four years old.[28]

Slaves, though, had no rights. The codes determined that anyone who could not prove he or she was a Christian in his or her home country was a slave in the colony even if the person converted to Christianity in Virginia. This rule meant that those who hailed from Africa, even if they came by way of the Caribbean colonies, were automatically slaves. Since the codes established that children followed the condition of their mother, racial slavery was now officially hereditary.[29]

Under the codes, enslaved individuals had no right to property, their bodies, or even their lives. Churchwardens were charged with seizing all cattle, hogs, and horses that had previously belonged to slaves, selling the animals, and using the proceeds to support the poor. There was no longer any such thing as upward mobility for black colonists. There was no longer any safety for their bodies, either. The Slave Codes established that runaways could legally be dismembered to discourage them from running away again. If a master happened to kill a slave in the process of "correcting" him or her, the codes established, the master was not liable for murder; he "shall be free and acquit of all punishment and accusation for the same, as if such an incident had never happened."[30]

The Slave Codes made it costly for white colonists to fraternize across race lines. People of color could not own white Christians, which meant that if any master married a person of color, his white servants would immediately become free. Any white person attempting to marry across race lines would be fined and sent to jail, and the minister performing such a marriage would be fined the astonishing price of ten thousand pounds of tobacco. White servant women who had mixed-race children either had to pay a whopping fine or have their term of service extended for five years. The child would be a slave until he or she was thirty-one years old.[31]

The codes also encouraged white servants to turn against their black comrades. Slaves could not hit any white Christian, including a servant, without facing a penalty of thirty lashes on his or her bare back. At the same time, a master could not whip a naked white servant. Nakedness was appropriate only for "savages," which, the law suggested, did not include white servants. The lives of white servants were still harsh, but at least they were treated as human. Their black neighbors were not.[32]

As leaders bound African Americans more tightly into slavery, they courted white Virginians into joining the cultural and social world from which they had previously been excluded. After Bacon's Rebellion, members of the elite jockeyed to solidify their position. The search for majorities always results in either greater disfranchisement or wider suffrage, and in this case, leaders reached out to poor white men for their victories. The assembly passed laws requiring masters to provide white servants with food and clothing, as well as money to set themselves up after they earned their freedom. This, combined with a booming tobacco market, enabled more white men to buy land. At the same time, the assembly reduced the poll tax, bringing more men into the body politic and giving them the vote.[33]

The Tidewater elite reached out to their less prosperous neighbors, rubbing elbows with poorer white men in taverns and welcoming them into their imposing homes to emphasize that they were all friends. Indeed, the needs of poor white landowners were not all that different from those of wealthier planters, and it was easy to believe that all Virginia voters had the same interests. They understood what it meant to be under the thumb of a tyrant, for they saw enslaved people and their enslavers all around them. They believed that owning land made a man independent, for that was their experience. And, unlike the royal officials who used their offices to enrich their friends, Virginia voters could argue that they had the best interests of the country at heart. They were free and independent. They were, one might say, equal.[34]

And there began the paradox. The very men who adhered most vigorously to the Enlightenment concept that all men were created equal held slaves. Indeed, their new, radical concept of freedom depended on slavery, for slavery permanently removed the underclass from any hope of influencing government. Virginia leaders had gotten rid of the problem of the poor in society: they had enslaved them. And, of course, they had gotten rid of the problem of women by reading them out of personhood altogether. What was left—ideologically, anyway— was a minority of people running the government, a body politic dedicated to the needs of men of property. And members of that body politic were—ideologically, anyway—identifiable by the handy metric of their skin color.

The pattern of division between black and white soon began to seem natural and proper, even God-given. White men began to believe that they were inherently superior to black men. They argued that the guidance of superior white men was all that kept black men from a savagery similar to that of animals. It was a burden for white men, to be sure, they thought, but it was their duty.

It was this mindset that southern leaders like Thomas Jefferson brought to their declaration that "all men are created equal." Since most white men could not conceive of a world in which men of color had rights equal to theirs—and they certainly didn't think women did—they believed that the fact white men had equal rights meant that the nation was dedicated to the ideal of human equality. When royal officials offered freedom to slaves who fought for the Crown during the Revolution and urged Indians to attack the revolutionaries, the gulf widened between white men, on the one hand, and Indians and slaves, on the other.[35]

That distinction was carried into the founding document of the American nation. Without irony, Virginian James Madison crafted the Constitution to guarantee that wealthy slaveholders would control the new government. Under the new system, which counted slaves as three-fifths of a person for purposes of representation, Virginia commanded an astonishing 21 electoral votes, 15.9 percent of the total votes in the Electoral College, the highest percentage of votes controlled by a single state in American history. Poor white men did not achieve actual economic and social equality with society's leaders, but those leaders did not have to worry about challenges to their privilege. Their lower-class white neighbors got the benefit of believing they were on the same level as rich men, because they shared the same racial identity. They would not revolt, because preserving the distinction between themselves and slaves was more important than seeking political power.

So in America, the radical idea that all men were created equal depended on the traditional idea that all men were created unequal and that a few wealthy men should control the government, and therefore the lives, of women and men of color. This is the paradox that sits at the heart of our nation. We have the radical capacity to "make the world anew," as Thomas Paine said, so that our government truly reflects human equality. But that idea assumed that some people were better than others, and that social hierarchies were natural—or even dictated by God. Natural leaders should govern the mudsills.

From its founding, America has stood at the nexus of democracy and oligarchy. And as soon as the nation was established, its history of conflating class and race gave an elite the language to take over the government and undermine democracy.

CHAPTER 2

The Triumph of Equality

At the time of the Constitution's ratification in 1787, it was not yet obvious that a contradiction lay at the heart of the nation's founding principles. For all its shortcomings, the accomplishment of white male equality under the law was extraordinary, and the concept of equality seemed to define the new country. Americans, or at least the white male Americans who dominated popular culture, rallied around the image of the independent farmer. They argued that their new system made their nation different from the Old World, which was split between a corrupt aristocracy and the lazy poor. The vast expanses of land to the west made Americans think they could avoid the class system of Europe and create the world anew on the basis of human equality. But the fundamental contradiction remained, and could not stay unaddressed forever.

Central to the question of how to create a successful government was the question "What then is the American, this new man?," as recent French immigrant Hector St. John de Crèvecoeur put it in 1782. Crèvecoeur declared that the American was the hardworking farmer who earned a living by the sweat of his brow. Since he could keep the rewards of his industry, Crèvecoeur wrote, such a man labored not because he was forced to but because it was in his own interest. Through their own hard work, he and his self-reliant neighbors enjoyed economic security.[1]

That self-reliance had political significance. Thomas Jefferson believed that farmers were central to democracy because they were independent. Merchants and wage workers depended on pleasing their customers or their employers, and thus could not vote freely. Farmers could. "Those who labour in the earth are the chosen people of God, if ever he had a chosen people," Jefferson wrote in *Notes on the State of Virginia*, the book in which he explained America to a French correspondent. In their "breasts he has made his peculiar deposit for substantial and genuine virtue. It is the focus in which he keeps alive that sacred fire, which otherwise might escape from the face of the earth."[2]

Neither Crèvecoeur nor Jefferson imagined that the ideal American might be a woman. For all that Abigail Adams reminded her husband, John, to "remember the Ladies" in that revolutionary year of 1776, because "all men would be tyrants if they could," and for all that women were as important to the economy as men were, the Founders did not really consider them equal citizens. Instead, they incorporated women into the body politic through their capacity as mothers, responsible for teaching their sons virtue and republican principles. This both gave women a social role in the maintenance of the republic and gave men a domestic foil against which they could define their public behavior. As a man worked in the fields, sold his goods at market, argued about politics, and voted, his wife nurtured national principles and his children both, beside the hearth at home.[3]

The outlines of the new American man really took shape after the War of 1812, largely because it wasn't entirely clear until then that the nation would actually become independent of England. After the Revolution, British officials simply pulled back to Canada and to western forts and bided their time, cultivating Indian allies and expecting the squabbling former colonists to tear their republic apart. But with independence finally secured in 1815, Americans embarked on a period of economic growth and political stability dubbed the "Era of Good Feelings." They set out to define the "national character," avidly reading what visitors wrote about the new nation: Frances Trollope's *Domestic Manners of the Americans* (1832), Alexis de Tocqueville's *Democracy in America* (1835), and Michel Chevalier's *Society, Manners and Politics in the United States* (1839).[4]

They also began to speculate on what made the nation different from European countries. In 1823, novelist James Fenimore Cooper's *The Pioneers* identified the American landscape as the key to the nation's identity. Two years later, in 1825, painter Thomas Cole launched the Hudson River School with sweeping landscapes that offered dramatic contrasts of shade and light, blasted trees and fertile fields, rugged mountains and tranquil waters, depicting a country that reflected the sublimity of God. Men fit naturally into Cole's landscapes, absorbing the spiritual qualities of the land as they nurtured fields and forged villages out of wilderness. Cole's friend Asher Durand, a painter in his own right, explained that the landscape showed God by revealing his creations.[5]

If God was manifest in the land, surely the political system built in that land was also divinely inspired. Most white Americans played down that they lived in a slaveholding republic, and instead celebrated democracy as the nation's unique contribution to the world. While Europe was mired in oligarchy, Americans had faith that God had made them capable of managing their own affairs. Democrats saw

Andrew Jackson, the hero of the Battle of New Orleans in the War of 1812, as the champion of the small farmer despite the fact he was, in reality, a wealthy slave-owning planter. In 1828, they elected him president to stand against established wealth and the mercantile men. Four years later, claiming to protect "the farmers, mechanics, and laborers" from "the rich and powerful," Jackson destroyed the national bank that stabilized currency and regulated credit. The rise of unregulated "wildcat" banks helped to push the nation into a full-fledged economic crisis by 1837, and it looked to worried observers as if enthusiasm for American democracy was losing ground to older notions of an economic and political system dominated by the wealthy.[6]

To hold back the tide, editor John O'Sullivan launched a magazine called the *Democratic Review* to create a self-consciously democratic literature that would promote American ideals. "We have an abiding confidence in the virtue, intelligence, and full capacity for self-government, of the great mass of our people—our industrious, honest, manly, intelligent millions of freemen," O'Sullivan wrote in October 1837. The men who worked directly with nature, the "sons of toil," had special access to wisdom, and they would enable America to lead the countries of the world toward "true theory of government": democracy. Published in New York, the *Democratic Review* tapped into the flourishing literary circles of the East Coast, featuring the work of William Cullen Bryant, Nathaniel Hawthorne, Herman Melville, and the young poet Walter (as he called himself then) Whitman. Theirs was the voice of a new, growing America, a Young America. "I hear America singing," Whitman crowed in one of his famous poems. He gave voice to mechanics, carpenters, masons, boatmen, and woodcutters, "young fellows, robust, friendly," the hard workers building the nation.[7]

The idea that American democracy was simply an exuberant celebration of the individual was wishful thinking, for the growing strength of slavery in the South told a different story. Slavery had bedeviled the nation since its founding, although no one had expected it to be a long-term issue. When the Founders wrote the Constitution, most of the new states practiced human slavery, but they thought the institution would eventually die out. And so it did in the North, where the short growing season meant enslaved labor was never particularly profitable. The South's long hot summers and rich, well-drained soil were perfect for cotton, though, and in 1793, only five years after the Constitution went into effect, Eli Whitney, a Massachusetts man gone south to make his fortune, invented the cotton gin, which made it easy to separate cotton fibers from the sticky seeds and increased cotton production tenfold. Suddenly cotton became an enormously valuable crop.

Under Jackson, southerners determined to get in on the cotton boom adjusted their vision of democracy to justify their seizure of vast swaths of land owned by the Cherokees and Chickasaws. The Cherokees had embraced formal education, adopted a constitution, and even developed a capitalist economy, including slave owning. They had launched their own newspaper, the *Cherokee Phoenix*, in 1828, and some of their leaders lived in plantation homes that rivaled those of local white elites. Jacksonians nonetheless defined their Indian neighbors as "savages," ignoring their assimilation and appropriating their land. In 1830, Congress passed the Indian Removal Act, forcing southeastern tribes to leave their lands and walk a thousand miles to Oklahoma on a journey known as the Trail of Tears. By the end of the 1830s, the frontier state of Mississippi was the nation's biggest cotton producer.[8]

Newly opened lands would create a feverish cycle of boom and bust, and land hunger continued. In 1835, revolutionaries split the Republic of Texas off from Mexico, and the following year asked Congress for admission to the Union. Most Americans opposed adding the slaveholding Republic of Texas, and pointed out that the lands there still belonged to Mexico. Southern Democrats backed the acquisition. Adherents of what was called the Young America Movement argued that Americans had a political, moral, and religious duty—a "manifest destiny"—to spread democracy around the world . . . and across the continent.[9]

Southern white men embraced a political vision based on individual hard work, and increasingly read all but themselves out of the equation. Americans were hard workers, earning their way in the world and creating a new form of government as they did so. The institution of slavery was an example of true democracy at work, they argued: the voting members of each state should determine the domestic institutions within that state. Slavery was emphatically a local question, so it was not a spoiler for the great triumph of democracy. They also ignored the rights of Indians, arguing that since democracy based in tilling the soil was the highest form of human civilization, it naturally overawed the "barbarians" with whom it came in contact. Indians would either be absorbed or die out. Texas and lands to the southwest, full of Mexicans, naturally belonged to America because they lay in the great Mississippi Valley. It was only a question of time until they joined the Union.[10]

By the 1840s, Americans had revised Crèvecoeur's new man. He was a white farmer, working hard to move up in society. He was the subject of poems, novels, travelogues, and lithographs. And he and democracy were tied together through America's special landscape. But in the South, that vision of democracy nourished oligarchy.

★

By the 1840s, the North and the South presented two very different economies. Most men in the North worked their own farms and made a living pulling wheat and corn out of the soil or cod out of the ocean, tending cattle and sheep, making shoes, cutting wood, or building houses, or they earned wages helping someone else do those things. Their wives and daughters spun thread and wove cloth, gardened, and tended children. The majority of Americans worked in professions tied directly to the land, or only a step from it, and youngsters could expect to do better than their fathers.[11]

But in the South, wealth was concentrating at the top. In an extractive economy, society revolves around the highly capitalized production of a single export. The cotton economy was an agricultural version: finance, politics, and society all revolved around cotton. Such an economy always creates a powerful elite, as ordinary people are either shut out of the market or reduced to working for those within it. Like other extractive industries, cotton required cheap labor, and lots of it. Cotton offered huge profits, but only to those who had enough money to monopolize large tracts of good land and to command gangs of workers. Rich planters monopolized both. Yet as they concentrated wealth and power in their own hands, wealthy southerners still insisted that they were simply farmers, and that their system embodied the equality the Founders intended. Any restrictions on their affairs, they said, infringed on their liberty. Increasingly, they defined American democracy as a fixed hierarchy.[12]

Tensions between slaveholders and non-slaveholders began in the early years of the Republic. The population in the North quickly outgrew that of the South, and in the House of Representatives, where each state's representatives are allotted according to population, the North called the shots. The South maintained parity in the Senate, where each state has two senators. After the War of 1812 ended, settlers in Maine wanted to break off from Massachusetts and become a state. Southerners insisted on balancing the statehood of Maine, where slavery was banned, with a new slave state, Missouri.

Opponents of the Missouri Compromise swamped Congress with petitions against admitting Missouri as a slave state, and they resented that slave owners in the Senate could hold the state of Maine hostage until they got their way. Tempers rose high enough that Thomas Jefferson wrote to Massachusetts (and later Maine) Senator John Holmes that he had for a long time been content with the direction of the country, but that the Missouri question, "like a fire bell in the night, awakened and filled me with terror. I considered it at once as the knell of the Union. It is hushed indeed for the moment, but this is a reprieve only, not a final sentence." To head off further trouble, Congress added another piece to the Missouri Compromise it passed in 1820: it drew a line just below Missouri and banned slavery above that line.[13]

After 1820, northerners who objected to slavery on moral grounds continued their petition drive, now trying to get Congress to whittle away at slavery where it could—by outlawing slave auctions in the nation's capital, for example. They focused on the immorality of slavery and never gained much traction in the general population—people tended to think of moral reformers as cranks. In the mid-1830s, these abolitionists adopted new tactics that did take hold. In 1831, a newspaper reporter who had taken part in the petition drive, William Lloyd Garrison, launched *The Liberator* out of Boston, pledging that he would be "as harsh as truth, and as uncompromising as justice." Garrison warned that slave owners were accumulating too much political power in the federal government.

For their part, as the economic system that was making a few of them so wealthy came under attack, white southerners who had once looked at slavery with distaste began to change their minds. In August 1831, enslaved Virginian Nat Turner led a rebellion that sped up that shift. Highly intelligent, deeply religious, and well educated for his time, Turner defied white definitions of a treacherous "savage." When he led seventy followers to kill more than fifty-five of their white neighbors, whites in slave states panicked. In the aftermath of the rebellion, courts and mobs executed 120 African Americans. Reaching beyond suspected rebels, state legislatures across the South also outlawed educating slaves and prohibited slaves from practicing religion without the supervision of white people.

Attacks from northern reformers and the Nat Turner Rebellion cemented white southern sentiment. Abolishing slavery once and for all would have solved the problem, and Virginia contemplated it, but that impulse died as cotton boomed in the 1830s. Land in Mississippi and Georgia taken from the Indians invited cotton speculation, and new textile factories in the North processed as much of the fiber as the South could produce. The price of cotton began to rise, and the industry spread. Rather than continuing to debate ending slavery, southern whites began to argue in favor of it.[14]

John Pendleton Kennedy's sketches of southern life, published in 1832 as *Swallow Barn; or A Sojourn in the Old Dominion*, helped to create the southern plantation myth. It offered a vision of a genteel world, where patriarchs oversaw their dependent slaves and indulged their wives and daughters, and was in part a reflection of the fact that the old world of the Virginia Tidewater planters was giving way to the speculative cotton boom in the Southwest, with its dicey financing, slave traders, and lower-class entrepreneurs. The patriarchs of this new society were modeled on the British aristocracy. They were not consumed by the desire to make money, as northerners supposedly were; they were chivalrous, skilled horsemen with fine manners and courage, who protected their dependents and defended their own honor.[15]

It was a portrait of a hierarchical society. Planters were planters and slaves were slaves, and slavery civilized black "savages" by placing them among good Christians. While abolitionists argued that slavery was immoral, southern ministers pointed out that slavery had precedents in the Bible and in ancient Greece and Rome, and that the Founders themselves had held slaves. They rejected the Enlightenment idea of human equality, arguing instead that God's law naturally created hierarchies in society, which should be modeled on a family structure based in paternalism. Increasingly, slaveholders bought into this vision and dehumanized their slaves, both brutalizing them in a constant demonstration of white men's dominance and caricaturing them as lazy, stupid, comical figures, stereotypes picked up in popular minstrel shows, where white men blacked their faces with burnt cork, sang catchy tunes like "Jump Jim Crow," and acted the parts of society's fools.[16]

Southern apologists also began to mythologize white women as pure beings to be protected from the world—a characterization that ignored the reality that most white women were wage workers—while also lumping them, too, at the bottom of the social hierarchy. In an 1836 novel written by a Virginia gentleman, a character named George Balcombe, one of society's elders, explains to a younger man with notions of equality that God has given everyone a place in society. Women and African Americans were at the bottom, "subordinate" to white men by design. "All women live by marriage," he says in one of his many long passages about women's proper sphere. "It is their only duty." Trying to make them equal was a cruelty. "For my part," says Balcombe, "I am well pleased with the established order of the universe. I see . . . subordination everywhere. And when I find the subordinate content . . . and recognizing his place . . . as that to which he properly belongs, I am content to leave him there." Women were made "to breed," as "toy[s] for recreation," or to bring men "wealth and position," leading South Carolina planter James Henry Hammond explained to his son in 1852. If women and black people were at the bottom, southern white men were an "aristocracy" by virtue of their descent from "the ancient cavaliers of Virginia . . . a race of men without fear and without reproach," "alike incapable of servility and selfishness." Any man outside that class was excluded because of his own failings or criminal inclinations.[17]

In the 1840s, the majority of white southern men, who worked their own fields alongside their wives and children and, if they were wealthy enough, owned one or two enslaved people, fell into the category Balcombe celebrated. These "plain folk" shared the democratic work ethic, believing they could rise if only they worked hard enough, and they shared the same sense of mastery over their dependents that wealthier men had. They disdained the landless whites, the "drones, vagabonds, bums, deadbeats, deadheads, nobodies, [and] damned rapscallions" who had a reputation for shiftlessness and an unfortunate fondness for hunting, fishing, and whiskey. They also outright rejected the idea of working for someone else, or menial work, which was "servile." Yet as the value of cotton continued to climb and the men at the top made enormous fortunes, the wealthiest southerners began to talk of their hardworking neighbors as "clodhoppers" who lacked brains, education, and money.[18]

By midcentury, cotton was the country's leading export by far, with the South producing almost 1 billion pounds of it in 1850 and more than 2 billion pounds in 1860. Southern cotton made up about four-fifths of all the cotton England processed in its mills, and all that northerners processed. Cotton was everywhere in the South—along wharves, on ships, on carts crowding southern towns, in piles as tall as houses. It dominated society, shaping labor, transportation, money, and religion around the demands of the region's richest cotton planters, who were also the richest Americans, with South Carolina's Wade Hampton, for example, netting more than $200,000 annually at a time when $300 was a good income. Planters drank French wine under their European masterpieces in one of their several homes; their wives had access to fine silks, novels, and even that exotic product olive oil.[19]

By 1853, a magazine called *The American Cotton Planter* was dedicated to cotton, the crop on which "the planter of the South, the farmer of the West and North-West, the manufacturer of the North, the merchants of the whole country, the Steamboat of the rivers, the coasting Vessel, the Rail Road and even the Telegraph" all depended. The wealth produced by cotton had dramatically upgraded living conditions, proving that enslaved labor conferred "inappreciable blessings" of "human progress and prosperity" on all of mankind, including the slaves themselves, who were "carried along with the onward current of improvement."[20]

Cotton depended on slavery—as did the valuable crops of sugar and coffee—and southern leaders recoiled at the idea of emancipation. Indeed, in the face of Great Britain's abolition of slavery in 1833, they set out to protect and spread slavery throughout the Western Hemisphere. They began at home, increasing punishments for anyone who questioned slavery. Distributing anti-slavery literature brought whipping, imprisonment, or death. Vigilante committees formed and worked alongside slave patrols to intimidate poor whites who talked about land reform or workers' rights, appeared to be insufficiently supportive of the slave system, or seemed too friendly with their black neighbors. Such men were accused of being closet abolitionists and were whipped out of town or lynched as an example to others.[21]

On March 4, 1858, prominent South Carolina slaveholder James Henry Hammond gave a speech in the Senate—to which he had been elected the year before despite the fact that his promising early political career had been nearly derailed when he admitted that for two years he had sexually assaulted his four young nieces, the daughters of the powerful Wade Hampton II (although he insisted he was being wronged because he should get credit for showing any restraint at all when faced with four such "lovely creatures"). Hammond embodied the hierarchy that enabled white planters to dominate their society, and his speech revealed how completely politics, society, and religion had come to spin around the southern oligarchy. The southern system, Hammond announced, was "the best in the world . . . such as no other people ever enjoyed upon the face of the earth," and spreading it would benefit everyone. If northerners persisted in trying to limit the extension of slavery, Hammond warned, it would come to war, one that the South would win. The South was the richest region in the world. It provided the world's key product. Southern leaders could bring any country on earth to its knees just by threatening to cut off its supply of cotton. "Cotton is king," Hammond declared.[22]

Still, the greatest strength of the South was not its economy, Hammond said, but rather "the harmony of her political and social institutions." Every society had "a class to do the menial duties, to perform the drudgery of life." Those people were the vast majority, and they made up the "mudsill" of society, supporting "that other class which leads progress, civilization, and refinement." The men in the latter group were intelligent and well connected, educated and wealthy; they recognized fine art and culture and understood the economy. In the South, whites had made an "inferior" race into the mudsills, dull but loyal people who were content to have their labor directed by their betters and to have no say in their government. The system operated in perfect harmony.

The North had no such happy arrangement. Northerners turned white men into mudsills, and then permitted them to vote. Since they could not comprehend what was best for society and simply wanted short-term gratification, they would vote to confiscate the wealth of their betters. They were a majority, Hammond warned, and if they combined politically, "where would you be? Your society would be reconstructed, your government overthrown, your property divided." It was only southern leaders who had kept mudsills from creating "anarchy and poverty" by insisting that the government could do absolutely nothing but protect property, no matter how many voters insisted that it take a more active role in society. Democracy did not mean that voters should actually "exercise political power in detail." They could simply elect one set of leaders or another.

Hammond concluded his address by warning northerners that— unlike them—slave owners were acting on principle "involving all our rights and all our interests." It was imperative that the South control the Union.[23]

★

The conviction among the elite slave owners that they were the nation's true leaders, the inheritors of the Founders' vision of equality, ran headlong into the reality that they were in a minority. In the years after 1825, when the Erie Canal had opened the Atlantic seaboard to the Great Lakes, the Midwest had grown at a fantastic pace. At the same time, the rise of industrial mills fed urban areas, and canals and nascent railroads had developed the northern countryside. By 1850, the North had more than 13 million people to the South's 9 million, of whom more than 3 million were enslaved. Even that didn't tell the whole story. In 1850, there were 347,525 slaveholders in America, out of a white population of about 6 million in slave states. But fewer than 8,000 slaveholders owned more than fifty people, and fewer than 1,800 owned more than a hundred. By 1850, then, large planters made up less than 1 percent of the slaveholding population and even less of the national population of 23 million. They knew they were in numerical trouble. To retain their power in the federal government, they began to attack the foundations of democracy, step by step, until they took over the Democratic Party and used it to try to take over the country.[24]

They started by censoring ideological attacks on slavery. When northern reformers tried to circulate anti-slavery literature to prominent southern white men through the federal mails in summer 1835, postmasters refused to deliver the packages, and mobs broke into the post offices, seized the mail, and burned it. The next year, when abolitionists flooded Congress with petitions asking it to curtail slavery in Washington, D.C., southern congressmen passed a "gag rule" in the House, automatically tabling all such petitions. Many people who didn't care much at all about the morality of slavery cared quite a bit about the ability of a political minority to censor the federal mails, and they took seriously the constitutional right of citizens to petition their government. Slave owners, now organized politically, seemed to be strangling white Americans' civil liberties.

Then slave owners stopped northerners from checking the spread of slavery. When southerners began to talk about annexing Texas after the 1836 Texas Revolution, northerners worried that new slave states would overawe the northern states in Congress and make slavery national. Northerners in the House of Representatives tried to ban slavery from any territory taken from Mexico with a proposal called the Wilmot Proviso, but southerners killed the measure in the Senate. The issue of the extension of slavery remained unresolved when the Mexican-American War ended in 1848 with the transfer of the Southwest—including what is now California, Nevada, Arizona, Utah, and much of New Mexico, Colorado, and Texas—from Mexico to the United States. Congress addressed rising tensions by cobbling together a complicated truce, but the Compromise of 1850 would not last.

The rush to organize the new western lands forced slave owners to up their game, pushing for the extension of slavery into lands that had previously been set aside for freedom. The arduous 1,500-mile journey to California shattered both wagons and people, and there was talk of building a transcontinental railroad to ease the trip. Democratic Senator Stephen A. Douglas of Illinois, an advocate of the Young America Movement, wanted the nation's central railroad hub to be in Chicago, which was still new and raw, instead of New Orleans, which was the obvious city for a railroad hub since it was established, wealthy, and located at the mouth of the busy Mississippi River. The differences in size and importance might be overcome, but New Orleans had an insurmountable advantage: legally, a railroad company could not build through any land that did not have an officially organized territorial government to approve the construction. The route from New Orleans to California passed through organized territories; the majority of the land west of Chicago was still controlled by Lakotas and Cheyennes.[25]

As chairman of the Senate Committee on Territories, Douglas introduced a bill to organize that land. It was above the Missouri Compromise line and thus should have been free, but Douglas's southern Democratic colleagues warned him they would never agree to admit another free territory unless it were balanced with a slave territory, and there was no more land available for one of those. So Douglas introduced the Kansas-Nebraska Act, separating the remaining unorganized part of the Louisiana Purchase—land that had been designated as free under the Missouri Compromise— into two large territories: Kansas (which included much of what is now Colorado) and Nebraska (including today's Nebraska, but also much of what is now Wyoming, Montana, North Dakota, and South Dakota). The status of slavery in those territories would be decided by the voters, though the senators' unstated expectation was that Kansas would have slaves while Nebraska would be free.

Outraged northerners pointed out that the South had gotten everything it could under the Missouri Compromise, and now that it was the North's turn, the rules changed.

The bill passed the Senate, in the face of extraordinary public outcry. Despite popular fury at the measure, Democratic president Franklin Pierce put enormous pressure on members of the House to pass it. They did, finally, on May 8, 1854. The passage of the Kansas-Nebraska Act turned the Democratic Party into the party of slaveholders. In the 1854 elections, voters in the North threw Democrats out of office; only those in the most extreme districts managed to hold onto power. By 1855, moderate Democrats were gone, and slave owners had taken control of the national party.

Their control showed in the way events played out over Kansas. The Kansas-Nebraska Act provided that the settlers would decide the status of slavery there, but didn't spell out when. Determined to maintain control of Congress, slaveholders resorted to fraud. In the first territorial election, pro-slavery men crossed the border from Missouri and swamped the polls, setting up a pro-slavery legislature. Since most Kansas settlers actually opposed the establishment of slavery, free-state men soon set up their own legislature. President Pierce declared the free-state legislature illegal and threw his weight behind the unpopular pro-slavery government.

On May 22, 1856, while a congressional committee tried to figure out whether the proslavery territorial government was legitimate, a southern Democratic congressman beat a northern senator nearly to death on the Senate floor. Massachusetts Senator Charles Sumner was sitting at his desk writing letters when South Carolina Representative Preston Brooks, a man famous for little aside from his violent temper, came up behind Sumner with a walking stick and beat him bloody as a number of Democratic senators looked on. Sumner had just delivered an inflammatory two-day speech against the Pierce administration's attempt to force slavery on an anti-slavery majority in Kansas, laying out the case that the nation was under siege by an oligarchy that was destroying the civil rights that American citizens had won in their revolution against the oligarchy of England. Only three days later, the front page of the *New York Times* declared: "HIGHLY IMPORTANT FROM KANSAS—THE WAR BEGUN." On May 21, pro-slavery men had attacked the headquarters of the Free-Staters at Lawrence, Kansas, looting the town. These two violent assaults, coming so close together that they seemed to be part of a concerted plan, proved to many northerners that a cabal—a "Slave Power," as its opponents put it—was going to war against democracy itself.[26]

In June 1856, the Democrats tried to sidestep their association with the slaveholding elite by nominating for president a political wheel horse who had been out of the country during the troubles of the past three years. As Minister to the United Kingdom, Pennsylvania's James Buchanan had not participated in the Kansas crisis. He won when a majority of voters split their ballots between the two candidates running who opposed the Slave Power. On March 4, 1857, in the Senate Chamber, Chief Justice Roger Taney swore Buchanan into office. In his Inaugural Address, Buchanan promised that a permanent solution to the question of slavery in Kansas was at hand, as the Supreme Court was about to hand down a decision in a case that had been postponed from the previous session. "To their decision, in common with all good citizens, I shall cheerfully submit, whatever this may be," Buchanan declared.[27]

Two days later, the Supreme Court handed down the *Dred Scott* decision, which gave slave owners everything they wanted. It declared that African Americans were not citizens and "had no rights which the white man was bound to respect," and that Congress could not prohibit slavery in the territories, because the Constitution required the protection of property, including slaves. Therefore, the Missouri Compromise, which had protected freedom in the Northwest, was unconstitutional. Northerners were outraged. "Any slave-driving editor or Virginia bar-room politician could have taken the Chief Justice's place on the bench and . . . nobody would have perceived the difference," wrote Horace Greeley in the *New-York Daily Tribune*.[28]

The mechanics of the decision seemed almost as corrupt as the ruling itself. It had been postponed until after the election, and Buchanan's willingness to endorse it two days earlier made it seem that he was in on Taney's scheme. This turned out to be true: the president had pressured a northern justice to side with the southerners.[29]

Even white southerners could see that an oligarchy was taking over America. The cotton boom of the 1850s left poor farmers' economic stability teetering, and in 1857, Hinton Rowan Helper, from North Carolina, noted that this growing class divide in the South could be resolved if only poor white southerners rose up to end slavery, not out of morality or concern for slaves but for their own self-interest. "Non-slaveholders of the South!" Helper wrote in his book, *The Impending Crisis of the South*. "Farmers, mechanics and working-men . . . the slaveholders, the arrogant demagogues whom you have elected to offices of honor and profit, have hoodwinked you, trifled with you, and used you. . . . They have purposely kept you in ignorance, and have, by moulding your passions and prejudices to suit themselves, induced you to act in direct opposition to your dearest rights and interests." Helper's book was a bestseller: between 1857 and 1860, 140,000 copies sold, about half as many as the phenomenon *Uncle Tom's Cabin* in the same period.[30]

Meanwhile, out in the frontier state of Illinois, a prosperous Springfield attorney was convinced that elite slave owners were trying to turn American democracy into an oligarchy. Abraham Lincoln had come from the dirt poverty of subsistence farming, cobbled together an education and connections, and risen to distinction in his adopted state. He had watched the rise of the Slave Power with trepidation and had recently thrown his lot in with the new Republican Party, whose members had come together after Congress passed the Kansas-Nebraska bill. In 1858, Illinois Republican leaders jumped at the chance to nominate him for Stephen A. Douglas's Senate seat.

In his speech accepting the nomination, Lincoln outlined his fears for democracy. The nation could not survive half slave and half free, he warned; it would soon become all one or all the other. He pointed out that at the beginning of 1854, half the states in the Union had been reserved for freedom. Then Douglas had argued that only settlers could decide the slavery question, and Pierce forced the Democrats to pass the Kansas-Nebraska Act. Taney's *Dred Scott* decision stopped Congress from banning the spread of slavery, and Buchanan sided with the pro-slavery minority in Kansas, ignoring the idea of majority rule so long as the Slave Power won. Lincoln warned, "when we see . . . timbers joined together, and see they exactly make the frame of a house or a mill . . . we find it impossible not to believe that Stephen and Franklin and Roger and James all understood one another from the beginning, and all worked upon a common *plan* or *draft* drawn up before the first lick was struck."[31]

Dogged by Lincoln, Douglas finally agreed to a series of joint debates before the 1858 election. They enabled Lincoln to press Douglas on how settlers could keep slavery out of the West when the *Dred Scott* decision said the opposite. Douglas answered that even though the Supreme Court had said that settlers couldn't exclude slavery, they really could, because they could simply refuse to pass local ordinances protecting slavery. Slave owners realized that he was right, and demanded that the federal government not just allow slavery in the West but protect it there as well. They wanted a federal slave code. In 1854, the federal government had defended freedom in the West. Now, four years later, southern slave owners were demanding the government defend slavery there. Lincoln did not unseat Douglas in the Senate in 1858, but he made clear to a national audience that the timbers in the oligarchic house of slavery were dropping neatly into place.

★

Now a national figure, Lincoln articulated a democratic vision for America, one that refuted the mudsill vision of Senator Hammond. On September 30, 1859, before farmers at the state fair in Milwaukee,

Lincoln explained that Hammond's "mud-sill theory" divided the world into permanent castes: capitalists driving the economy and workers stuck at the bottom. But there was another theory: that workers, not capitalists, drove the economy, and hardworking men could—and should—rise. This latter "free labor" theory articulated the true meaning of American democracy for northerners and for the non-slave-holding southerners, who, as Lincoln reminded his listeners, made up a majority in the South. "The prudent, penniless beginner in the world, labors for wages awhile, saves a surplus with which to buy tools or land, for himself; then labors on his own account another while, and at length hires another new beginner to help him," he explained. Unlike in the mudsill theory, those at the bottom were there not because of a caste system, but because of improvidence, folly, or singular bad luck. If able, they were free to move up.[32]

In the election of 1860, voters decided whether America should embrace the mudsill theory or the free labor theory. Worried when the Democratic Party itself refused to adopt their vision—in 1860 it split in two, and the more moderate wing backed Stephen Douglas—southern planters were terrified they would lose control over the government. So they bolted from the official Democratic Party to nominate their own presidential ticket, calling for the federal government to protect slavery throughout the West—just as Lincoln had predicted. Then they wrote ballots that excluded Lincoln's Republicans, kept poor white voters from the polls, and flooded media with warnings that if Republicans won, they would free the slaves, who would both take white men's jobs and attack their women. Andrew Henry, the editor of the *West Alabamian* newspaper, wrote that white men would have to "submit to have our wives and daughters chose [*sic*] between death and gratifying the hellish lust of the negro!! Submit to have our children murdered, our dwellings burnt and our country desolated!!"

In this formulation, anyone who did not support the southern extremists—including fellow Democrats who preferred a more moderate Democrat for president—was dangerous and must be harried out of town and kept away from the polls. It was a "reign of terror," the British consul reported. "Persons are torn away from their residences and pursuits; sometimes 'tarred and feathered'; 'ridden upon rails,' or cruelly whipped; letters are opened at the Post Offices; discussion upon slavery is entirely prohibited under penalty of expulsion, with or without violence, from the country." When Lincoln won nonetheless, making it clear that the federal government would no longer defend the interests of the slaveholders alone, southern leaders took the ultimate step to destroy democracy: they railroaded their states out of the Union to form the Confederate States of America.[33]

In this, southern leaders insisted they were defending the will of God. According to the Confederacy's Vice President, Alexander Stephens of Georgia, the nation's Founders had made a grave error by thinking that "all men are created equal." Addressing an audience on March 21, 1861, he explained that "our new government is founded upon exactly the opposite idea . . . its foundations are laid, its cornerstone rests, upon the great truth that the negro is not equal to the white man; that slavery subordination to the superior race is his natural and normal condition." The Confederacy was the first government in the world to be, as Stephens put it, "based upon this great physical, philosophical, and moral truth," and "if we are true to ourselves, our destiny, and high mission, will become the controlling power on this continent."[34]

Three weeks later, at 4:30 on the morning of April 12, 1861, southern forces began to lob mortar rounds at the federal fort in Charleston Harbor. Thirty-three hours of Confederate shelling with more than 3,000 rounds of ammunition took not a single life on either side (two Union privates died during the formal surrender when a spark exploded a stack of ammunition), but it launched a war that over the course of four years would involve more than 2 million men and cost the government more than $5 billion. (The entire 1861 budget had originally been projected at $62 million.)[35]

In the years before 1860, southern leaders arranged for the government to protect slavery. They kept its functions small to keep it from interfering with what they claimed was an economic institution, except when they wanted the government to exert authority to defend their property rights. When poorer men advocated roads or the dredging of harbors to spur economic growth, Democrats insisted that any federal assumption of economic activity threatened to crush American liberty. The federal government should simply deliver the mails, manage foreign affairs, collect the tariffs, maintain a small military force in the West to push back against Comanches, and, of course, protect slavery. For that, they reversed their position and wanted a powerful government. But when southerners left the Union, they left the nation in the hands of those who believed that the government should do what individuals could not: open the way for poorer men to rise—as Lincoln had called for.

Republicans created a new kind of government, beginning by shifting the nation's finances away from bankers and toward ordinary Americans. At first, Treasury Secretary Salmon P. Chase borrowed from the nation's major bankers to fund the war. But as costs rose to more than $2 million a day and bankers balked at more loans, Chase hired a young financier named Jay Cooke to market government bonds directly to the people. Cooke's campaign was a roaring success; northern men, women, and even former slaves bought $2.5 billion worth of them.[36]

Congress also created a national currency and national banking system that replaced capitalists with popular funding. When bankers demanded control over national financial policy, Congress responded by authorizing the issue of government currency (printed with green ink on the back—hence their nickname, "greenbacks") based not on bankers' capital but instead on the nation's ability to redeem it. Small farmers and wage workers, especially those in the West, loved that the government's solvency now rested with them, and grabbed at the new money "like a duck at a worm," as one congressman put it. But the value of the greenbacks fluctuated, and to stabilize the currency, Congress created national bank notes—currency circulated by new national banks. To establish a national bank, owners had to invest their capital in United States bonds, then issue money secured by those bonds. Because the bonds paid interest in gold, that money didn't fluctuate. Westerners generally liked the inflationary greenbacks and eastern businessmen preferred the stable national bank notes, but both currencies pumped energy into the economy by making it easy for people to do business across state lines.[37]

Congressmen knew that making the nation's finances dependent on the bankers or simply printing money would either bankrupt the country or lead to ruinous inflation, so they also set out to pay for the war by transforming America's tax system. Before the war, America had no national system of taxation. During the Civil War, Congress placed taxes of 5 percent on virtually every item made in America. Since that gave untaxed foreign products an unfair advantage over those made at home, Congress also put new comprehensive tariffs—essentially taxes on imports—on every imported product representatives could think of. "If we bleed manufacturers we must see to it that the proper tonic is administered at the same time," said the author of the tariff bill, Vermont Representative Justin Smith Morrill, "or we shall have destroyed the goose that lays the golden eggs." By the end of the war, tariff rates were pegged at about 47 percent of a product's value.[38]

These taxes and tariffs hit all Americans equally, so the Republican Congress did something truly novel to make sure that "the burdens will be more equalized on all classes of the community, more especially on those who are able to bear them," as Morrill put it. It created an income tax, and a government bureau, the Internal Revenue Bureau—the forerunner to the IRS—to collect it. By the end of the war income taxes stood at 5 percent for incomes from $600 to $5,000, 7.5 percent for incomes from $5,000 to $10,000, and 10 percent for incomes over $10,000. When circumstances warranted it, Morrill explained, the government could demand 99 percent of a man's property. When the nation required it, "the property of the people . . . belongs to the Government." Taxes paid for about 21 percent of the war's cost.[39]

The new federal taxes were overwhelmingly popular. Paying them signaled support for the government and democracy. Even conservative newspapers declared that "there is not the slightest objection raised in any loyal quarter to as much taxation as may be necessary."[40]

Financial legislation was just the start. If Congress was going to tax people, it must also help them make money to pay those taxes. So the Republicans in Congress turned free labor theory into laws. They encouraged immigration and passed the Homestead Act, giving citizens—or immigrants who announced their intention to become citizens—a western farm of up to 160 acres of land after they had lived on it for five years. Congress also brought western territories and states into the Union at rapid-fire pace, both to spread farming and to open up mines. It organized Colorado, Nevada, and Dakota Territories in 1861, Idaho and Arizona Territories in 1863, and Montana Territory and Nevada as a state in 1864. Congressmen planned for the labor of hardworking men to rouse the "giant energy of productiveness" in the West and "pour the wealth of empires at our feet," Horace Greeley wrote in the *New-York Daily Tribune*.[41]

To make sure poor farmers had the latest information and the best seeds, Congress established the Department of Agriculture in spring 1862. "Seed money" was not a waste during wartime, Republicans argued, for, as William Pitt Fessenden, the Chairman of the Senate Finance Committee put it, the country would be "richly paid over and over again in absolute increase of wealth. There is no doubt of that." Then, to make sure that a poor man's son and a rich man's son had the same access to education, Congress passed the Land Grant College Act, providing western land to states to sell in order to fund public colleges. This farsighted law was the basis for the nation's public universities.[42]

Since even educated young men couldn't use western land unless they could get to it, Congress assumed the power to found corporations and created the Union Pacific Railroad Company to bring together the many branch railroads reaching into the western plains and to connect them to the nascent lines in California. Railroad men were reluctant to invest in track heading across barren plains controlled by powerful Indian tribes, so to encourage the project, Congress gave to the company alternate sections of land alongside the track. The Union Pacific directors could sell this land to settlers to raise money. Congress also permitted the Union Pacific to sell bonds up to a certain amount per mile of track laid—more over the mountains, less over the plains—and guaranteed interest costs on the bonds. After a slow start, the project took off in 1864.[43]

The war tied the government to the American people, but it did far more than that. It expanded the definition of who was included in "all men are created equal." On January 1, 1863, Lincoln signed the Emancipation Proclamation, freeing slaves in the lands still under the Confederacy's control. He freed them out of military necessity, since he was trying to weaken the South by taking its manpower, but he went a step further, asking freed slaves to "to abstain from all violence, unless in necessary self-defence; and . . . in all cases when allowed, [to] labor faithfully for reasonable wages." He also declared that African Americans were welcome in the U.S. Army and Navy. The Emancipation Proclamation established that America's free labor economy was indeed open to men of all races, and that black men could fight for the government, traditionally a crucial step toward citizenship.

In his 1863 address at the dedication of a national cemetery for the soldiers killed in battle at Gettysburg, Lincoln acknowledged that the United States was in the midst of "a new birth of freedom." He explicitly tied the nation not to the Constitutional principle of the protection of property, on which slaveholders had based their right to spread slavery across the land, but on the Declaration of Independence, which gave birth to "a new nation, conceived in liberty, and dedicated to the proposition that 'all men are created equal.'" The Gettysburg Address reminded Americans they were engaged in a great test of "whether that nation, or any nation so conceived, and so dedicated, can long endure." He urged them to rededicate themselves to the great cause of America: "that government of the people, by the people for the people, shall not perish from the earth."

They did. When Lincoln was assassinated in 1865 as the war came to an end, the United States government answered to the people rather than to wealthy slave owners. Republicans had brought to life an economy based on the theory of free labor and had destroyed an oligarchic society based on wealth accumulated through enslaved labor. To kill the old system once and for all, Congress wrote and sent off to the states for ratification the Thirteenth Amendment to the Constitution, ending slavery or involuntary servitude except as punishment for a crime. It was the first amendment that increased, rather than decreased, the power of the federal government.

The success of the free labor experiment would change the nation's definition of citizenship. Before the war, the ideal "new American" was a white man with property, but that model had cost the nation 600,000 lives and more than $5 billion. Impoverished black men had fought for the Union and died at higher rates than white Americans. Shouldn't they have a say in that new government of the people, by the people, and for the people? And what about women, who had given their money, muscle, and men to the cause?

Immediately after the war, aided by Lincoln's replacement, President Andrew Johnson, former Confederate leaders tried to reestablish their control over the government and to reinstate their prewar society. They remanded southern African Americans back into a form of quasi slavery with laws called the Black Codes, requiring former slaves to sign year-long labor contracts with white employers and giving them no legal rights to defend their interests. Republicans defended their new vision of America. They crafted the Fourteenth Amendment to the Constitution, declaring that anyone born in America was a citizen entitled to equal protection of the laws.

When southern whites refused to ratify that amendment and instead rioted against their black neighbors and the federal government in Memphis and New Orleans in the summer of 1866, Republicans gave black men the right to vote for delegates to new constitutional conventions charged with writing new constitutions for the southern states. In March 1867, the Military Reconstruction Act put the federal government in charge of protecting black Americans in the South and enrolling voters there. The law explicitly included all men over the age of twenty-one, without regard to "race, color, or previous condition." Leading Republican politician James G. Blaine acknowledged that the Military Reconstruction Act was of "transcendent importance and . . . unprecedented character," a "far-reaching and radical" measure that "changed the political history of the United States."[44]

Under the Military Reconstruction Act, southerners wrote new state constitutions that weakened the power of former elites and included African American men in the body politic. The governments organized under those constitutions ratified the Fourteenth Amendment and were readmitted to the Union, where their representatives had a voice in the national government. When, after readmission, the white members of the Georgia legislature expelled all of their black colleagues, arguing that state laws prohibited African Americans from holding office, Congress protected black equality in government with the Fifteenth Amendment to the Constitution. This amendment guaranteed that the right to vote—and, by extension, the right to hold office—could not be denied or curtailed according to "race, color, or previous condition of servitude." Georgia was required to ratify this amendment as a condition of its restoration to the government in 1870.

The Fifteenth Amendment represented the high-water mark of equality, embedding the principles of the Declaration of Independence into the Constitution. All men were created equal and had a right to have a say in a government that responded to the needs of all, rather than just to the wealthy. It included all American men under the same umbrella, a breathtaking expansion of the democratic idea.

But while the right to vote could not be abridged by race, the amendment said nothing about other restrictions. The United States government could not have prevailed in the Civil War without the support of women, who took over production in the fields and factories when the men went to war, blessed their sons and husbands as they turned soldier, nursed the wounded, and bought bonds to finance the war effort. Surely they had earned a right to a say in the nation's new birth of freedom. But they were not included in the Fourteenth Amendment, and with that amendment the word "male" was added to the Constitution for the first time. When women protested, allies warned them that it was "the Negro's hour," and that women's rights must wait until black men had secured theirs.

Julia Ward Howe, the author of "The Battle Hymn of the Republic," complained that although the male slave had been "not only emancipated, but endowed with the full dignity of citizenship," women were not to be treated the same way. "The women of the North had greatly helped to open the door which admitted him to freedom and its safeguard, the ballot," she continued. "Was this door to be shut in their face?" Elizabeth Cady Stanton and Susan B. Anthony formed the National Woman Suffrage Association, admitting women only and demanding a wide range of legal reforms as well as the vote. Months later, Lucy Stone and Howe herself formed the American Woman Suffrage Association, a more moderate group that admitted men and wanted only the vote for women, believing that, once they could vote, women could defend their own interests by electing representatives who would make sure the laws stopped privileging men.[45]

Briefly, it seemed women might also win equal voices in the American government. In 1869, Wyoming Territory gave women the vote, and the next year Utah followed suit. In 1870, the nation appeared to be on the threshold of a new era of inclusiveness. On July 15, 1870, on the morning of the day it adjourned for the session, Congress readmitted the state of Georgia. The United States government had been restored. The country had been reconstructed.[46]

In the middle of the nineteenth century, Americans were forced to address the ideological contradiction that lay at the heart of their nation. In the 1850s, wealthy southern planters explicitly denied that all men were created equal, arguing that most people were fit only for menial work, and that society worked best when a few rich men ran it. They insisted that their oligarchic view was the proper vision for America, and they set out to make slavery not regional but national by looking to the West. Empowering an elite class, they said, would benefit everyone, as leaders drove the economy and advanced culture.

By 1860, those men had taken over one of the two major political parties and came close to taking over the government. But when their dominance threatened to destroy the ability of ordinary citizens to rise to economic stability, those citizens rallied and went to war to preserve the nation. The war made Americans reconceive the government, using it to promote the good of all rather than to protect the wealth of a very few. When Andrew Johnson tried to resurrect the prewar government, making northerners confront the question of who, exactly, they meant by "all Americans," a majority sided with the Declaration of Independence and threw their weight behind the proposition that all men are created equal. And they used the might of the newly powerful federal government to guarantee that equality.

By 1870, Americans had given the nation a new birth of freedom. They had destroyed the oligarchic threat that ran through their society and ensured that theirs was a country where all men, regardless of their race or background, were equal.

CHAPTER 3

The West

The triumph of equality, the new birth of freedom, was an illusion. The oligarchic principles of the Confederacy did not die; timing and geography would give them a new lease on life. At the very moment that eastern Republicans were erasing racial categories from American law and toying with the idea of women's rights as they tried to base the country on the fundamental principle of human equality, settlers were moving westward across the Mississippi River. And there, in vast lands of the American West, hierarchy was even more deeply ingrained than it had been in the East. The postwar settlers in that region picked up and reinforced the belief that equality would destroy liberty.

The West has its own founding story, separate from that of the East. It begins not with the idea of small farmers pushing back the forests but with frontiersmen Kit Carson and Davy Crockett and the Alamo— brave white men bringing commerce and religion to savage lands. The regions to the west of the Mississippi River had a long history based upon the civilizations of their Indian inhabitants, and then the Spanish settlers who conquered it in the 1500s, and then the Mexicans who revolted against Spain's colonial rule and created their own country in 1821. But when Americans began to arrive from the East in great numbers in the 1850s, they brought a worldview that would create a new history.

The West began to loom in the American imagination even before the Revolution. One of the chief grievances colonists held against England was that royal officials had forbidden them to cross the Appalachian Mountains. Virginian Daniel Boone had repeatedly defied the law, and in 1775 he brought settlers over the Appalachians to establish a foothold in what was then western Virginia. In 1784, three years after the Revolutionary War ended, a land speculator named John Filson, eager to convince settlers to try their luck in the frontier area known as "Kentucke," wrote a book portraying Boone as a rough, strong, intelligent, but undomesticated western hero. Filson gave Americans their first version of the "West" as Boone portrayed it: a land of unspoiled nature, riches, savagery, and, most of all, opportunity.[1]

Thomas Jefferson was from the western part of Virginia and had been drawn to the land beyond the mountains since boyhood. He and Boone served together in the Virginia state legislature in the early 1780s, and, as curious as he was, he must have listened to Boone with fascination. In 1786, as Minister to France for the United States under the Articles of Confederation, Jefferson persuaded the explorer John Ledyard, originally from Connecticut, to cross Russia and make his way across North America from the Pacific to the Atlantic to explore the West. That expedition failed when Russian authorities under Catherine the Great deported Ledyard, who eventually died in Cairo.[2]

Jefferson revisited the scheme after he became president in 1801. In January 1803, he wrote a secret message to Congress asking for money to fund an expedition to travel from the Mississippi River up the Missouri River to the Pacific, making contact with Indians along the route and trying to persuade them to stop trading their furs with the British and start trading instead with Americans. Congress funded the request in February of that year, and Jefferson tapped his personal secretary, Meriwether Lewis, to lead the expedition. In April, Lewis began to prepare for the journey by studying medicine and natural history.

While Lewis was at his books, the ground was shifting under the expedition. Government officials were formalizing the first of the three major acquisitions that would shape the American West. At the end of the 1790s, settlers along the Mississippi River had threatened to throw in their lot with Spain so they could trade at the Spanish port of New Orleans. In 1801, American officials set out to buy trading rights at the port. They discovered that Spain had secretly transferred the entire huge Louisiana region to France. France, meanwhile, had been stretched thin by the combination of its wars in Europe and the Haitian Revolution, which had cost the lives of thousands of soldiers, largely from disease. With French leader Napoleon Bonaparte desperate to raise money to fight England, he was happy to dump Louisiana in exchange for cash. To their surprise, the Americans ended up buying the entire Louisiana territory, a huge chunk of land (some 827,000 square miles) equal to the size of the United States at the time, from France for $15 million. The purchase was concluded so quickly even the French negotiators didn't really know where the boundaries lay. So by the time Lewis chose William Clark to share the leadership of his expedition, much of the land they were to explore had become American territory.

The official announcement of the Louisiana Purchase came on July 4, and the next day the Lewis and Clark expedition set out. Jefferson did not wait the two years it would take for the expedition to come back before sending out more men to explore the new territory. In 1805, he dispatched an Army expedition headed by Zebulon Pike to find the headwaters of the Mississippi River. Jefferson was equally happy to send men to explore land that didn't belong to the United States. In 1806, he dispatched another expedition under Pike to explore the northernmost settlements of the Spanish in Texas. That same year, he also sent an expedition up the Red River, but the Spanish turned it back.

So thrilled was Jefferson with the stories and specimens the Lewis and Clark expedition and Pike brought back from their travels that he turned the Entrance Hall of the White House into a museum of the West. The White House slaves hung arrowheads, skins, and animal heads on the walls, and Indian pots and pestles stood on a table just inside the door. Jefferson considered the Executive Mansion the people's house, open to the public. Visitors who came to the Entrance Hall could marvel over these exotic artifacts of a distant world. They could also gawk from a distance at the pair of live grizzly bears Jefferson kept penned up on the lawn.[3]

The focus on expanding to the west created a new kind of political leader. The British continued to trade with the Shawnees in the Ohio Valley, known as the Old Northwest, and Indians gathered together under Tecumseh to stop American settlers from moving into their region. Furious at being shut out of western lands, young southerners organized to elect thirty-four-year-old slaveholder Henry Clay of Kentucky to the House of Representatives in 1810, and then, in an unprecedented—and never repeated—move elected him Speaker of the House on his first day in Congress. Clay and his fellow "War Hawks" backed a strike on Tecumseh's people, and in November 1811 General William Henry Harrison defeated the Shawnees at the Battle of Tippecanoe in what is now Indiana. The War Hawks also demanded that the government push England out of America once and for all. The ensuing War of 1812 was primarily a naval war, but its conclusion did give Americans full access to the land to the west, as well as a political champion: Andrew Jackson, a rough, rule-breaking southern slaveholder who defeated the British in 1815 at the Battle of New Orleans. The fact that Jackson fought the battle after the war was over did not mar the fact that he represented the new western hero.

The end of the War of 1812 brought an economic boom, and Americans embraced the idea that they were destined to flow westward. With the Indians and British out of the way, they continued to move into the Mississippi region, setting up new cotton plantations across the American South. In the 1820s, they moved across the Mississippi River. Their first corridor was the Santa Fe Trail, a trade route that led from Independence, Missouri, to Mexico. An eastern traveler got to the trail by crossing Missouri from St. Louis, on the Mississippi River at the eastern side of the state, to Independence on the west, the same jumping-off point that pioneers would later use to launch their journey west on the Oregon Trail. From Independence, they picked up the Santa Fe Trail, crossed the whole width of what is now Kansas, touched the southeast tip of Colorado, then crossed half of what is now New Mexico to reach Santa Fe. From there, Mexican trails headed due south. The Santa Fe Trail took travelers from the East into the Missouri River basin, with its forests full of game, then across the vast Great Plains of Kansas and southern Colorado before swinging down into the dry tablelands of New Mexico. The open land must have looked exotic to travelers who had grown up in the green swamps of Mississippi, closed in on all sides by the Spanish moss, or in the scrub hills of Tennessee. As they headed west, they met new peoples, too: Mexicans and Apaches, and Comanches who used the trail to trade horses and captives.

From the Santa Fe Trail, fur trappers like Kit Carson branched off to follow the streams in the Missouri River basin, going after the beavers, minks, and otters that were the main source of the furs for European top hats. Carson never learned to write, but he picked up Spanish, French, and nine Indian languages as he traveled through the region. Others moved across the Mississippi River into Texas.[4]

Eager to stabilize their northern borderlands, Mexican officials permitted American settlement in what is now Texas, but just a year after Jackson became president in 1829, Mexico banned slavery there. Americans had come to the area to make a killing in the cotton boom, and they couldn't do that without enslaved labor. In October 1835, Americans and Mexican opponents of President Antonio López de Santa Anna's government—known as Texians—went to war against Santa Anna's troops. By December, the Texians had pushed Mexican troops out of Texas, and they hunkered down in the Alamo Mission near what is now San Antonio. In January, Texian reinforcements arrived, including James Bowie, a Kentucky man famous for killing a sheriff with a knife when he lived in Louisiana. By 1836 he was a Mexican citizen, married to the daughter of a high-ranking Mexican government official. Davy Crockett, a former congressman from Tennessee, famous for his tall tales, also came. They stood with around 200 other Texians when about 1,800 of Santa Anna's troops laid siege to the Alamo on February 23, 1836. On March 6, Santa Anna's troops attacked, killing almost all of the defenders.[5]

The last stand at the Alamo became the foundational event for western American history, offering a vision of self-sacrifice and heroism. It prompted the formation of the Republic of Texas, and inspired the Texians under Sam Houston to defeat Santa Anna's troops in April at the Battle of San Jacinto. In the retelling of what happened at the Alamo, what got lost was the reality that the defenders were rebelling against the Mexican government in Mexican territory, and that they were fighting to defend their right to enslave other people. The myth also ignored the fact that many of the defenders were Mexican opponents of Santa Anna, and that some of the defenders—including Davy Crockett—surrendered.[6]

Nonetheless, "Remember the Alamo!" became a cry that justified the annexation of Texas, particularly by leaders from the new Democratic Party that had formed around Andrew Jackson. They developed the concept of "Manifest Destiny": that it was the inevitable,

God-ordained future of America to take over the entire continent. Settlers, they said, would bring political, economic, religious, and cultural enlightenment to the Mexicans and Indians who lived in the West.

In 1846, after officially annexing Texas and settling the nation's northwestern border with England along the 49th parallel, America declared war on Mexico. U.S. troops marched south. They met little resistance. Mexican settlers had fled from the Comanches, who claimed the region and raided settlements for goods and captives to trade. Unaware that Comanches had cleared the way for them, Americans cheered at the ease with which they pushed all the way south to Mexico City.

President James K. Polk had sent negotiator Nicholas Trist to secure Texas and California, which put Trist in the extraordinary position of negotiating to give up land that American troops already occupied. In 1848, the Treaty of Guadalupe Hidalgo gave the United States the huge chunk of land that would become the states of California, Nevada, Utah, Colorado, New Mexico, and Wyoming, in exchange for assuming some of Mexico's debt and $15 million. But there was something that no one negotiating the deal was yet aware of: ten days before the treaty was signed, workers discovered gold in the stream at Sutter's Mill in California, in the land that was about to change hands.

As men rushed to the gold mines, newspapers ran one piece after another about the exotic land and the great wealth there. Interest in the West produced popular stories about the "mountain men," fur traders who had gone west in the 1820s and 1830s and had fought and bred with Indians: half-wild American heroes. In 1849, the first dime novel about mountain man Kit Carson gave readers a hero straight out of James Fenimore Cooper's novels. Carson was "erect and lithe as the pine tree of his own forests; his broad, sun-burnt face developing a countenance, on which a life of danger and hardship had set its weather-beaten seal, and placed in boldest relief the unerring signs of a nature which for reckles[s] daring and most indomitable hardihood, could know scarce a human superior." Carson was "the hero of prairie and forest, the prince of backwoods-men."[7]

★

In addition to their own mythology about the West, easterners brought with them into that multicultural region the conflict between democracy and oligarchy that was raging back home. In the 1850s, the newly acquired western lands forced a crisis between the two systems, which had reached an uneasy truce in the East. When news of the gold in California broke in 1849, men eager to make their fortunes set out on the brutal 1,500-mile overland journey from St. Louis, braving the dry plains, two mountain ranges, and a desert, or they took their chances on the ocean voyage around Cape Horn at the tip of South America. Those who survived the journey poured into California, and their mining camps made the need for order and law obvious.

The reality was that power in the West came from social networks and kinship ties rather than from individual prowess, but these men saw the West as a land of unparalleled opportunity, where a man willing to swing a pick could make a fortune literally out of the dirt. It was the stuff of hope and legends, and offered an enviable future to even the most downtrodden easterner. But western migrants made sure that opportunity was limited to them. Much as American democracy in the East depended on slavery and male supremacy, the racism and sexism that were always inherent in the idea of a white man taking on the wilderness became a primary part of a western individualist's identity. Eastern migrants may have sought new lives, but they carried the American paradox west.[8]

Miners and settlers believed they had a right to appropriate the resources in the lands around them, and they did not take kindly to the Indians who had a different opinion. In the East, Americans had clashed with native tribes weakened by smallpox, influenza, chicken pox, measles, and typhus, which often swept through tribes all at once. These epidemics caused death rates of up to 90 percent, throwing tribes into social, political, and economic chaos. Plains Indians came into contact with Spanish explorers at roughly the same time that eastern Indians came into contact with European fishermen, and they, too, suffered horrific losses. But by the nineteenth century, Plains tribes had adjusted to the disruption caused by disease and stabilized. They were not as weakened as their eastern counterparts.

Even more important, Plains Indians had adopted horses by the time emigrants arrived in significant numbers. Horses are not native to America; the Spanish conquistadors brought them, and the animals thrived on the southwestern plains. Indians in what is now Texas had started to adapt to horses by about 1500, and the animals had spread to what is now the border of Canada roughly by the time of the American Revolution. Plains tribes who depended on the buffalo for survival were poor when they were limited to hunting on foot, but the arrival of horses gave some tribes wealth and power. With horses, Comanches, Kiowas, Cheyennes, and Lakotas could kill large numbers of buffalo and trade their hides east to America or south to Mexico. Horses also made them dangerous warriors. Aside from the Confederacy, they were the most powerful fighting force the U.S. Army would encounter until World War I.[9]

As emigrants to the West collided with Apaches, Comanches, Cheyennes, and Lakotas who controlled their own empires in the region, the identity of western Americans became tied up with the idea of defeating and then dominating Indians. Kit Carson, for example, was as famous for his fighting as he was for his fur trapping. The Santa Fe Trail ran through Apache land, and while Apaches generally had a good relationship with Americans because of their mutual dislike of Mexicans, in the 1840s they began to push back against those moving across their territory. In October 1849, a band of Jicarilla Apaches and allied Utes in what is now New Mexico requested payment for the use of the trail from a trader named James White traveling with his wife, child, an enslaved African American, and a number of others. When the travelers refused, the Indians attacked, killing all but Mrs. White, her daughter, and the slave, then killing Mexicans who happened on the scene later. When the story made it back to an army garrison near Taos, soldiers set out to punish the Jicarillas and rescue the Whites. To find the Indians, they hired Carson, who had no qualms about shooting Indians. Carson led the soldiers to the band. In the fracas that followed, Mrs. White and an Indian were killed. The rest of the Indians fled.[10]

News of the "White massacre" inflamed settlers, and for the next several years tensions between settlers and Apaches simmered. In March 1854, when a beef contractor blamed Jicarillas for stealing his cattle, the U.S. Army set out to end the raiding once and for all. Skirmishes culminated in the Battle of Cieneguilla near Pilar, New Mexico, when about 250 Apaches and Utes routed 60 soldiers, killing 22 and wounding another 36, while losing about 20 of their own warriors. A week later, army scouts—including Kit Carson—found several hundred Jicarillas in Ojo Caliente Canyon. Soldiers chased them from their hot springs winter encampment. Without heat and supplies, many of the Indians died. The Battle of Ojo Caliente ended the full engagements of the Apache Wars, but enough fear of war remained that in 1856 the U.S. Army, under Secretary of War Jefferson Davis, imported thirty-four camels from the Mediterranean to carry provisions in the Southwest to support the troops in the Indian wars.

Shortly after the Battle of Ojo Caliente, Congress passed the Kansas-Nebraska Act, opening the West to slavery, and the battle over the nature of the American West was on. The terms of the 1848 Treaty of Guadalupe Hidalgo transferred land from Mexico to the United States, and the Mexican citizens living in the transferred territory could either stay where they were or sell out and move south into Mexico. They had one year to decide if they were staying or going. Anyone who stayed had a year to opt to retain their Mexican citizenship, but if they didn't, authorities would assume they wanted to become American citizens. Congress would admit those people to citizenship, with all its rights and duties, "at the proper time." Regardless of their choice, liberty and the ownership of property in the exchanged land either by those who chose to be Mexican or those who chose to be American was to be "inviolably respected."

The terms of the treaty were clear . . . and Americans ignored them. Soon after the land exchange, as word spread of the gold discovery in California, prospective miners rushed west to become part of the boom. There were already 150,000 Indians on the land in and around the diggings, and many of them were going after the gold. As many as 25,000 Mexicans were also either there or on their way, as eager to get in on the gold rush as Americans were. Mexico and Chile had a long history of mining, and many of the Mexicans and Chileans who arrived in California knew their trade and did better than the untrained Americans.

Americans resented these miners, whom they saw as interlopers. After an initial period of working alongside the Indians and Mexicans, they began to adopt the practice of Indian slavery from the Mexicans in the region, then began to hunt Indians down, blaming them when their own luck in the mines didn't pan out. They tried to get rid of the Mexicans first by stealing their mules and money, then by threatening them, and finally by violence. At least 163 Mexicans were lynched in California between 1848 and 1860, a rate comparable to that of black Americans in the American South in the early part of the twentieth century. The mobs often mutilated the corpses, cutting out their tongues, hacking them into pieces, or burning them after the hanging, practices that underscored that they did not see Mexicans as fully human.[11]

Chinese miners escaping the devastation of the First Opium War of 1839–1842 also came to what they called "Gold Mountain," and they, too, ran afoul of white miners. Chinese men hoped to make money in America and then return to China, from which they could not legally emigrate. Expecting to go home again, they did not try to assimilate to American culture. They retained their languages, their culture, and their habits of dress. They wore their hair in long braids called queues. They tended to work the mines Americans had cleaned of their biggest deposits, focusing on meticulous reworking of the gravel, and they, too, did better than Americans thought they should.

In 1850, a legislature charged with establishing the legal framework for the proposed state of California guaranteed that white men would dominate the region. It adopted the federal law enacted a half-century earlier, in 1802, that limited citizenship to "free white persons," and prohibited both African Americans and Indians, or people with black or Indian blood, from testifying in court against white people. It also prohibited marriage between "white persons" and "negroes or mulattoes." But to white men it was quite generous. It extended suffrage to "every white male citizen of the United States, and every white male citizen of Mexico who shall have elected to become a citizen of the United States." When Congress admitted California to the Union on September 9, 1850, America had its first western state. Its legal code set a precedent for the American West.[12]

The laws of the new state codified the racial lines forming in the gold fields, but unlike in the East, these laws focused not on black slaves, who were prohibited from California by virtue of its status as a free state, but on Indians, Chinese, and Mexicans. The legislature "protected" Indians by allowing Americans to take their land, but only so long as they set aside other, unprofitable land for them. They permitted Indian children to be enslaved until they were grown: men at eighteen, women at fifteen. They permitted Indians to testify in court, but "in no case shall a white man be convicted of any offense upon the testimony of an Indian, or Indians." Because American men were taking possession of land on the grounds that they had married Indian women, the legislature made such transfers legal, provided that the woman was told that she was handing over her property and had acknowledged "on examination apart from and without the hearing of her husband" that she was doing so "freely and voluntarily, without fear or compulsion, or undue influence of her husband." The laws permitted police officers to punish tribal leaders for the transgressions of any Indian in their tribe. If an Indian was fined for a crime and couldn't pay, a white man could pay the fine and the Indian would have to work it off. Indians could be punished with whipping. And any able-bodied Indian "who shall be found loitering and strolling about, or frequenting public places where liquors are sold, begging, or leading an immoral or profligate course of life," could be arrested and sold to the highest bidder for four months.[13]

State laws also went after Chinese and Mexicans, initially by prohibiting anyone who was not a U.S. citizen or a native California Indian from mining without a license that cost $20 per month. Failure to have such a license bore a penalty of up to three months in jail and a $1,000 fine. When this drove foreign prospectors out of business, in 1852 the state dropped the cost; a new foreign miner's tax required a payment of $3 each month. Then, in 1854, a white man successfully challenged his conviction for murdering a Chinese miner by arguing that Chinese testimony implicating him should have been excluded under the statute forbidding nonwhites from testifying against white men. The following year, the legislature tried to stop Chinese immigration altogether by passing a $50 tax on shipmasters for each person ineligible for citizenship they brought to the state.[14]

Just two days after the legislature passed the shipmaster tax, it adopted a vagrancy law that targeted anyone apparently unemployed, punishing them with ninety days of hard labor. The legislators made it clear whom they meant with the next provision, which permitted lawmen to disarm and arrest for vagrancy "all persons . . . commonly known as 'Greasers' or the issue of Spanish and Indian blood . . . who go armed and are not known to be peaceable and quiet persons."[15]

Mexican subordination would leave a lasting cultural legacy. Under Mexican rule, wealthy landowners oversaw large plots of land that were worked by others under a paternalistic system. Ignoring the assurances the government had made to Mexican property owners, Americans moved onto the large ranches. Local courts tended to side with the American squatters rather than the original owners. In 1851, Congress passed a law to validate Mexican land claims, but the process of litigating ownership while squatters destroyed fields and killed cattle impoverished most of the landowners. By the time the Supreme Court validated Mexican ownership, most had already been forced to sell off their lands. Adding insult to injury, the landowners had to pay the squatters for any improvements they had made to the lands while they lived on them.[16]

Furious at the loss of their lands, Mexicans pushed back, pleading with the government to protect their rights. On the new border, the son of a wealthy Mexican cattle rancher finally turned against the politicians and judges who were taking advantage of American laws to appropriate Mexicans' lands. Juan Cortina's family owned large tracts near Matamoros and Brownsville but repeatedly faced challenges to their ownership. In 1859, after leading a raid against Brownsville officials, Cortina issued a proclamation warning that "our enemies . . . have connived with each other . . . to persecute and rob us, without any cause, and for no other crime on our part than that of being of Mexican origin." He gathered a band to push back against the Anglos. Skirmishes turned to outright battles as Cortina took over the town of Brownsville. He issued another proclamation: "Flocks of vampires, in the guise of men," had robbed Mexicans of their "property, incarcerated, chased, murdered, and hunted [them] like wild beasts." First Texas Rangers and then U.S. troops forced Cortina and his men to flee to the Burgos Mountains. With the turmoil on the border, Americans developed the idea of the "Mexican bandit," a term Cortina embraced as the definition of a man who fought for his neighbors' rights.[17]

Indians and Mexicans were fierce defenders of their land, for sure, but American settlers in the Southwest had an incentive to exaggerate their ferocity. Having troops in the area created markets for local goods. In 1859, when army commanders decided to abandon Fort Brown, near Brownsville, Texas, settlers petitioned Congress, insisting that they needed protection because if the troops left, they were "liable to be descended upon by the merciless savages." "Bands of Mexican armed soldiers, highwaymen, and Indians," they claimed, "would cross into our Territory, plunder our commerce, murder our citizens, and make desert our frontier." The officer who had made the call to leave the fort expressed his opinion to the head of the army: "There is not, nor ever has been, any danger of the Mexicans crossing on our side of the river to plunder or disturb the inhabitants, and the outcry on that river for troops is solely to have an expenditure of the public money."[18]

The pre–Civil War West might have been a place of opportunity for white men, but even without the issue of black slavery, the government there acknowledged a hierarchy of men according to their race.

★

A memoir from the period illustrated that power in the West was not simply about skin color but also about making money and dominating others. In the winter of 1854–1855, fur trapper Jim Beckwourth dictated his life story to a man who cleaned it up and got it into print. Beckwourth's yarns committed to paper the mythological stories of the American mountain man. The son of a wealthy southern slave owner, Beckwourth claimed to hate Indians because he had witnessed a massacre as a child. He went to the Rocky Mountains in 1824 to work as a horse wrangler for Rocky Mountain Fur Company founder William Ashley, and despite his professed biases, he settled with the Crows, possibly at Ashley's instigation, to facilitate trade with the tribe. There he would stay for the next eight years, fighting with the warriors against their traditional enemies the Blackfoots, and taking at least two wives, one of whom he boasted of hitting in the head with a battle-axe after she joined a dance celebrating the murder of three white men.

In his account, Beckwourth comes across as the quintessential western hero, earning leadership over those he called "savages." He shot, traded, loved, dominated, and survived better than any other man. But while Beckwourth let his readers assume he was a white man— describing the murdered white men as "my people," for example—in fact, according to the usage of the day, he was black. His father was indeed a prominent southern slaveholder, as Beckwourth claimed, but his mother was not his father's plantation mistress wife. She was his slave. In Beckwourth's West, a black man could literally become a white man, so long as he made money and dominated women and the men below him.[19]

Westerners were following the lead of what was happening back east. Southern slave owners were defending their "peculiar institution" by developing the idea that white men were society's natural leaders. In the North, the Irish Potato Famine was driving impoverished Irish to New England, and in Massachusetts especially, native-born Americans pressed for laws against the new immigrants. Members of the newly formed American Party, dubbed "Know-Nothings" because when asked about the party they claimed to know nothing about it, defined Irish immigrants as an inferior race. They were lazy, drunken, and prone to crime. Know-Nothings insisted on laws requiring the deportation of those Irish deemed to be likely to be a public charge; on the daily reading of the Protestant Bible in schools; and on laws keeping Irish from voting. These "n——rs turned inside out," as they were popularly known, were consigned to a place below white Americans in the law.[20]

By the 1850s, those who believed in democracy in America watched the rise of racial categories with dread. Abraham Lincoln recognized that enshrining racial distinctions in the law would destroy the Republic. Musing privately about the issue in 1854, he worked out his ideas on a piece of scratch paper: "If A. can prove, however conclusively, that he may, of right, enslave B.—why may not B. snatch the same argument, and prove equally, that he may enslave A.?" Lincoln demolished the idea that categories should be based on race: "You say A. is white, and B. is black. It is *color*, then; the lighter, having the right to enslave the darker? Take care. By this rule, you are to be slave to the first man you meet, with a fairer skin than your own." He also tore down other permanent categories: "You do not mean color exactly? You mean the whites are intellectually the superiors of the blacks, and, therefore have the right to enslave them? Take care again. By this rule, you are to be slave to the first man you meet, with an intellect superior to your own."[21]

Lincoln got to the heart of the matter: "But, say you, it is a question of *interest*; and, if you can make it your interest; you have the right to enslave another. Very well. And if he can make it his interest, he has the right to enslave you."[22]

Lincoln recognized that creating human categories admitted the principle that any man could enslave another. The following year, when his friend Joshua Speed asked him where he stood politically, a disgusted Lincoln replied: "I am not a Know-Nothing. That is certain. How could I be? How can any one who abhors the oppression of negroes, be in favor or degrading classes of white people? . . . When it comes to this I should prefer emigrating to some country where they make no pretence of loving liberty—to Russia, for instance, where despotism can be taken pure, and without the base alloy of hypocr[is]y."[23]

In 1860, as Democrats embraced the language of oligarchy, with its permanent castes, Lincoln's Republican Party cited the Declaration of Independence in its party platform, reminding Americans that preserving the principle that "all men are created equal" was "essential to the preservation of our Republican institutions." In addition to excoriating the attempts of slaveholders to use the federal government to protect slavery everywhere in the nation, the platform's drafters committed the party to opposing any change in the laws that would hedge the "rights of citizens hitherto accorded to immigrants from foreign lands." It called for "giving a full and efficient protection to the rights of all classes of citizens, whether native or naturalized, both at home and abroad."[24]

The newly acquired American West had become the center of the fight between democracy and oligarchy, and as soon as the Civil War broke out, Republicans moved as quickly as possible to establish their worldview there. As the southern senators and representatives left, in January 1861, Congress admitted Kansas to the Union as a free state.

Over the next four years, Congress organized governments in the West as fast as it could. In February 1861, it organized Colorado Territory; in March, Nevada Territory and Dakota Territory. In 1863, Congress organized Idaho Territory and Arizona Territory. In 1864, it organized Montana Territory and admitted Nevada to the Union as a state. In 1861, the Great Plains were largely unorganized land dominated by the Indians who lived there. Four years later, the U.S. Congress had carved them into a political form that looked much like it does today. And at least one north-south boundary of Kansas, Colorado, Nebraska, New Mexico, Montana, Wyoming, Dakota Territory, Utah, Arizona, and Idaho were all measured from the newly declared American meridian of 0° 0′ 0″ that ran through Washington D.C. Washington was literally the epicenter of the new West.

Congress had worked quickly to spread the free labor economy into those newly organized lands and had shut slave owners out of them. To easterners generally, and certainly to those in the federal government, the West appeared to be the successful laboratory of democracy. Using the government to promote the interests of ordinary men was remarkably successful. A wartime agricultural boom kept prices high as farmers scrambled to provide food both for the troops and for a drought-stricken Europe. By 1865, observers could readily believe that the West had made equality in America a reality.

★

But while Congress's efforts to bring a free labor economy to life transformed the East, they did not eliminate the legal and cultural structures that dominated the West. Instead, even as the region was brought into the Union, the Civil War exacerbated the racial lines that were already in place. Beginning in 1861, Indian wars broke out across the plains. The timing of those conflicts, coming in the midst of a war for the very survival of the Union, made them increasingly savage.

In January 1861, Coyotero Apaches stole cattle and kidnapped a boy from John Ward's ranch at Sonoita Creek in Arizona. Lieutenant

George Bascom set out to retrieve the child and the animals, but mistakenly blamed Chiricahua Apaches for the raid. When Chiricahua leader Cochise met with Bascom and offered to find the culprits, Bascom instead imprisoned Cochise and his party, including his wife and two children, his brother, and two nephews. Cochise used a knife to slash his way out of the back of a tent and escaped, but the others were caught. When Bascom refused to release Cochise's family, Cochise and a band attacked a group of traders, killing nine Mexicans and offering to trade three captured Americans for his family. When Bascom refused, Cochise killed the Americans and mutilated their bodies for Bascom to find. In mid-February, army officers hanged Cochise's brother and nephews. This marked the start of an all-out war between the Apaches and the American settlers. Within a year, Cochise had allied with legendary Apache leader Mangas Coloradas and the much younger Geronimo to drive Americans out of their land.

Settlers in the Southwest had a long history with Apaches, Comanches, and Kiowas, but easterners had little experience with Plains Indians. Their introduction set a pattern for the future. In 1851, Dakotas in Minnesota Territory had given up 24 million acres of their land in exchange for a narrow strip of land along the Minnesota River and promises of food, supplies, and cash payments forever. In 1862, the cash-starved U.S. government reneged on its treaty obligations and refused to provide Dakotas with food. Starving Indians fought to retake their lands.

In late summer, just as Union prospects on the battlefields of the South were at a low ebb, Dakotas killed between four hundred and eight hundred Minnesota settlers. Whites portrayed the Indians as savages determined to destroy the nation, and howled for their blood. This "uprising," coming at a moment when the Union's military fortunes were grim, convinced observers that western Indians posed a profound threat to the nation itself. One evangelical Christian publication wrote of "children with their heads cut off, women ripped open, and men with their skulls dashed in and their throats cut." Military officers wanted to execute every one of the surrendering Dakota men and arranged kangaroo courts-martial to hand down death sentences. Lincoln recognized that executing men for engaging in a war against the government would set a dangerous precedent in the midst of the Civil War. He commuted the sentences of anyone convicted of murder on a battlefield, letting them stand only for those convicted of rape or murder of civilians. On the day after Christmas, December 26, 1862, the U.S. military hanged thirty-eight Dakotas in the largest mass execution in American history. Survivors fled west to their relatives, the Lakotas (known by their enemies as the Sioux), who lived in the country stretching from what is now South Dakota to the land around the Powder River Basin in what is now Montana and Idaho.[25]

A similar dehumanization of Indians played out in the Southwest, where the struggle between the Union and the Confederacy was in full force. In July 1861, only four days after the First Battle of Bull Run, Lieutenant Colonel John Baylor of the 2nd Texas Mounted Rifles advanced into New Mexico Territory to take Fort Fillmore, on the Rio Grande, from federal forces. After a skirmish in the nearby town of Mesilla, the Union troops abandoned the fort and set off overland across the mountains to nearby Fort Stanton. They soon collapsed from dehydration—possibly brought on because they chose to fill their canteens with liquor rather than water when they abandoned the fort—and surrendered to Baylor. The victory at Mesilla prompted Confederates to recognize their own Territory of Arizona in August 1861; this comprised the southern halves of current-day Arizona and New Mexico, with Mesilla as its capital.[26]

In February 1862, the Confederacy launched the New Mexico Campaign, hoping to gain control of the West and its mines. As Rebel troops traveled along the Rio Grande, the Union rushed men from California under Colonel James Henry Carleton to push them back. In March 1862, the 1st Colorado Infantry met the Confederates at Glorieta Pass in New Mexico. The Confederates won the battle, the high-water mark of the Confederacy in the West. They also lost so many supplies that they were forced to retreat. With New Mexico and Arizona now apparently safe from the Confederacy, Union officers relocated most Union troops back to the East.

They left behind a smaller group of troops overseen by General Carleton, who had risen through the military ranks in California before arriving in Arizona and New Mexico to secure that region against the Confederacy. Apaches and Navajos were taking advantage of the chaos in the wake of the struggles between Confederates and U.S. soldiers to raid. In late 1862, Carleton ordered the construction of Fort Sumner to protect settlers. Next to it he laid out a 1,600-square-mile reservation that came to be known as Bosque Redondo, where he planned to turn Apaches and Navajos into farmers.[27]

Enlisting none other than Kit Carson as a guide, Carleton went to war with Apaches under Cochise and Mangas Coloradas, ordering Carson to kill all Apache men for their treachery and crimes, even if they asked for a truce: "This severity, in the long run, will be the most humane course that could be pursued toward these Indians." In 1863, his men took him at his word and killed Mangas Coloradas while under a flag of truce that should have guaranteed the Apache leader safe passage for peace negotiations. Fascinated by the legendary figure, the army surgeon boiled his head and sent his skull to famous New York City phrenologist Orson Squire Fowler, who concluded that the skull proved phrenology was a true science, because its shape showed a man that was "simply monstrous."[28]

With Apache resistance literally decapitated, Carleton moved about five hundred Apaches onto Bosque Redondo and then turned to fight the Navajos, some of whom had been raiding settlers in New Mexico. Once again, he turned to Kit Carson for help. With the aid of Ute scouts, Carson forced the Navajo to surrender at their home in Arizona's Canyon de Chelly by destroying their homes, sheep, and crops. While some managed to evade the army, about ten thousand of them handed themselves over to Carson and army officers during the winter of 1863. At the end of the year, Carleton praised the zeal of settlers who "have shown a settled determination to assist the military in their efforts to rid the country of the fierce and brutal robbers and murderers who for nearly two centuries have brought poverty to its inhabitants and mourning and desolation to nearly every hearth throughout the Territory." In early 1864, Carleton ordered his troops to march groups of malnourished and poorly clothed Navajos about three hundred miles to the Bosque Redondo reservation near Fort Sumner. At least two hundred died on the way to what amounted to internment at a prison camp, one with far too little food and fuel.[29]

Trouble in Colorado Territory would cement the dehumanization of Indians. In 1851, the U.S. government had recognized Cheyenne and Arapaho ownership of a vast swath of land, including most of what is today eastern Colorado. But a gold rush to the Rockies brought settlers, and in 1861, American officials pressured Cheyenne and Arapaho leaders into ceding most of their land. The younger men of the bands refused to acknowledge the new agreement and continued to hunt on their lands, skirmishing with the Americans cutting through it. Colorado settlers got more and more nervous, especially as men went east to fight in the Civil War. Meanwhile, the territorial governor, John Evans, had ambitions for elective office when the territory became a state. He promised settlers he would protect them from Indians. On August 11, 1864, he issued a proclamation authorizing citizens "to kill and destroy as enemies of the country wherever they may be found, all . . . hostile Indians."[30]

A militia unit under Colonel John Chivington took him at his word and, following a common pattern, set out to hunt down peaceful Indian camps, because they were far easier to find than hostile ones. On November 28, 1864, James Beckwourth guided Chivington and more than four hundred soldiers to a group of peaceful Cheyennes camped near Sand Creek, Colorado, where they had been relocated by the Army. Most of the men were out hunting; those in the camp were mostly women, children, and the elderly. The next morning, the soldiers fell on the Indians, who instantly raised a white flag. The signal didn't matter. Soldiers killed as many as they could, ultimately cutting down about 105 women and children and 25 men.

This massacre was different from its predecessors. The soldiers didn't simply attack and kill unarmed Indians; they butchered their victims, taking body parts as trophies. Both the military and Congress held investigations of what had taken place, and their discoveries were chilling. One soldier told the investigators that "men had cut out the private parts of females and stretched them over their saddle-bows, and some of them over their hats."[31]

News of these atrocities spread back to the East, but rather than sparking widespread outrage, the outcome of the Sand Creek Massacre hardened American perceptions of Plains Indians. Westerners resented congressional disapproval and the condescension of those who recoiled from the bloody realities of life there. Easterners simply didn't understand the conditions in the West, didn't get just how bad Indians were. The massacre forced easterners, too, to adjust their ideas about Indians. In 1864, most Americans had a son or a brother or a father wearing an army uniform. No one wanted to believe that a soldier—someone who could be their kin—would cut off a man's testicles to use them as a tobacco pouch. So they dehumanized the victims of the massacre. Indians were not people; they were savages who had forced the soldiers to kill them and treat them so brutally.

In spring 1865, northerners were celebrating that they had not only saved the Union but also saved the West from slavery, and that the concept of human equality was now spreading. Westerners were celebrating the fact that they had finally secured their region from Mexicans and Indians. In the North, the war had bolstered democracy. In the West, it had reinforced a society in which the oligarchic ideas of the defeated South would thrive.

CHAPTER 4

Cowboy Reconstruction

The surrender of General Robert E. Lee to General Ulysses
S. Grant at Appomattox Courthouse on April 9, 1865, seemed to
ensure that the principles for which the U.S. government had fought
would prevail across the nation. Although there were still two major
southern armies in the field, it was clear that the Confederacy's days
were numbered. Yet while slave owners did not win the war, it turned
out they had surrendered only on the battlefields. Over the next few
years, they would set out to recover their lost power by advancing a
new narrative that drew on old fault lines. They divided supporters
of democracy by binding race to class, and by constraining women

into roles as either wives and mothers or prostitutes. This would not have been possible in the war-torn East, of course, where those who championed the Confederate oligarchic ideology had lost. But they found a home for their worldview in the West, where there was a fresh example of Crèvecoeur's "new American" to embody it: the cowboy.

The process of constructing a new nation based on the idea that all men—and possibly women—were created equal would require the deft hand of someone like Abraham Lincoln. But on April 14, at Ford's Theatre in Washington, the actor John Wilkes Booth shot him in the back of the head in one last, desperate attempt to protect the oligarchic world of the Old South. As he jumped to the stage from the president's box, Booth shouted, "Sic semper tyrannis" (thus always to tyrants)— Virginia's state motto and the line Brutus speaks in Shakespeare's *Julius Caesar* to justify his murder of the emperor. Booth's bullet put southern Democrat Andrew Johnson into the White House.

Johnson wanted no part of the Republicans' new birth of freedom. A rough, brash man in the mold of Hinton Rowan Helper, he deeply resented the rich slaveholders who controlled the South, but he shared their conviction that people of color were not quite human. Johnson opposed slavery because it consolidated wealth in the hands of a very few. Once slavery was gone, he had no interest in using government to promote equality of opportunity for anyone other than white men. Johnson set out to restore the country's Democrat-dominated 1860 political system, minus slavery. Under his influence, the hierarchical society the Confederates had tried to impose on the country would gain new ideological power. He would articulate the corollary to the American paradox in new terms, ones that incorporated the popular changes of the Civil War years into the vision of the antebellum oligarchs.

The timing of Lincoln's murder gave Johnson an extraordinary amount of power to stop the spread of the Union's democratic vision. Congress had adjourned for the summer on the morning of Lincoln's second inaugural address, and it was not scheduled to reconvene until early December 1865. The exhausted congressmen had hurried to their far-flung homes. Just a month later, as news spread of Lincoln's death, they rushed back to Washington, fully expecting that Johnson would call them into emergency session, just as Lincoln had in 1861. But Johnson had no intention of sharing power with Republicans as they set out to advance democracy. He ignored Congress and took it upon himself to rebuild America alone.

Johnson shifted General William Tecumseh Sherman to the West to oversee the Indian Wars, then turned his attention to the devastated South. White refugees searching for shelter jostled along country roads with formerly enslaved people trying to find lost family members. All of them trudged past fields that had gone to weeds, where the carcasses of horses and mules—and an occasional body, buried too shallowly—rotted in the sun. Destitute southerners of all stripes made their way toward towns where they hoped the Army might feed them. Once there, they had to reckon with ruined buildings and with broken men who would rob them with impunity, for there were no police officers to stop them. It was imperative that someone restore order in the South and see that seeds for food and cotton got planted before the season passed.[1]

To rebuild the South, Johnson turned not to the Army, or to the ex-slaves who had supported the Union, but to former Confederates. He offered pardons to all but about 1,500 Confederate leaders and asked the southern states to ratify the Thirteenth Amendment, declare secession illegal, and essentially declare bankruptcy so that no one would ever again bankroll rebellion against the United States government. The states agreed—more or less—but then codified the racial violence that swept across the South in the summer of 1865. As employers cheated workers out of wages, gangs beat and raped African Americans into submissive behavior, and whites attacked their black neighbors, southern state legislatures created the Black Codes.

These laws prohibited African Americans from meeting in groups and from owning weapons. They forced former slaves to sign yearlong labor contracts with white employers and gave them no legal rights to defend themselves or their interests; they could not testify against white people. Breaking the codes could lead to whipping or hefty fines. When impoverished freedpeople could not pay, sheriffs were charged with hiring out the prisoners to anyone who could, giving preference to their employers. The Black Codes reinstated a form of slavery, but tied it to class rather than race.[2]

Terrorized African Americans turned to the U.S. Army stationed in the South to protect them. In March 1865, Congress had created a temporary bureau within the Army to help starving southerners and start the work of repairing the region. Eager to jump-start the southern economy, officers of the Bureau of Refugees, Freedmen, and Abandoned Lands began to intercede with southern whites on behalf of freedpeople. When officers decided in favor of freedpeople—which, according to records kept in 1865–1866, was about 68 percent of the time—southern whites howled. Despite the fact that about a third of the rations distributed by the bureau went to white southerners, they derogatorily dubbed it the "Freedmen's Bureau," and called for it to end. Energized by Johnson's support, white southerners laid down a new ideological marker for the postwar years. They began to argue that they had fought the Civil War not over slavery—despite the many state secession declarations and speeches saying exactly the opposite—but rather to keep an intrusive federal government out of their lives.[3]

When Congress reconvened in December 1865, Johnson met the new members with the astonishing news that what he called the "restoration" of the states had been completed. As soon as Congress seated the senators and representatives who had been elected under the new southern governments, reunification would be complete.[4]

Republican congressmen were apoplectic. The South had virtually reenslaved the only people in the region who were loyal to the U.S. government, then elected to Congress some of the very men who had been responsible for trying to destroy the United States in the first place—including Alexander Stephens, the former vice president of the

Confederacy, who would soon arrive to take his seat as a senator from Georgia. The strength of white southerners in Congress would only increase, since for the first time the 1870 census would count African Americans as whole people rather than as three-fifths of a person. Only nine months earlier, northerners had been fighting on the battlefields to save the United States government from destruction by slave owners; under Johnson's plan, Confederate leaders would wield more power in the Union than they had had before the Civil War.

The Republicans refused to seat the southern senators and representatives gathered in Washington, and appointed a committee of thirteen senators and representatives to come up with their own plan for reconstructing the nation, a plan that would eventually become the Fourteenth Amendment. While the committee met, Congress tried to combat the violence taking place under the Black Codes by giving southern African American men equal standing before the law. It passed the Civil Rights Act establishing that any person born or naturalized in America was a citizen and thus gave freedmen the right to sue, hold property, and testify in court. In case state courts did not cooperate, Congress also expanded the Freedmen's Bureau to provide federal courts in the South, so that black men could be guaranteed the right to testify.

Republicans thought these laws were uncontroversial, as well they should have been, but Johnson vetoed them. He insisted that Congress could not legislate without southerners represented—a bombshell right there—and went on to lay out a political argument that echoed slaveholder James Henry Hammond's ideology. He warned that Congress was dangerously expanding the federal government to give privileges to black men that white men did not have. This, he said, would destroy America, because a big government would require tax levies, which would fall on white men who had worked hard for their property. That money would be spent on government officials providing services for African Americans, like those working for the Freedmen's Bureau. Republicans believed their policies leveled the playing field between former slaves and white Americans. Johnson argued that they were a redistribution of wealth that undermined American liberty by taking a man's property.[5]

Johnson's rejection of Lincoln's vision began the process that would resurrect American oligarchy.

★

President Johnson's support energized white southern Democrats, who set out to reduce their black neighbors to subservience. When white southerners rejected the Fourteenth Amendment and Congress passed the Military Reconstruction Act to put biracial conventions in charge of rebuilding the South, the Ku Klux Klan organized to prevent southern Republicans—black and white both—from voting in favor of the new state constitutions. The Ku Klux Klan murdered nearly a thousand Unionists before the 1868 elections, terrorized their neighbors, and undercut democracy in the South. Even more effective than Ku Klux Klan ropes, clubs and bullets, though, were the new tactics to which white Democrats turned when they realized that the violence of the Klan simply hardened Republican resolve. Echoing Johnson's argument that government policies promoting black equality were simply a redistribution of wealth, Democrats set out to break down national support for inviting all Americans to have a say in their government. They linked race to class in an explicit acknowledgment of the devil's bargain the Founders had made a century before.

The story began to play out as soon as voters turned Andrew Johnson out of the White House in 1868. Southern Democrats had put their faith in Johnson's promise that northern Democrats would take the 1866 midterms and reinstate his lenient terms for their return to the Union. When voters instead elected Republicans, giving them the power to rebuild the South as they saw fit, including black suffrage, and then readmit the southern states on those terms, Democrats could only hope to win control of the government in 1868. But voters across

the country elected to replace Johnson with the very man who had defeated the Confederacy, General Ulysses S. Grant.

Grant's election would change political calculations in the South.
He won in large part thanks to 70,000 southern African Americans,
whose votes threw the Electoral College to him. Democrats recognized
that Republicans were going to make sure that laws applied equally
in the South. When Ku Klux Klan violence affected the 1870 midterm elections, Congress in April 1871 passed a bill making it a crime
to keep African Americans from exercising their civic rights: voting,
holding office, or sitting on juries (which were picked from the voting
lists). The bill authorized the president to declare martial law in places
where the Ku Klux Klan held power, and in October 1871, Grant
did precisely that in nine South Carolina counties. Troops arrested
hundreds of Klansmen and as many as 2000 fled the state guilty, as one
testified, of "whipping and killing" to "tear down the party in power
and build up the other party."[6]

With the muscle of the federal government now enlisted against
racial violence, Democrats tried a new approach, echoing Johnson's
claim that government enforcement of black rights meant a redistribution of wealth. They denounced black participation in government
by arguing that black men were too lazy to work, and thus used their
ballot to vote for policies that took money from hardworking white
taxpayers and redirected it to themselves.

This concern resonated in the North, where workers were beginning to organize to oppose measures that favored industrialists.
Northerners had fought the Civil War to defend the idea that the
government should treat every man equally, but the reality of fighting
such an all-consuming war meant that the government had given
contracts primarily to those who could produce large orders—mule
shoes, rain slickers, and hardtack, for example—uniformly and quickly.
Industrialists like Andrew Carnegie and financiers like Jay Cooke
made fortunes during the war from contracts that were funded largely
by tax dollars paid by workingmen. At the same time, wartime inflation

cut into workers' wages. As soon as the war ended, workers organized to demand reforms, including better wages and shorter hours.[7]

Leveling the playing field between workers and employers seemed to many people to be the logical outcome of a war for democracy against oligarchy. After all, what difference did it make if oligarchs owned plantations or factories? In public, leading Republican Benjamin F. Wade, a senator from Ohio, mused, "Property is not equally divided, and a more equal distribution of capital must be worked out." But businessmen recoiled in horror from what they interpreted as a war on property, and their spokesmen, including the editor of the *New York Times*, hammered home the idea that any hardworking man could make it in America. Labor agitation convinced many observers that workers had turned lazy. By the end of 1870, an article in *Scribner's Monthly* claimed that workers had become demoralized: "The good workman has lost his incentive to be better than his companions, and the poor workman grows poorer by being raised, without effort of his own, to an equality of wages with his superiors."[8]

Americans were not the only ones speculating about the relationship between labor and capital in an industrial society. The International Workingmen's Association had organized in Europe in 1864 under the leadership of Karl Marx, who theorized that human history had five stages. Capitalism was the fourth stage, he wrote, and would finally collapse under pressure from the fifth, when workers would seize the means of production and usher in a just and free society. Marx urged laborers to organize to take over control of the state and speed up the pace of history. The International had come to America by 1867 and had established a headquarters in New York City.[9]

Northerners were already nervous about workers organizing to take over the government when in March 1871, that very thing seemed to happen in France. In the wake of the Franco-Prussian War, Parisians who thought their leaders had sold them out in the peace treaty rejected the treaty's terms and organized their own government. American newspapers trumpeted the notion that the Paris Commune was a regime of workers run amok. According to one article, they were a "wild, reckless, irresponsible, murderous mobocracy" that murdered priests, burned the Tuileries Palace, and bombed buildings. They were overturning all of society, and their intent was to confiscate all property—money, factories, and land—and give it to associations of workingmen.[10]

Although French national troops crushed the Commune at the end of May, most Americans shuddered at the threat posed by the "Communists of Paris" and worried that lazy men at home were hatching similar plots. Throughout 1871, the American press speculated that the country was on the verge of a revolution in which mobs would try to destroy any "mechanic who honors religion and law, and by a superior skill, industry and economy acquires a little property, or who comfortably feeds, clothes, and educates his children." The *New York Times* commented, "Possibly the very extravagances and horrible crimes of the Parisian Communists will, for some years, weaken the influence of the working classes in all countries. The great 'middle-class,' which now governs the world, will everywhere be terrified at these terrible outburst[s] and absurd[ities;] they will hold a stronger rein on the lower."[11]

These growing northern fears about a radicalized lower class meshed easily with southern racism. The Paris Commune had organized in 1871, the year after the Fifteenth Amendment had guaranteed black men the right to vote. White men in South Carolina took advantage of this confluence and began to attack the idea of black voting not on racial grounds—although all the men involved had been vocal in their dislike of African Americans—but on the grounds that it gave poor men control over the states' government, and that they were using that majority power to redistribute wealth.

Their proof was in South Carolina's new legislature, which had met in July 1868. African Americans made up the majority of South Carolina's population, and eighty-eight blacks and sixty-seven whites held seats in the first legislature to sit after the introduction of black suffrage. The black legislators were typically men with some education and some property, and they tended to work with white legislators to protect property in the state. Despite the fact that a disgusted observer sneered, "The colored man standeth forth in his dignity as a freeman, a citizen, a voter. And so doeth the 'white trash,'" the legislature did not lean toward reflecting the interests of former field hands or the poor white workers who wanted radical policies in South Carolina.[12]

Nonetheless, opponents focused on new taxes levied by the majority-black legislature. Rebuilding the state would require money, and to raise the funds for new schools, hospitals, roads, and prosthetics for veterans—a necessity after the butchery of the Civil War— the legislature placed taxes on all property at its full value. Before the war, wealthy landowners in the legislature had consistently undervalued land for tax purposes, placing the burden of taxation on urban professionals, merchants, and bankers. The new tax valuation meant that landowners, especially large landowners, faced higher taxes at a time when their land had lost significant value and their cash reserves were at an all-time low. Then the legislature voted to use state funds to buy land that it would in turn sell to settlers on easy terms. In South Carolina, those poor farmers would usually be freedmen.[13]

South Carolina Democrats howled that the "monkey-show," the "crow-congress," was deliberately plundering white property owners to redistribute wealth to black men. They organized a "Taxpayer's Convention" to meet in Columbia to protest the new taxes—although black taxpayers noted that they were not welcome at the convention. Convention delegates called former slaves "ignorant, superstitious, semi-barbarians," who were "extremely indolent, and will make no exertion beyond what is necessary to obtain food enough to satisfy their hunger." Republicans had given these lazy louts the vote and, since they held the balance in elections, they had "absolute political supremacy," which they were using to plunder the state's taxpayers. "The most intelligent, the influential, the educated, the really useful men of the South, deprived of all political power," were being "taxed and swindled by a horde of rascally foreign adventurers, and by the ignorant class, which only yesterday hoed the fields and served in the kitchen."[14]

In the end, the Taxpayers' Convention concluded only that the South Carolina legislature should be careful with money, but their argument spread throughout the North, where Democrats were eager to undermine the legitimacy of the southern Republican governments, and Republicans were eager to silence the voices of northern workers, who tended to vote for Democrats. What was going on in South Carolina was also going on in New York City, the *Chicago Tribune* said; both were being ruled by "irresponsible non-property-holders." The Republican *New-York Daily Tribune* published an interview with former Confederate Secretary of State Robert Toombs, a Georgia Democrat, who explicitly compared former slaves to the Paris Communards. A property qualification for voting was imperative, Toombs said, otherwise "the lower classes . . . the dangerous, irresponsible element," would control government and "attack the interests of the landed proprietors." Toombs insisted that "only those who owned the country should govern it, and men who had no property had no right to make laws for property-holders."[15]

It was no surprise that a former slaveholder and staunch secessionist had resurrected the slaveholders' prewar philosophy. More surprising was that by 1871 many northerners now shared it. The popular magazine *Scribner's Monthly* used italics for emphasis when it warned: "*The interference of ignorant labor with politics is dangerous to society.*"[16]

★

Democrats got as much traction as they did in part because they contrasted what they saw as a system of race-based wealth redistribution taking hold in the East with an image of the American West where hardworking men asked nothing of the government but to be left alone. The cowboy era and Reconstruction overlapped almost exactly, and to oppose Republican policies, Democrats mythologized the cowboy, self-reliant and tough, making his way in the world on his own. Cowboy life was actually harsh and decidedly unromantic, but that didn't matter to those seeking to use the cowboy's image to undermine the growing federal government.

While Congress focused on putting farmers on the western plains, Texans had tried farming in the wide expanses of the short-grass prairie, and they knew it was a losing battle. The landscape was one of stunning beauty: buffalograss, pink coneflowers, yellow and brown black-eyed Susans, orange and red blanket flowers, and purple lavender hyssop blew in the incessant wind. But that beauty thrived under a burning sun and with so little water the grasses stretched their roots down six feet or more. Southerners had moved into Texas in the 1830s to establish cotton plantations there. They soon discovered that the Great Plains, which start at about the 98th meridian that runs close to the southern tip of the state, were far too hot and dry for cotton. They were, however, perfect for grazing animals. Native bison, horses, and the Texas longhorn cattle, descended directly from the animals that arrived with the Spanish, thrived.

In the 1840s, Americans began to dabble in the cattle trade, which was dominated by Mexicans, who had run cattle along the Santa Fe Trail since the Mexican Revolution. Cattlemen would drive the beeves to a railhead at St. Louis, where they would be shipped back east. The trade broke down during the Civil War, when the United States Navy isolated Texas by taking the Mississippi River and blockading southern ports, and southern railroads deteriorated so badly that cattlemen couldn't move animals east by rail. Trapped in Texas, cattle multiplied until observers estimated there were eight beeves for every person in the state. By early 1865, Texas cattlemen were so desperate to get rid of the animals that they offered them to Confederate President Jefferson Davis for free, if only he would take them. The Confederacy could not, and so southern troops ate parched corn while cattle ran wild in Texas.[17]

When the Confederate government collapsed in April 1865, what was left of state law enforcement fell with it. Texas was full of desperate, despairing men, who were as willing as not to run stock off and murder anyone who objected. "It looked like everything worth living for was gone," former Texas Ranger Charles Goodnight told a sympathetic biographer in the 1920s. "The entire country was depressed—there was no hope. We could not see what the Reconstructionists would do, nor how long they would hold out." Cattle offered a way out. In 1865, a man could buy a fattened beef for about $4 in Texas—if he bothered to buy it rather than simply running it off— and that same animal would sell for $30 to $40 in a booming city like Chicago.[18]

In 1866, Goodnight and another Texan, Oliver Loving, gathered a herd of cattle and fourteen hands: former Confederate soldiers who had lost everything but their ability to shoot a gun and ride a horse, and former slaves eager for work. They traveled north along the Pecos River to Fort Sumner in New Mexico, where federal officers paid eight cents a pound for beeves to feed the Indians held at Bosque Redondo. Arriving back in Texas with $12,000, they sparked the cattle rush. From 1866 until 1886, when seemingly endless blizzards devastated herds that were already weakened by drought and overgrazing, cattlemen with money hired men to corral large numbers of cattle and drive them north to market—to railheads, to Indian reservations, to mining towns—across the Great Plains.[19]

To white southerners, the West beckoned. Their own land had been ruined by the war: the roads churned to ruts, homes burned, cities smashed, fields gone to weeds, and survivors scarred in body and mind. To rebuild meant reaching an accommodation with former slaves, who now held far more power than most white southerners thought they should. The West, seemingly beyond reach of the war's aftermath, offered a new start. White southerners began to move into the Great Plains.

The myth of the American cowboy was born of Reconstruction and carried all the hallmarks of the strife of the immediate postwar years: he was a hardworking white man who started from nothing, asked for nothing, and could rise on his own. The reality was that about a third of all cowboys were men of color—black or Mexican, and sometimes Indian—and that few rose to prosperity. From the moment a young man signed on to a crew for a workingman's wage, his life was guided solely by the task of getting those cattle alive to market. That meant days and nights in the saddle, rubbing tobacco in his eyes to stay awake, breathing dust, braving storms, and avoiding the cottonmouths that nested near river crossings. And those were the dangers a man could see coming. Worse was that cattle were easily spooked. A sudden noise at night—a wolf howl, a gunshot, or a flash of lightning—and they might stampede. So, in the dark, cowboys sang soothing songs, in part to keep the cattle calm and in part so that crew members could try to turn stampeding cattle away from their partners before they were flattened—literally—by terrified beeves. Despite all their hard work, most of the profits went to the cattlemen. Their low wages, dangerous conditions, and lack of access to upward mobility made cowboys a western version of industrial workers in the factories back east.

That's not how they looked to eastern Democrats, for whom the young men on horseback were the image of ideal Americans, fun-loving and honest boys in an all-male world, protecting their employer's interests from attacks by barbaric Indians and cunning Mexicans. They didn't need regulations or a handout; they were individualists, working to make it on their own.

In reality the federal government was more active in the American West than in any other region. In the postwar period it provided settlers with land, fought and then corralled Indians, bolstered markets through contracts to feed and clothe Army personnel and hundreds of thousands of reservation Indians, and funded and protected the railroads that got western products—including cattle—to eastern markets. The mythologized cowboy embodied the resentment of southern Democrats and their northern compatriots, who believed that the Republicans were using the federal government to give lazy black people benefits white men did not have.[20]

A political fight in Missouri brought the link between western individualism and anti-government activism to popular attention. A slaveholding Union state, Missouri had been torn apart by the Civil War. To harass Union supporters, Confederate William Quantrill organized a guerilla band to launch surprise raids: riding their horses into a town at full speed, firing revolvers with both hands, and then riding out before the Unionists could scramble for their weapons. When Missouri Republicans rewrote their state's constitution in 1865, they were so angry at Confederate sympathizers that they essentially erased their civic identity. No one who had ever helped the Confederacy in any way—even by mailing a letter or feeding breakfast to a relative who was a soldier—could vote, hold office, teach, preach, or practice law in the state. Named for the leader of Missouri's Republican Party, Charles Drake, the Drake Constitution—or the "draconian constitution," to its opponents—turned the state over to Republicans, seemingly for all time.[21]

Because Missouri was a northern state and did not fall under the Military Reconstruction Act, Democrats there could not vote even after Georgia was readmitted to the Union in 1870. While most Americans considered the nation's government restored to normal, Democrats in Missouri were still disfranchised. They argued that Republicans were monopolizing the government to make sure they would always stay in power.

A newspaper editor who was eager to return Democrats to control in Missouri developed this theme by creating a sympathetic figurehead for it. Former Confederate John Newman Edwards used his newspaper, the *Kansas City Times*, to attack the Drake Constitution by defending Jesse James, a former member of Quantrill's Raiders. After the war, James turned the talents he had developed as a guerilla to a spree of robberies and murders. In late 1869, James and some of his men robbed a bank in Gallatin, Missouri, and James murdered the cashier. The governor of the state put a price on his head.

In 1870, Edwards began to print letters from Jesse James insisting that he was innocent of the crimes laid to his account (though he wasn't) but that he couldn't turn himself in because he was a former Confederate and a Democrat. Since the Drake Constitution prohibited Democrats from becoming lawyers or voters, the state's lawyers, judges, and jurors, as well as the governor, were all Republicans and, he said, they would send him to his death no matter what the evidence before them. Edwards's columns turned the outlaw Jesse James into the symbol of a hardworking man persecuted by a corrupt government.[22]

This was a powerful image, and a Missouri Republican looking for a platform made it national. Newspaperman Carl Schurz had wrested a senatorship out of the hands of Charles Drake himself by echoing the complaints of Missouri Democrats about Republican attacks on the individual. Schurz wanted to get rid of President Grant as the head of the Republican Party, so he began to echo and promote the argument that, under the president's leadership, the party was simply buying black votes with taxpayer-funded handouts.

In 1872, to challenge Grant's reelection, Schurz and his friends launched a new political party: the Liberal Republicans. The government had no role in adjusting inequalities in American life, they argued. They were willing to accept the Reconstruction Amendments, but beyond that the government must not go. Policies that helped African Americans cost tax dollars that amounted to a redistribution of wealth. Amplifying the Democrats' critique of the Republican government, Liberal Republicans highlighted the idea of the western individual eager simply to be left alone. The Liberal Republicans merged with the Democrats and lost in a landslide when they put newspaper editor Horace Greeley up as their presidential candidate. But they had brought most of the nation's journalists to their campaign, and their western version of what it meant to be an American stuck.[23]

By 1880, the cowboy had become an iconic image of the American individualist whose eastern counterpart was under attack.

★

Just as the prewar eastern independent farmer had depended on slavery, the cowboy depended on racial and gender hierarchies. In the mythologized West, Americans who were increasingly defined as "white" stood against the "other." Despite the Fourteenth and Fifteenth Amendments, the federal government and western state and territorial legal systems kept people of color at the margins, using treaties, military actions, and territorial and state laws that limited land ownership, suffrage, and intermarriage. Racial distinctions might be disappearing in the move toward equality in the East, but in the West they were very much alive. There the hierarchical lines were as crucial to the image of the prosperous white western individualist as they had been to the image of the rising yeoman farmer in the East after the American Revolution. And just as the image of the farmer had helped pave the way for the rise of wealthy southern planters, so the image of the independent rising westerner helped pave the way for the rise of industrialists.

The end of the Civil War did not mean peace. When the U.S. Army stopped fighting in the South in 1865, it simply turned its attention to the wars on the Great Plains against the Apaches, Kiowas, Comanches, Cheyennes, and Lakotas. Government officials had already settled the question of whether or not Indians were equal to white men during the Civil War, when Santees were hanged, Navajos force-marched to Bosque Redondo, and Cheyennes massacred and mutilated. During the war, Americans saw Indians as enemies of the Republic; after the war, the government codified that perception.

There was special urgency to the Indian Wars in 1865, for postwar Americans were eager to push their way into the West and Indians were stopping them. In the Southwest, Kiowas and Comanches were raiding the Union Pacific Railroad as the workers hammered their way through Kansas, and in the Northwest, Lakotas were attacking the miners traveling up the Bozeman Trail that cut from the old Oregon Trail in Wyoming to the gold fields in Montana. Americans had just won a war to spread the economic system of free labor across the West, and they were not going to turn back because a few savages on horseback wanted to hunt buffalo rather than work for a living.

General Grant dispatched his best fighter, William Tecumseh Sherman—"Cump" to his friends—to oversee the conflicts simmering on the Great Plains, but Sherman's guidance was not of much use in the Southwest, where Apaches, Kiowas, Comanches, Mexicans, and Americans had rubbed elbows for a generation. There, local officers seemed to be able to handle the necessary negotiations. So Sherman turned his attention to the Northwest, where the Bozeman Trail had only recently brought significant numbers of Americans, Lakotas, and Cheyennes into contact, and the collision meant that tempers were hot. Lakotas insisted on protecting their hunting grounds from the miners snaking their way through it. The U.S. government insisted on protecting those miners from Indian attacks.

The Army had established Fort Reno near the Powder River on the Bozeman Trail in 1865, then strung forts along the trail. Fort Phil Kearney in what is now Wyoming went up in July 1866. Then, a month later, soldiers began to knock together Fort C. F. Smith in Montana on the Bighorn River. The new forts were hastily built, understaffed, and plagued by rats that ate stored grain and undermined the fort walls. They also were manned by soldiers who had come west with little respect for Indians. In December 1866, Colonel Henry B. Carrington, who was in command of Fort Phil Kearny, ordered Lieutenant Colonel W. J. Fetterman and eighty men under his command to protect men gathering wood, but warned Fetterman to stay close to the fort. Fetterman, who thought Carrington was weak, boasted that he could whip the Lakota once and for all. Lakota warriors Red Cloud and American Horse lured

Fetterman away from the fort and into a trap, where they killed the entire party.[24]

"This massacre should be treated as an act of war and should be punished with vindictive earnestness," General Sherman wrote, "until at least ten Indians are killed for each white life lost." He urged his men to kill any Indians they found, to "destroy all of the same breed." He told them to consider all Lakotas in the Powder River region hostile, and to "punish them to the extent of utter extermination if possible."

For the next two years, the conflict, dubbed Red Cloud's War, raged, with the Lakotas quickly gaining the upper hand. In August 1867 they attacked men haying near Fort C. F. Smith, then attacked again near Fort Phil Kearny, where the men threw together wagon boxes for defense. A few days after the "Wagon Box Fight," Lakota warriors attacked a Union Pacific freight train in Nebraska.

Congress rejected Sherman's plan for extermination of the native peoples, and instead sent a peace commission to push the Indians onto two giant reservations, one on the southern plains and one to the north. In October 1867, the commissioners met with tribal leaders near Medicine Lodge Creek in Kansas, where they persuaded a critical mass of Apaches, Comanches, Kiowas, Cheyennes, and Arapahos to sign a series of treaties known collectively as the Treaty of Medicine Lodge. The Indians agreed to stop attacking railroad crews and settlers, and to exchange claims to about 90 million acres of land for firm titles to about 3 million acres in what is now Oklahoma. The government promised to provide the Indians with food, clothing, medical care, teachers, and the professional guidance they would need to turn to farming.

Up north, Red Cloud sent word to the commissioners that he would not negotiate until the troops were removed from Forts Phil Kearny and C. F. Smith. Concluding they could not protect both the railroads and the Bozeman Trail, government officials abandoned the forts. Red Cloud's people burned them down and then, victorious, rode into Fort Laramie to negotiate. Having demonstrated that he held the upper hand over the U.S. Army, Red Cloud signed a peace treaty primarily to gain trading rights at the fort in exchange for promises to stop killing settlers.[25]

The 1868 Treaty of Fort Laramie was a mirror of the Treaty of Medicine Lodge. It established a 22-million-acre tract of land in the western half of what is now South Dakota, along with a piece of Nebraska. In return for their cooperation, the government promised the Lakotas food, clothing, farm animals and tools, seeds, clothing, and a yearly annuity, along with a doctor, a carpenter, a sawmill, and teachers to help them transition from hunting to farming. These provisions didn't interest Red Cloud much, because the treaty also gave the Indians the right to hunt bison in the Black Hills, a right that Indians interpreted as meaning "forever." Sherman knew better. "It will not be long before all the buffaloes are extinct near and between the railroads, after which the Indians will have no reason to approach either railroad," he wrote to his brother, Ohio Senator John Sherman, in June 1868.[26]

By 1868, the western wars had made many easterners revise their belief in the concept that "all men were created equal." When Congress hammered out the Fourteenth Amendment, the members explicitly excluded "Indians not taxed"—that is, those either on reservations, still fighting the U.S. Army, or considered too poor and undesirable—from being counted for a state's representation in Congress. That would avoid the problem apparent in the South, where not-yet-enfranchised black voters would swell a state's population for the purposes of representation but would not have a say in their actual government. By cutting Indians out of the equation, Congress hoped to make sure that what was happening in the South wasn't replicated out west. But counting Indians out of representation both distinguished them from other Americans and guaranteed that few politicians would work on their behalf. They had nothing to gain from it.

There was an additional and uncodified loophole in the Fourteenth Amendment. It confirmed citizenship for "all persons born or naturalized in the United States and subject to the jurisdiction thereof." This excluded Indians fighting the United States. It also excluded another crucial group: Chinese immigrants. Westerners were not terribly concerned about black Americans—there were only 4,272 African Americans in California in 1870, while there were almost half a million white Americans—but they wanted no part of allowing Chinese men to be part of American society. When Congress wrote the Fifteenth Amendment to protect the rights of southern black men to vote and to hold office in the South, members of the Nevada legislature refused to ratify it until they were assured that Congress had deliberately worded it to permit the exclusion of Chinese, and legislators in California and Oregon rejected it outright (Oregon went so far as to reject it after it was already ratified). In the wake of the racist uproar over the Fifteenth Amendment, Democrats won control of California and Oregon. A year later, in Los Angeles—then a cattle town of 5,800 or so residents—a mob of Americans and Mexicans lynched more than fifteen Chinese.[27]

While the Fourteenth Amendment was designed to erase legal distinctions among men of different heritages in the East, it never did so in the West, where states and territories enshrined those distinctions in their legal systems, based on laws written in the previous century to distinguish between white settlers and imported slaves. The country's early naturalization laws permitted only "free white persons" to become citizens. At the time, Congress was trying to distinguish between imported slaves and voluntary European immigrants. The Fourteenth Amendment overrode these laws for African Americans but not for immigrants. Western states and territories fell back on the early naturalization acts, finalized in 1802, to exclude Chinese from citizenship.[28]

The image of the western individual also reinforced traditional eastern gender norms. When the first Wyoming Territorial legislature met in 1869, its Democratic members, furious at the idea of black voting, passed a law giving women the vote, which, its secretary bragged, put "the youngest territory on earth in the vanguard of civilization and progress." Their hope was to bring women to the territory to "civilize" it with their superior values as wild bachelors settled into marriage and as women reared children. In February 1870, Utah Territory followed suit. But after women there voted to support polygamy, Wyoming legislators, suddenly unsure that women were such a "civilizing" factor after all, tried unsuccessfully to revoke female suffrage. When Congress crafted the Fifteenth Amendment in 1870, it left women out.[29]

Suffragists decided to test their right to vote under the Fourteenth Amendment in the 1872 election. Certainly they fell under the native-born designation, as they pointed out, and thus should also be citizens able to vote. In New York, Susan B. Anthony voted and was later tried and convicted—in an all-male courtroom in which she did not have the right to testify—for the crime of voting illegally. In Missouri, where the question of who would have a right to have a say in society was still hotly contested because of the Drake Constitution, a registrar named Reese Happersett refused to permit suffragist Virginia Minor to register to vote. Minor sued Happersett, and the case went all the way to the Supreme Court. When the justices finally handed down a unanimous decision in 1875, they codified a constriction on the postwar idea of democracy. Yes women were citizens, the justices concluded. But citizenship did not necessarily mean the right to vote.

Only a decade after the Civil War, the underpinnings of democracy, which the war had been fought to uphold, were under attack. The mythology of the self-made "new man," the cowboy, depended on the racial and gender hierarchies of the West, much as the iconography of the independent eastern farmer had a generation earlier. Western states and territories maintained racial categories in their cultural and legal systems: the cowboy was a white man. The cowboy image also had no role for women except as good wives, dependent on their men, or as prostitutes; working women in the West disappeared from popular view. Class lines in the West were much like those in the East, but white men could see themselves as superior to everyone around them. So while Republicans in the East had fought the Civil War to banish the idea that a few wealthy white men should rule society, Democrats in the West after the war were fighting for precisely that principle.

CHAPTER 5

Western Politics

For all that the Civil War had been fought over controlling the West, the political system before the war involved easterners almost exclusively. The Republican Party had formed in the 1850s as a northern party, and it had largely stayed in the North. When Congress readmitted the former Confederate states to the Union between 1868 and 1870, though, Republicans had to figure out how to build a national party, one that could keep hold of the White House. At first, they hoped that black voters would make the party competitive in the South. Those hopes faded quickly as white supremacists kept black voters from the polls. The last election in which Republicans were competitive in the South was 1876. Even then, it took four months of complicated negotiations to swing the Electoral College behind Republican candidate Rutherford B. Hayes to give him the presidency.

In 1880, Republicans ran the popular former Union general James A. Garfield on a platform in which he promised, quite eloquently, to protect black rights. Garfield won, but by only 8,355 votes out of almost 9 million cast. Ominously, the South went solidly against the Republicans, and it would stay that way until Tennessee broke ranks briefly in 1920.

So Republicans began to look west to resurrect their fortunes. They began with California, which had gone Democratic in 1880, but just barely—by only 144 votes out of more than 160,000 cast. Democrats there were capitalizing on white workers' hatred for the Chinese. The completion of the Union Pacific Railroad in 1869 increased racial tensions when the linking of the West Coast to the East pushed California into an economic recession. Men thrown out of work blamed the Chinese, who, they believed, competed for their jobs, especially as now-unemployed Chinese workers moved from the rail lines back to coastal cities.

In San Francisco, Irish-born Democrat Denis Kearney had built a successful business as a drayman, moving goods around the city by wagon. But he could only go so far, because the businessmen who ruled San Francisco controlled the freight-moving business, and they refused to fix the streets' potholes. In 1877, Kearney began to speak to workingmen in the city, urging them to rise up. At first he spoke highly of Chinese workers, but within a year he began to blame them for the plight of the white worker. His speeches became increasingly racist, and soon he was ending them all with a signature tagline: "The Chinese must go."

In 1879, Republican Senator James G. Blaine, who had an instinctive sense of which way the political winds were blowing, backed the idea of ending Chinese immigration. Fellow eastern Republicans lambasted him for giving up on democratic principles, but the majority of the party was willing to sign on to nativism to attract voters. In 1882, Republicans bowed to western sentiments and passed the Chinese Exclusion Act, a law that prohibited Chinese workers from immigrating to America (although it permitted businessmen, scholars, and diplomats). *Harper's Weekly* lamented Republican willingness to prohibit "the voluntary immigration of free skilled laborers into the country, and . . . to renounce the claim that America welcomes every honest comer."[1]

With the Chinese Exclusion Act, the western legal system that discriminated between individuals based on race became national law. Hierarchies were back on the table and, as always, that idea led to dehumanization. In the wake of the new law, western violence against the Chinese got worse. In 1885, white miners in Rock Springs, Wyoming, became convinced that Chinese workers were undercutting their wages, and murdered as many as fifty of them.

The Republicans had surrendered Lincoln's key point, but it still was not enough to help them win in 1884. Voters who believed the Republicans had sold out to big business put a Democrat into the White House for the first time since the Civil War. Grover Cleveland promised to curb the power of the rich, and his election revealed a sea change in American politics. Republican operatives recognized they were going to have to adjust their electoral strategies: because they could not compete in the South, they would have to find votes in the West.

In 1888, when Cleveland won the popular vote again by about 90,000 votes, Republican operatives maneuvered the Electoral College to award victory to Benjamin Harrison. (When Harrison, a devout Presbyterian, mused that Providence had given him the victory, his political manager, Mark Hanna, grumbled, "Providence hadn't a damn thing to do with it. [A] number of men were compelled to approach the penitentiary to make him President.")[2]

With Republicans back in control of the federal government, Republican operatives turned to the West, where the territories the Republicans had admitted more than twenty-five years earlier were still sitting in limbo. This long-term territorial status was unprecedented. Generally a territory gained enough population to become a state within a year or two, and was admitted to the Union shortly thereafter. The western territories, though, had been organized quickly during the Civil War and gained population very slowly. By then, politicians were entrenched in the new territories, and back in Washington, D.C., each side blocked the admission of states they thought would favor their opponents and called for the admission of states they thought would swing in their favor. Republicans expected they could take the Dakota and Washington Territories, while the Democrats expected Montana and New Mexico would be theirs. Things had dragged on until early 1888, when Congress debated admitting all four states to- gether. Harrison's election, along with a Republican Congress, sud- denly changed the equation. The Democrats had to make the best deal they could get, and fast, or the incoming Republican Congress would simply cut Democratic territories out of statehood altogether.[3]

On February 22, 1889, just before he left office, President Cleveland signed an omnibus bill that cut the giant Dakota Territory into two pieces: North Dakota and South Dakota. The bill enabled the people there, along with those who lived in the Territories of Montana and Washington, to write state constitutions and elect state governments. The bill provided that those four new states would be admitted to the Union on the following July 4. Cutting the Democratic New Mexico Territory out of statehood, the bill promised to give the Republicans three new states and the Democrats one—Montana (gleeful Republicans boasted that they could take that state, too). *Frank Leslie's Illustrated Newspaper*, operated by President Harrison's ne'er-do-well son Russell, bragged that the new states would send eight new Republican senators to Washington and provide enough Electoral College votes to keep New York, which usually put its 36 elec- toral votes behind a Democrat, from determining the next president.[4]

When the admission of these new states still didn't secure Republicans' hold on power, they added Wyoming and Idaho to the nation as well, rushing to bring them in before the 1890 midterm elections. Since there were too few people living in them to qualify as states, Republicans insisted that the 1890 census would reveal that they had grown dramatically since the census of the previous decade. They were in such a hurry to admit Idaho that they ignored the usual procedures and simply called for volunteers to write a state constitution, which voters approved only months later. Opponents pointed out that Democratic New Mexico and Arizona had far more people than Wyoming and Idaho, and that the fast admission of these two empty western territories was intended to stack the political deck.[5]

In rushing the admission of western states, eastern Republicans intended to create additional votes for their own policies, but it didn't turn out that way. Instead, they created a new political bloc that would change the course of American history. In the 1890 midterm elections, western voters joined with southern Democrats to oppose eastern Republicans' economic policies. A tight money supply, high tariffs, and a refusal to fund public works projects might have helped eastern businessmen, but they hurt the nation's underdeveloped regions. In 1890, westerners organized as the Farmers' Alliance and the Silver Party gave control of Congress to Democrats.

After their midterm defeat, eastern Republicans tried desperately to pass a bill protecting African American voting in the South, a bill that would give them a shot at regaining the power they had lost there. The Federal Elections Bill had passed the House with Republican votes before the election, but when the Senate took up the bill after it, western Republicans joined Democrats to kill the measure, noting that the West and the South both wanted to keep nonwhites from power. Western white men had no desire to share power with Chinese or Indians, so why should southern whites share it with a similarly degraded race? Thanks to the admission of the new states, the nine Pacific and Rocky Mountain states, with fewer than 3 million people, had eighteen senators, while the six New England states, with almost 5 million people, had only twelve. The weight of the new western states killed the Federal Elections Bill. It would be seventy-five years before Congress again attempted to protect black voting.[6]

On the heels of this show of strength, in 1891 westerners explicitly organized as a political bloc. Leaders from western states and Louisiana formed the Trans-Mississippi Congress to promote the interests of the

West as a region without regard to party. Former Colorado governor Alva Adams told delegates to an early meeting that their mission was "to convey to our government, to our friends in the East . . . that we are growing, that we are developing, that we are increasing in strength, and that the new Empire of the West is being consolidated and that we are fast becoming a commercial, political, and intellectual center." He called for westerners to forget about political affiliations and to work with one another. "Let us unite and concentrate for the accomplishment of our purposes and then we shall become a power that will be irresistible; and the West will soon become omnip[o]tent in the affairs of our nation."[7]

Delegates to the Trans-Mississippi Congress were excited about their region's future. They believed that the West would ally with the Canadian West as well as South America and take the Pacific Islands, becoming the world's driving commercial force. Two things were key to that success: easier access to money and water development, including a canal across the Isthmus of Panama. To strengthen their hand, westerners wanted the admission of the rest of the western territories. They began to push for the admission of Utah, New Mexico, Arizona, and Indian Territory, or Oklahoma. In 1894, after the Mormon Church outlawed polygamy, California businessman Isaac Trumbo, who was interested in developing mines and a railroad in the region, helped Utah boosters get Congress to set their territory on the road to statehood. Westerners managed to add Utah as a state in 1896, mainly because Republicans believed they could snag it for their own (they did get one senator, and managed to block the other appointment), but they would have to wait until 1907 to get Oklahoma, and until 1912 to get Arizona and New Mexico admitted.[8]

★

The new western states were far more in line with the hierarchical structure of the South than with the democratic principles of the Civil War Republicans. Their political orientation reflected the reality of the western economy, which looked much more like that of the antebellum South than that of the antebellum North. By 1890, a few extractive industries dominated the West. Just as in the antebellum South, those industries depended on poor workers—often migrant workers—and a few men in the sparsely populated western states controlled both the industries and politics. They had far more sympathy for the ideology of former plantation elites—who had ruled much the way they did— than for that of the common man.

When they first came to the West in significant numbers, Americans inherited a society shaped by the Spanish and Mexicans. Grafted onto a similar Spanish system, the Mexican tradition of giving large land grants to favored leaders who had accumulated wealth and power through trade on the Santa Fe Trail meant the development of a society that circled around a few powerful men. That, in turn, buttressed a caste system, including debt peonage and slavery, although of Indians rather than African Americans. American fur traders perpetuated this caste system, and when Americans acquired the West in the 1840s, their hunger for access to resources gave them no inclination to change anything. In fact, just the opposite: settlement of the West tended to reinforce the dominance of a few men, rather than to challenge it.[9]

Over the course of his career, for example, William Sharon earned the nickname "the Great King." Sharon had arrived in Sacramento, California, from the Midwest in 1849 to sell merchandise to the miners swinging their picks after gold. When a flood washed away his tent and his goods, the fiddle-playing, cockfighting, womanizing gambler made his way to San Francisco, still a raw town into which an occasional grizzly bear wandered, where he made a fortune in real estate, married, and entered politics. He lost his money gambling in stocks of mines on the newly opened Comstock Lode in Nevada, but in 1864, his friend William Ralston, head of the Bank of California, made him manager of a Bank of California branch in Virginia City, located in the midst of the legendary Comstock gold and silver mines. He moved to Virginia City with his servant Ah Ki, an immigrant from China, who would stay with him until Sharon's death twenty-three years later.[10]

About the time Sharon arrived in Nevada, Congress welcomed the state to the Union as one of the western territories and states Civil War Republicans were admitting quickly in the 1860s, in hopes of reproducing the North's system of independent farmers and small towns. But that system never worked particularly well on the dry prairies. Instead, the need for large amounts of capital meant that men like Sharon, rather than individuals wresting a living from nature, dominated the postwar West. Mining, cattle, and railroads all demanded deep pockets, a requirement that made them turn to bankers. When Sharon set up the Bank of California branch in Virginia City, the Comstock mines appeared played out. Sharon first loaned money to mining and milling companies, then took over the bankrupt businesses when they couldn't repay the loans. What Sharon did in Virginia City looked a lot like what happened across the rest of the world. Even after the advent of irrigation systems in the late 1890s, small farmers did not take root in the West; rather, large-scale agribusiness did. And then came the oil industry.[11]

These new western industries looked much more like the extractive industry of antebellum cotton than like northern subsistence farming. While popular magazines touted the freedom and independence of the miner and the cowboy, working conditions and upward mobility for westerners mirrored those of the industrial workers in eastern factories. Mining, for example, quickly moved from panning at the surface into deep shafts, expensive to dig and expensive to work; as the expression had it, it took a gold mine to develop a silver mine. In Virginia City, William Sharon quickly figured out that the real fortune to be made from the Comstock Lode was not in digging the rock, but in the steady work of grinding it down to extract the ore. After taking possession of local mills in 1867, Sharon boasted he made $250,000 in six months. Between 1863 and 1874, the Yellow Jacket mine yielded more than

$13 million worth of gold; more than $10 million went into milling costs.[12]

The money in the region's other major industries was also at the top, and the low wages and poor conditions miners suffered were similar to those of cowboys, farm workers, railroad laborers, and oil workers. The cowboys made little for their dangerous work with the half-wild cattle in the extremes of hot and cold, crossing rivers, risking death during stampedes or from Indian battles. Agribusiness used migrant workers from the beginning: Mexican Americans and Japanese Americans picked sugar beets and, later, fruits and vegetables. Oil production, too, used primarily inexpensive wage workers. Indeed, the region's corporation-heavy economy was possible in large part precisely because employers could draw on a population of cheap laborers, often immigrants, who moved around the area under the control of labor bosses. And then there were the railroads. The nation's first private big business, the railroad industry dominated the American economy after 1870, but the men who built the railroads did not get rich from them. They were poor wage workers, including Chinese and African Americans.[13]

The power of western business leaders grew with the country. They expanded their holdings: Sharon, for example, worked with his partners to monopolize local water supplies to feed his mills, and then took over lumber production to build the mines. As their pockets got deeper, they pushed their interests by putting pressure on local governments and state legislatures. Recognizing that there was money to be made transporting gold out of the Comstock region to a railhead, for example, Sharon organized a railroad company in 1867, then in 1869 became president of it and got the Nevada legislature, local mining companies, and stockholders to back construction. Largely completed by 1870, the railroad turned a huge profit. It was only later that locals realized they were stuck paying off the bonds that funded the project, while Sharon lobbied to undervalue the railroad so that he would not have to pay anywhere near the taxes he had promised it would produce.[14]

As early as 1870, Sharon and his partner had discussed the benefits of Sharon going to the Senate, where he could advance their interests. By 1872, he had moved back to San Francisco, but he guaranteed the money that enabled a friend to buy a local newspaper to support Sharon's candidacy for one of Nevada's two senate seats. In that year, he abruptly withdrew from the race when the *Territorial Enterprise* ran exposés of his career. In 1874, though, still determined to win a Nevada senatorship "regardless of the expense," Sharon finagled the temporary retirement of Nevada's other senator, bought the *Enterprise* for five times its value, and set out to rebuild his public image. When his key opponent defended "the paramount dignity and honor of labor," Sharon called him a communist trying to corrupt the government, while noting that he had "for years given thousands of men steady employment . . . I have expended . . . millions in your midst—in building mills and hoisting works and in opening our mines and improving the country."[15]

Sharon's campaign was overtly racist. His opponent, Adolph Sutro, was a Prussian Jew who had arrived in America after the Revolution of 1848, and Sharon's operatives hit all the anti-Semitic themes they could, concluding that Sutro was "a liar . . . a villain . . . a traitor to the people by whose sufferance he lives and urges his nefarious schemes in free America." Sharon also assured voters that Chinese were inferior to white men, although he had hired them to build his own railroad. While Chinese could be "employed as cooks and at certain kinds of labor in households," he said, "I do not wish you to understand . . . that I am in favor of inviting an inferior people to our shores."[16]

Sharon won the Senate seat, which he would take shortly after his partner Ralston, financially embarrassed by the duo's speculations, committed suicide. Sharon then saved the Bank of California, making him even wealthier than he had been before.[17]

Sharon was an extreme example of a postwar western pattern. The unique territorial years of the postwar West reinforced the power of a few wealthy men, as the population stayed sparse and politics centered around those who could deliver capital to the region through railroad contracts, banking ties, government contracts, or Indian land cessions. Those men continued to hold power as they passed favors on to their sons or acolytes, creating political dynasties. Sharon, for example, encouraged his daughter to marry a young lawyer named Francis G. Newlands, whom he brought into the family business. Newlands would move to Nevada in 1888, and in 1892, with the help of Senator William Morris Stewart—another longtime Sharon attorney—and his own $50,000 investment, he would win a seat in the House of Representatives. A decade later, Newlands would trade the House for a prominent career in the Senate.[18]

At the time Newlands was running for the House, it seemed as if the arrival of six new states in 1889–1890 might democratize the western system. In 1890, the first election in which the new states would vote, farmers and miners who had watched the rise of industrialists with dismay organized to break their hold on the West. In the midterm elections of that year, they allied with Democrats to take the House by a margin of two to one, and challenged big-business Republicans in the Senate. By 1892 they had come to believe they were leading a new birth of democracy, and they formed a new political party, the People's Party, to advance their cause. Delegates met in Omaha, Nebraska, to launch the 1892 campaign. "The fruits of the toil of millions are boldly stolen to build up colossal fortunes for a few, unprecedented in the history of mankind; and the possessors of these, in turn despise the Republic and endanger liberty," the party platform declared. Delegates wanted "to restore the government of the Republic to the hands of the 'plain people,' with which class it originated." In 1892, the Populists, as they were now dubbed, helped to put the Democrats in power for the first time since before the Civil War. But their hopes did not pan out. By the 1890s, western leaders were the poles around which society spun, and their interests were the ones that western politicians favored. Populism flourished on the small farms of the West, but the towns and cities supported a power structure that favored the concentration of wealth.[19]

Rather than being the year that Populists took back the government for the people, 1892 was instead the year that demonstrated the power of the wealthy to use the government against ordinary people. In Wyoming, a conflict that had begun thirteen years before ended in 1892 with a shocking demonstration of government intervention in favor of wealthy men. Large cattle operators had organized in 1879 as the Wyoming Stock Growers' Association (WSGA) to systematize the industry by registering brands, planning the spring roundups, and hobnobbing with state officials. After the horrific winter of 1886–1887, when epic snowstorms killed up to 90 percent of cattle, already weakened from malnutrition on the overgrazed plains, cattlemen needed lots of grazing land and plenty of water to recoup their losses. So the cattle barons tried to push homesteaders and smaller cattlemen from the federal lands and water they needed, accusing the smaller operators of being rustlers.[20]

In spring 1892, members of the WSGA hired fifty Texas gunmen to murder their competitors, giving them a written list of seventy "rustlers" they wanted dead, all of them small-time cattlemen and settlers in Johnson County. The gunmen killed two of that group's leaders after setting fire to a cabin where they were hiding. Later that night, outraged settlers surrounded the ranch where the gunmen were staying and threatened to hang them all. It turned into a standoff. When local law enforcement officers sided with the settlers, the stock growers appealed to the governor, who in turn appealed to President Benjamin Harrison, who sent in the army to break up the "insurrection" in the county. Army officers rounded up the WSGA men, but the governor ordered them held near Cheyenne, the state capital and the headquarters of the WSGA. They were not locked up and were allowed to carry their guns, and they openly boasted of going back to

Johnson County to finish their job. Over the next four months, key witnesses for the settlers and smaller cattlemen suddenly went quiet, and the case against the WSGA men fell apart. The big stock growers literally got away with murder.[21]

In the same year, an industrial standoff in Idaho, this one between miners and mine owners, turned out similarly. After a long strike, the owners of the mines in the towns along Idaho's Coeur d'Alene River got a federal injunction to stop the strikers from interfering in the operation of the mines, an injunction that would have let the operators bring in non-union labor. Miners objected, and local governments, again, sympathized with the miners, so the owners appealed to the governor for support. Harrison mobilized the Idaho National Guard and declared martial law, claiming that the strikers were engaged in a "domestic insurrection." The U.S. Army arrested three hundred members of the union and got rid of the local sheriff on the grounds that he "was acting in the interest of his friends, the strikers, to whom he owed his election."[22]

By the end of the nineteenth century, western leaders had internalized the idea that democracy was, in fact, a perversion of government—exactly as southern leaders had done in the immediate postwar years. They argued that small farmers, cattlemen, and miners were not promoting American prosperity and voting legitimately for policies that answered their needs. Instead, they were illegitimately skewing government in their own interests and against what their employers were sure was best for the nation. It was what southern Democrats had said about African Americans during Reconstruction. In that era, race had become class; now class had become race.

Western leaders like William Sharon and Francis Newlands also echoed what eastern industrialists said about their own dominance. After the Civil War, big businessmen had demanded that Congress retain the sweeping tariffs that protected their products, long after their industries had become well established. That protection kept out foreign competition and enabled industrialists to collude to raise prices. At the same time, rising immigration was weakening the labor market and driving down wages. New white-collar workers for whom the new system provided higher salaries and shorter hours denigrated the workers—often non-English-speakers from Italy or Poland, who practiced Judaism or Catholicism—as lazy misfits who refused to work for their own success. When these workers attempted to organize to win higher wages, better conditions, and shorter hours, many dismissed them as socialists or communists trying to game the system to redistribute wealth.

As capital rose to the top and more and more Americans fell behind, leaders justified their control of the economy, politics, and society. In 1889, steel magnate Andrew Carnegie published *The Gospel of Wealth*; in it, sounding much like the pre–Civil War slave owners, he wrote that civilization depends upon "the sacredness of property." The elite were better able to put accumulated wealth to best use. The alternative was "Communism," which killed initiative and destroyed prosperity. "The best interests of the race are promoted" by the system of individualism, "which inevitably gives wealth to the few."[23]

Westerners wholeheartedly endorsed those sentiments. A friend of William Sharon's, Supreme Court Justice Stephen J. Field, helped to write them into American law. A Forty-Niner like Sharon, Field rose quickly in legal circles in California, and Abraham Lincoln appointed him to the Supreme Court in 1863 to represent the important new region. Field was a Democrat who shared the racism of his party. He was also an advocate for mining leaders like Sharon, who had once loaned him $25,000—Field never repaid it—and put him up in a fancy hotel for free whenever he came back to San Francisco. In his thirty-four years on the Court, Field wrote more opinions than almost any other Supreme Court justice in history, insisting that the primary law in America was not the promotion of equality but rather the protection of property.[24]

★

Like the redefinition of former slaves as dangerous socialists, the redefinition of regular Americans as lazy weaklings who wanted a handout was possible because of the postwar image of the western individualist. At meetings of the Trans-Mississippi Congress, which attendees almost immediately renamed the Trans-Mississippi Commercial Congress, speakers lionized the Alamo, that "shrine of Texas liberty," and declared that the West was settled by men who had, as the president of the congress put it in a speech in 1892, "the instinct which nature has planted in the breast of the individual, and which causes him to brave all the dangers to which mankind are subject . . . led him across the scorching desert, and caused him to brave the dangers of Indian warfare; sent him up the mountain slopes and down the canyons in search of silver and gold."[25]

The image of the western individualist had taken hold. In 1883, William F. Cody, who had gained the byname "Buffalo Bill" when he killed bison for the Kansas Pacific Railroad to feed its workers, figured out that there was more money, and easier money, to be made as a showman than as a frontiersman. Cody was not the first, nor the only, one to monetize the cowboy mystique. Cowboys used to pit their roping and riding skills against each other in contests when they got to a town, and from those informal events had developed the western rodeo. Enterprising individuals had started to take "Wild West shows" back east, to pull in money from easterners hungry for a taste of the western experience.

Buffalo Bill went one bigger and better. He brought together former cowboys and Indians to create Buffalo Bill's Wild West Show, repackaging the region as one of romance—full of buffalo hunts, wild Indians, and brave white men who could tame horses and Indians and women and the land. There were no government contracts in Buffalo Bill's Wild West, nor army campaigns to protect railroads, nor mining barons, nor stock growers. Instead there were Pony Express riders who made the short-lived business of delivering private mail look glamorous, and cowboys, whom Buffalo Bill dubbed the "Rough

Riders." In Buffalo Bill's telling, these men were homespun heroes, braving harsh conditions to defend civilization against stagecoach robbers and murderous Indians. The romance of Cody's show made it the entertainment event of the era. The show crisscrossed the East, and by 1887 Cody was bragging, "I kick worse than any quartermaster's mule ever kicked if I don't clear a thousand dollars a day."[26]

By the end of the century, the western individualist became the face of American democracy thanks to historian Frederick Jackson Turner, who delivered a paper at the American Historical Association's annual meeting in 1893 that reinterpreted the nation from the perspective of the post–Civil War West. The historians had decided to meet that year at the Columbian Exposition in Chicago so that scholars would have a chance to see the great exhibits of American machinery, inventions, art, and agricultural products on display at what was popularly known as the "White City," after its gleaming glass and white stucco buildings. The truth is that the historians were probably more interested in the Columbian Exposition than in the work of a young scholar, so probably few of them went to hear what he had to say. Turner's parents were in town for the fair, and even they didn't go to hear him.[27]

Turner did nothing less than reinvent American history. Before him, most people who had bothered to think about the origins of their democracy had chalked it up to the intellectual principles of Thomas Paine, John Adams, Thomas Jefferson, and the rest of the Founders. But Turner argued that it was born on the frontier, as Europeans—and later Americans—constructed a society on the wild edge of savagery, taming the wilderness with civilization. Turner's actors in this drama were not a few eastern elites; they were ordinary men building democracy in the West as they tried to make a living.

Turner rewrote American history to conform to the western mythology. In reality, the West had always been characterized by a multitude of peoples who traded with settlers as well as fought them, but Turner defined the frontier as a line between the civilization of whites and the savagery of Indians. That line gave birth to American individualism, Turner explained, as a man making a homestead in the wilderness looked only to his family and thoroughly resented any control over his actions. In that individualism lay the true roots of American democracy, Turner theorized, for the land permitted men to support themselves, and thus to exercise independent political power.

Just a year or two after western farmers had organized and tried to wrest control of the government out of the hands of big businessmen and give it back to ordinary citizens, Turner attributed democracy to an older time and to iconic heroes. It was not through social movements like Populism that democracy was born, according to Turner, but on the frontier, crafted by individuals like Daniel Boone and Kit Carson, both of whom Turner mentioned by name. With its wealthy leaders and its Trans-Mississippi Commercial Congress, the West of Turner's day looked much like the East, characterized by growing extremes of wealth and poverty. Turner ignored the modern reality and instead harked back to the ideology of the early 1800s, asserting that, from the beginning, "America has been another name for opportunity," and it had called out men's restlessness, energy, practicality, inquisitiveness, invention, and ability "to effect great ends."

Turner's frontier mirrored and reinforced the image of the cowboy as the quintessential individualist. It also reflected the cowboy's imagined world. Turner's thesis not only erased the multiculturalism and the mechanics of trading in the regions where cultures met, it also erased everyone but white men. In Turner's telling, much like in the vision of Young America in the 1840s, slavery was "an incident," and not a terribly important one at that. There were no people of color in Turner's version of the country. Enslaved African Americans lived on the fringes, and there were no free blacks. Neither were there Chinese or Mexicans. The immigrants who became Americans on Turner's frontier were Germans and Scotch-Irish.

And there were no women. Turner's male individualists built their society around "family," but the women in those communities were invisible. In late nineteenth-century America, women worked, studied, labored in factories, went to college, and became teachers, writers, nurses, government clerks, and, increasingly, secretaries. In the West, women worked, farmed, raised money for schools and churches, and, increasingly, voted. They were as central to western life as they were to society in the East. But on Turner's frontier, just as in the mythic version of the cowboys' world, the women were invisible, offstage: the wives who supported the men and nurtured the children, or the painted ladies who wore striped stockings and lived above saloons in the cow towns.

The frontier "carried with it individualism, democracy, and nationalism," Turner argued, qualities he and his peers associated with white men. It was the frontier that had produced the principles of the American Revolution, and which continued to preserve "republican principles pure and uncontaminated." But as the Revolution had showed so pointedly, he explained, the West's power threatened more settled eastern societies. As the frontier expanded, the communities left behind got more complex; they developed government, regulations, and taxes, and sought to control the free men in the West. Easterners tried to regulate westerners with religion, through education, or by limiting their political rights. Westerners, in turn, resented the East, seeing its attempt at control as a threat to their freedom. In a virtual echo of the early Reconstruction years, Turner noted that on the frontier, "the tax gatherer is viewed as a representative of oppression."

Turner claimed that the genius of American democracy had moved west after the Civil War, and there individualism still reigned. There, he said, all people became Americans and regional peculiarities were washed away in a great tide of nationalism. Even slavery, that central rift in the country's life, had been destroyed in the West, where democracy had come fully to life. It was there, then, that America was fulfilling her true destiny.

Turner's vision of the frontier and the role of the West after the Civil War was a triumphant celebration of the nation, a declaration that the promise of the Founders' experiment had come to full flower. In

Turner's view, this nation was different from any other. Unlike countries in the Old World, which were fully settled and where more complex societies had been established for ages, America had the landscape to continually reform democracy. The growing power of wealthy men at the moment Turner wrote his influential article made it more convincing, and his theory burrowed deep into the nation's ideology. Even today, when politicians talk about how America is exceptional, they are, consciously or unconsciously, echoing Turner's Frontier Thesis.

While Turner summed up his generation's thinking about American democracy and the western individual, his famous thesis was not only about triumph. Rather, it issued a dark warning. Turner lived in a time where large corporations were rising in the West, and he pointed out that the director of the 1890 United States Census had recently dropped a significant statistic. Noting the westward sweep of settlement, the director wrote: "There can hardly be said to be a frontier line" any longer. The truth was that the census director was in a tearing hurry because the 1890 census had been such a complete disaster that the first director had resigned, leaving his replacement to try to cobble something together. The poor man had cut where he could. Turner nonetheless took the director at his word, and to him this presented a dire scenario. If democracy was continually remade on the frontier, what would happen to America if the frontier was gone?

★

This concern inspired New York politician Theodore Roosevelt to re-create western individualism in government. "I owe more than I can ever express to the West," he wrote in his autobiography in 1913. The young widower had moved from his native New York to his ranch in Dakota Territory in 1884, to recover from the deaths of his wife and mother on the same day in February of that year. There, according to his memoirs, he lived the life that Frederick Jackson Turner described. Roosevelt was disgusted with eastern politicians, who were all trying to game the system. He saw westerners, in contrast, as hardworking, helpful, independent, and loyal. "Everybody worked, everybody was willing to help everybody else, and yet nobody asked any favors," he wrote. Roosevelt believed that he had earned the respect of the ranch hands by pitching in no matter what chore was at hand, and insisted that the rough conditions made him, a thin bespectacled Harvard man, equal to poor, uneducated cowhands, and vice versa. "They soon accepted me as a friend and fellow-worker who stood on an equal footing with them, and I believe the most of them have kept their feeling for me ever since."[28]

Returning to the East and to politics after the hard winter of 1886–1887 had decimated his herds along with everyone else's, Roosevelt brought the image of the West back home with him. After an unsuccessful run for New York City mayor in 1886, he settled down to memorialize his Dakota adventure in a history of American westward expansion called *The Winning of the West*, which he published three years later. This book influenced Turner and, in exchange, Turner's 1893 Frontier Thesis spoke to Roosevelt. "I think you have struck some first class ideas, and have put in to definite shape a good deal of thought which has been floating around rather loosely," Roosevelt wrote to the young historian.[29]

Roosevelt worried that modern society had become what Turner had warned about: Americans were too absorbed with making money and were too eager to limit individual rights and opportunities. Oligarchs were rising. In 1889, Roosevelt had accepted a position on the U.S. Civil Service Commission, charged with appointing men to political office on merit rather than connections. He found the task tough going in an era when "To the victor go the spoils" was a vital political principle. Roosevelt worried about the drift of the government. He still believed that American democracy depended on public virtue. Regaining that virtue—and thus democracy—depended on bolstering the western cowboy.

In 1897, Roosevelt became the Assistant Secretary to the Navy. The following year, he found the perfect avenue to restore American values in the face of machine politics. The opportunity arose on the nearby Caribbean island of Cuba, a Spanish colony only about a hundred miles from the tip of Florida. Cubans had been struggling to throw off Spanish rule repeatedly since 1868, and by 1878 the island was in ruins. Crops had been destroyed, and between 30,000 and 50,000 Cubans had been killed alongside 80,000 Spanish troops. To pay for the war, Spanish officials tripled the island's taxes. In 1895, desperate Cubans launched another strike for independence in the form of a guerilla war. To pacify the island, Spanish governor Valeriano Weyler "reconcentrated" all Cubans into fortified towns guarded by soldiers and surrounded with barbed wire. Anyone who refused to come in was considered a rebel and hanged.

Weyler's concentration policy precipitated a humanitarian crisis. The towns were ill equipped for the influx of 300,000 refugees, leaving the crowded people to starve or die of disease. In 1898, U.S. Secretary of State John Hay (once Lincoln's secretary) issued a plea to American citizens to send relief: clothing for women and children, blankets, medicine, flour and beans, and "large quantities of condensed milk, as many person are . . . too feeble for any other nourishment." As newspapers trumpeted stories about the destruction in Cuba, playing heavily to stories about the suffering of women and children, Roosevelt joined the clamor for intervention. He began to work with congressmen who shared his convictions. He focused, he said, on representatives "from the West, where the feeling for war was strongest." A war with Spain, Roosevelt believed, "would be as righteous as it would be advantageous to the honor and the interests of the nation."[30]

But business interests did not want to go to war for starving Cubans. Cuba's plantations had produced valuable sugar and tobacco before the troubles, and businessmen were eager for the restoration of Spanish control and the stability it brought. The more businessmen urged President McKinley not to go to war, the more popular enthusiasm for it grew. Sneering at "those who go at midnight, behind closed doors, to point out the views of the plutocrats and submit them as the voice of the people," Ohio Democrat John J. Lentz reminded the president, "This is a Government yet 'by the people and for the people,' and it will remain so." The fight boiled over at a public dinner at Washington's Gridiron Club, where journalists traditionally roasted politicians. Leading Republican operator Mark Hanna objected to the war, explaining to the dinner guests that a conflict would be expensive and deadly. Roosevelt and the other attendees wanted none of it. Roosevelt growled at Hanna over the dinner table: "We will have this war for the freedom of Cuba in spite of the timidity of the commercial interests."[31]

The U.S. sent the U.S.S. Maine to Havana to protect Americans there, and on February 15, the ship blew up. The disaster was probably caused by the spontaneous combustion of coal dust in the bunker beside the powder magazine, but those eager for war with Spain believed the ship had been mined by Spanish agents. "Remember the Maine," they insisted, and on April 25, 1898, Congress declared war on Spain in a drive to reassert American democratic values. Determined that businessmen would not swoop in and scoop up the valuable sugar plantations on the island, Congress also put into law that the United States would not keep Cuba, but would "leave the government and control of the Island to its people."

Engagement in Cuba was an extension of cowboy individualism. As Roosevelt later explained it, Congress authorized the creation of "three cavalry regiments from among the wild riders and riflemen of the Rockies and the Great Plains." Secretary of War Russell Alger, a lumber baron and former railroad president, offered Roosevelt the command of one of the regiments. Roosevelt instead gave the colonelcy to a friend with more experience and took the lieutenant colonelcy for himself. To raise his "cowboy regiment," Roosevelt called for "men who can ride, fight, shoot, and obey orders." Newspapers picked up the romance of his quest. The *New York Times* celebrated his "dashing band of Western cowboys" as "sturdy frontier heroes" who "have their own mounts, their own arms, and, what is more, know how to take care of themselves, live under any circumstances, and fight all the time. They need no drilling or inuring to hardship, but can give lessons in endurance and soldierly qualities to the veterans of the regular army." The press dubbed Roosevelt's men "Rough Riders," after the heroes in Buffalo Bill's Wild West Show.[32]

When he wrote about them after the war, Roosevelt used his Rough Riders to reinforce the idea that while the West remained the refuge of individualism, the qualities associated with it were in good citizens everywhere. His initial charge had been to recruit men only in the remaining western territories, but he got permission to take recruits from all over. He claimed that they were both penniless frontiersmen and Harvard scholars, Indians and Indian-hunters, northerners and southerners, whites and blacks. Leadership and discipline turned them from a "valueless mob" to America's finest.

Young men across the country were rallying to this image, setting out to recover American values from the businessmen who had taken over the country. They would take up arms to fight a foreign oppressor on behalf of their Cuban neighbors and protect suffering women and children. McKinley had asked for 125,000 volunteers, but the Army was swamped with them. The 200,000 volunteers who eventually served were generally poorer men from small towns, farmers, laborers, and clerks, with only a few merchants and professionals thrown in. Roosevelt later wrote that these men were not interested in a commission or their social standing in the regiment, but instead were trying "to show that no work could be too hard, too disagreeable, or too dangerous for them to perform, and neither asking nor receiving any reward in the way of promotion or consideration." All they wanted was to do their duty.[33]

Seventeen thousand American troops landed in Santiago on June 30, 1898. After the Spanish garrison surrendered on July 17, Secretary of State Hay wrote to Roosevelt that it had been "a splendid little war; begun with the highest motives, carried on with magnificent intelligence and spirit, favored by that fortune which loves the brave."[34]

Like western individualism itself, however, America's experiment with imperialism had a dark side. Spain controlled not just Cuba but also the Philippines, a group of islands in the Pacific Ocean to the south of China, on the opposite side of the globe from Cuba. U.S. secretary of the Navy John Davis Long happened to be away as tensions with Cuba escalated, leaving his assistant in charge. Roosevelt ordered the commander of the American Asiatic fleet to attack the Spanish in the Philippines as soon as war was declared. On May 1, Commodore George Dewey attacked the Spanish fleet in the Battle of Manila, opening the battle with the famous line to the captain of his flagship, USS *Olympia*: "You may fire when ready, Gridley." In six hours, the U.S. Navy sank the entire Spanish fleet.

Filipino insurgents under Emilio Aguinaldo had been trying to push Spanish rule off their islands, and at first American soldiers joined forces with them. After Spanish troops surrendered on August 13, however, the alliance quickly fell apart. Filipino representatives were not admitted to the peace negotiations, where Spain gave the Philippines to the United States for $20 million.

Taking the Philippines was the underside of Americans' reflexive humanitarianism in Cuba. If business interests had objected to intervention in Cuba, they were positively quivering with excitement at the idea of expansion into the Pacific. Not only were the islands way stations to Asia, but also they produced sugar—more than 200,000 tons of it in 1897. At the insistence of the enormously powerful Sugar Trust, which controlled 95 percent of the U.S. sugar market, the 1890 McKinley Tariff had put duties on foreign sugar, and sugar growers wanted a way to avoid those tariffs. In 1893, sugar growers on the Sandwich Islands in the Pacific (Hawaii) staged a coup to overthrow the Hawaiian queen and asked for the islands to become an American state, a move that would exempt them from the tariff. McKinley's friend and confidant President Harrison had cheerfully backed annexation, and westerners had been calling for the islands for years. But before the treaty could be approved, Grover Cleveland took office. With Hawaiians furiously protesting against the machinations of an American business cabal, Cleveland insisted on an investigation, and Hawaiian statehood stalled.

When the Spanish-American War broke out, the Senate still did not have enough votes to admit Hawaii, so Congress annexed it by a joint resolution—called the Newlands Resolution after its sponsor, Francis G. Newlands, Sharon's son-in-law and an avowed white supremacist—and McKinley, now president, signed it. America was swallowing "sugar plums," as the popular magazine *Harper's Weekly* put it: the 1899 Treaty of Paris that ended the war gave the United States the sugar islands of Cuba, the Philippines, and Puerto Rico, as well as a number of smaller islands, including Guam.

Those in favor of taking these islands, valuable not just for their sugar but also for their location, did not want to argue that they took the land for private gain, as European colonial powers did. Instead, they fell back on the rhetoric of individualism. The American system was superior to any other, they said, and the country had a duty to export democracy and the capitalism that supported it to benighted peoples. Ignoring the Filipinos' long history of Catholicism and education, pro-annexationists argued that they were savages unable to govern themselves. The Filipino government was illegitimate, Brigadier General Thomas M. Anderson said from his post in Manila, a "revolutionary" junta that did not truly represent the people; they simply wanted to control politics so they could confiscate the wealth of their betters, as well as take over the railways, tramways, electric plants, and waterworks. An Illinois man wrote to *Harper's Weekly* that permitting Filipinos to govern themselves would be like turning "over the entire West to Geronimo and his band of Apache cutthroats when in 1885 they claimed that territory, and pressed their claim, as Aguinaldo is doing to-day, killing, butchering, devastating any and every thing in his path!"[35]

If this was a "part of 'the white man's burden' which we can not now lay down," as one man declared, it presented a problem. The inhabitants of the territorial islands were people of color who had been defined as savages. How could the United States "provide a safe government for the Philippines, without granting that degree of citizenship in such a colony as will permit actual voting powers in the United States"? Beginning in 1901, the Supreme Court, consisting of all but one of the justices who had handed down the *Plessy v. Ferguson* decision in 1896 maintaining that racial segregation was constitutional so long as accommodations were "separate but equal," decided the issue with a number of cases collectively known as the Insular Cases. Focusing on the nation's history of allowing "white" people to be citizens—the same foundation western states used to deny rights to Chinese and Indians—the court created a new legal doctrine in America. It concluded that the newly acquired islands were not the same as previous territories. Rather than assuming that any new acquisitions would automatically begin the process of becoming states incorporated into the Union, as had been the case since the signing of the Constitution, the Supreme Court decided that the islands were "unincorporated territories"; that is, they were, to paraphrase the southern Democratic Justice Edward Douglass White, "foreign in a domestic sense." Sugar growers could bring in their product without paying tariffs, but the land was not fully American.[36]

This immediately raised the question of the status of the inhabitants of the newly acquired islands. When a pregnant twenty-year-old Puerto Rican woman named Isabel Gonzalez arrived in New York City in 1902 to join her fiancé, the immigration commissioner turned her away on the grounds that she was an "alien" who would require public support. Gonzalez sued. When her case reached the Supreme Court, it concluded that Gonzalez was not an alien, and indeed that she should not have been denied entry to the United States. The justices went on to create a new category of personhood for the islands' inhabitants. They were not aliens, but they were not citizens, either. Instead, they were "noncitizen nationals." As such, they had some constitutional protections but not all. They could travel to the American mainland without being considered immigrants, but they had no voting rights. In short, the Insular Cases meant that exactly what Lincoln had feared in the 1850s—that America would sort people according to categories— had become national law.[37]

The resurgence of the South's prewar ideology came from the nation's new political bloc: the western states. Eastern Republicans had made the mistake of thinking that westerners would join their coalition, only to discover that with their peculiar history and extractive economy, westerners had more in common with antebellum white southerners than with postwar easterners. By the 1890s, a few wealthy men dominated western society. Poor white men had little opportunity, people of color and women had even less, and leaders worked to keep it that way. Still, as in the East before the Civil War, the myth of the individualist convinced Americans that the West was the land of opportunity. Turner's Frontier Thesis and Roosevelt's war record took the western ideal and put it on the national stage. By the end of the century, Americans embraced the cowboy image and vowed to spread it across the globe, putting into law that some people were better than others. Once again, freedom was hierarchical.

CHAPTER 6

The West and the South Join Forces

B y the turn of the twentieth century, inequality was written into American law. That inequality did not spell the triumph of oligarchy, though, for the simple reason that the emergence of the western individualist as a national archetype reengaged the paradox that lay at the core of America's foundation. Denigrating people of color, organized workers, and independent women actually weakened the ability of oligarchs to cement their power: they could not convincingly argue that government activism was designed to redistribute wealth from hardworking white men to the undeserving poor. Indeed, the progressive legislation of the early twentieth century was possible because it privileged upwardly mobile white men. As in the days of the Founders, democracy was attainable only so long as it was exclusive.

With this boundary back in place, westerners and southerners joined together to expand opportunity for white men and, eventually, for those women who defined themselves as wives and mothers, rather than as independent actors with rights equal to those of men. Even as progressives relied on the government to regulate business and level the economic playing field, they retained their idea that "the American, this new man," wanted nothing from the government. In that, they drew on the myths of self-reliance embodied in both the cowboy and the Confederate soldier.

Theodore Roosevelt was crucial in translating western individualism into national politics. In 1898, he parlayed his stint as a Rough Rider into the governorship of New York, where he promised to defend the rights of hardworking men by cleaning up corruption and taking government out of the hands of corporations. Party operatives set out to neutralize him by convincing him to take the vice presidential slot on the 1900 Republican Party ticket behind William McKinley. The vice presidency was the place political careers went to die, a backwater from which they thought Roosevelt would never reemerge.

Then, in September 1901, an unemployed young steel worker who believed the Republican Party was replacing democracy with oligarchy shot McKinley in the stomach. McKinley, who had survived the Battle of Antietam, died eight days later. Members of the Republican Old Guard were appalled. "I told McKinley it was a mistake to nominate that wild man at Philadelphia," Mark Hanna moaned. "I told him what would happen if he should die. Now look. That damned cowboy is president of the United States."[1]

Roosevelt brought his western brand of democracy to the White House. He embraced the idea that the United States was the greatest nation on earth and must export its system around the world. If America was really that extraordinary, he thought, it must also make sure that all of its people had the opportunity to reach their full potential. The nation must support democracy overseas and at home by creating healthy, educated, and prosperous citizens. Roosevelt worried that the oligarchs of industry had taken the place of oligarchs of slavery, but that didn't mean his vision included people of color and union organizers. With them excluded from the body politic, he was perfectly willing to make sure everyone else was treated equally. He would use the power of the federal government to protect the ordinary white man's ability to be treated according to his own merits.[2]

Until Roosevelt, oligarchs had gamed the system by insisting that the government must not intrude on their ability to amass wealth. As soon as Roosevelt was installed in the White House, he set out to use the government to regulate the economy. His first step was to break up several powerful industrial trusts. In February 1901, financier J. P. Morgan had brought two-thirds of the nation's steel production under the control of one firm, U.S. Steel, which was capitalized at $1.4 billion—a sum almost three times larger than the nation's annual budget. Nine months later, Morgan brought the nation's major railroad companies together into the Northern Securities Company, a giant conglomerate designed to circumvent antitrust laws. Roosevelt's administration filed suit against Northern Securities, and when an astonished Morgan complained that government officials had not told him about the suit ahead of time, Roosevelt responded that that was the point. " 'Justice for all alike—a square deal for every man, great or small, rich or poor,' is the Roosevelt ideal to be attained by the framing and the administration of the law," noted the *Boston Globe* with obvious approval. "And he would tell you that that means Mr. Morgan and Mr. Rockefeller as well as the poor fellow who cannot pay his rent."[3]

Like Lincoln, Roosevelt intended to use the government to foil oligarchs. There was, however, a crucial difference between his version of democracy and that of his martyred predecessor. Lincoln divided the world largely into two groups: workingmen and the powerful few. Roosevelt also divided the world in two, but he divided it between hardworking men who wanted nothing from government, and those who wanted everything from it. While Lincoln called for a government that helped workingmen rather than oligarchs, Roosevelt's vision inherently privileged upwardly mobile white men over people of color, independent women, or anyone mired in poverty.

Roosevelt and his fellow progressives called for a very specific kind of reform. They did not want to protect everyone. Rather, they wanted to make it possible for those they saw as true Americans to succeed. This meant they wanted to make sure workers had safe workplaces, reasonable hours, and fair pay, but not unions. They wanted to ensure that corporations both paid taxes and could not monopolize public resources, but were otherwise left alone. Progressives worked to clean up the cities and to make sure children got educations and had space to play. They also cleaned up food and drug production, making it possible for mothers to know what contaminants were coming into their homes. And, finally, they limited the hours women could work, out of concern that overworked mothers would produce weak children who would not make good citizens. For a vast number of white Americans, progressive legislation filed the deadly edges off industrialization and made it possible for them to survive.[4]

Roosevelt expanded democracy to anyone who embraced his own particular notion of individualism. Since its egalitarian beginnings, women's suffrage had lost its radical faction and sought respectability, with suffragists demanding access to the vote not from a sense of absolute right, but rather to enhance their roles as wives and mothers. They marched in white gowns, pushing their babies in strollers, and promised to clean up American politics, using their ballots to outweigh those who wanted government handouts. Some supporters explicitly noted that women would be better voters than African Americans, other people of color, or organized workers. By 1912, Roosevelt openly endorsed women's suffrage, in the belief that women would support his progressive reforms.

Roosevelt often insisted as well that African Americans and American Indians should all have the same rights as any white man. "In the last analysis," he told an audience of settlers and Indians in Idaho in 1903, "what America stands for more than for aught else is for treating each man on his worth as a man." And, much to the distress of white supremacists, he illustrated this principle by defending black veterans and inviting educator Booker T. Washington to the White House. He also established ties with Comanche leader Quanah Parker, who hosted a wolf hunt for the president, and with Geronimo, who marched in Roosevelt's inaugural parade.[5]

Crucially, however, Roosevelt's definition of hardworking Americans in the western mold excluded people of color, many immigrants (including Asians), organized workers, and independent women, all of whom had come to be seen as "special interests" wanting government benefits. Roosevelt was as dead set against government "by the mob" as he was against government by plutocrats. He kept America from turning into an oligarchy at the beginning of the twentieth century, but he did so the same way the Founders had: by creating an ideological underclass.

★

The rise of the individualist resurrected the legitimacy of racism. Western settlers had reinforced racial distinctions rather than abandoning them, and their laws went far beyond the citizenship restrictions based on the 1802 naturalization law. By adopting elaborate laws against racial intermarriage, they advanced the pre–Civil War social categories that had established hierarchical racial lines to prevent the corruption of white blood. And they expanded the list of "races" that must not intermarry with "white" people to include Indians, Chinese, native Hawaiians, and anyone with "negro" blood.[6]

Such racial categories resurfaced in the South after Democrats solidified power in 1880. First southern Democrats fought to rid themselves of the black voters they insisted were corrupting the government by voting for policies that redistributed wealth; they kept black voters away from the polls through intimidation. Then, when Republicans at the national level tried to protect black voting in 1889, a new generation of white southern men turned political objections to black voting into a social argument. Black men were corrupting southern society by corrupting politics, opponents argued, and they must be purged. Lynching, which had fallen dramatically in the South since the early heyday of the Ku Klux Klan in the 1870s, exploded after 1890.

To legitimize this erasure of black lives from the body politic, fourteen southern congressmen wrote a book in 1890, dedicating *Why the Solid South? Or Reconstruction and Its Results*, "to the business men of the North." In it, they explained that black voting was simply a way for lazy people to enrich themselves with government aid, and preventing them from having access to the ballot would restore government to its proper form. To justify this voter suppression, they rewrote the history of the postwar years, describing what had happened as a perversion of government in which former slaves had exercised "negro domination" and given their votes to Republicans in exchange for government largesse. Although most people who lived through the postwar years tagged the end of Reconstruction as July 1870, when Georgia was readmitted to the Union, *Why the Solid South* identified the end of Reconstruction as the end of Republican rule in each southern state. Reconstruction, it said, should be defined as the period of terrible misrule enabled by black voting, and could be remedied only by the return to power of Democrats and good government. In this telling, southern Democrats had "redeemed" democracy by ending it in the South.[7]

In 1890, Mississippi undertook to prevent blacks from voting altogether by putting into place a new constitution that limited suffrage by education, lack of criminal record, and proof of taxpaying. That was only the start. The determination to purge society of those corrupting the body politic gave way to the nation's first blatant political coup. In Wilmington, North Carolina, in 1898, about two thousand armed white Democrats overthrew a government of black Republicans and white Populists. The Democrats agreed that the town officials had been elected fairly, but they rejected the outcome of the election nonetheless, insisting that such people had no idea how to run a government. In a "White Declaration of Independence," they announced that they would "never again be ruled, by men of African origin." It was time, they said, "for the intelligent citizens of this community owning 95 percent of the property and paying taxes in proportion, to end the rule by Negroes." They accused the white men who had worked with the black Republicans of exploiting black voters "so they can dominate the intelligent and thrifty element in the community." Indeed, the Democrats later maintained, they had not had to force the officials to leave their posts; the officials recognized that they were not up to the task and left of their own accord. As many as three hundred African Americans were killed in this "reform" of the city government.[8]

After Wilmington, the political argument against black voting quickly became a social one that tapped into generations of mythmaking. If black men could hold political office, they would give jobs to men who could vote for them. White women who wanted to become teachers had no votes to offer, so they would have to find some other way of persuading black school superintendents to hire them. Pundits turned their arguments about political corruption into fears of sexual predation, and then white mobs turned that equation into the age-old idea that black men were rapists.[9]

In 1902, North Carolina writer and Southern Baptist minister Thomas Dixon popularized this revision of the past with his book *The Leopard's Spots: A Romance of the White Man's Burden*, which portrayed black voters as tyrants out to redistribute all the wealth and power in the South from white landowners to themselves. At the climax of the novel, a gathering of leading white men, in an echo of the Wilmington coup, issued "a second Declaration of Independence from the infamy of corrupt and degraded government. The day of Negro domination over the Anglo-Saxon race shall close, now, once and forever." The book sold more than 100,000 copies in its first few months. In 1905, Dixon published *The Clansman*, which was even more popular than its predecessor.[10]

In the early part of the twentieth century, southern towns began to erect statues to Confederates, making them into western-style heroes and individualists. No longer were Confederate soldiers fighting for slavery. Instead, as the dedication speaker for the statue that stood on the University of North Carolina campus put it, they fought for states' rights against "consolidated despotism." Their heroic individualism had preserved democracy for northerners, who were finally coming around to see the light. Confederate wives, sisters, and mothers had nurtured the soldiers, cheered them on, remained devoted to the cause, and kept alive the memory of the dead.[11]

This rewriting of the past created momentum for women's suffrage. After a long fight for the ratification of a constitutional amendment to guarantee women the right to vote, the Nineteenth Amendment finally became part of the Constitution in 1920. In 1922, Georgia put a women's suffrage advocate in the Senate for a day. Rebecca Latimer Felton was a reformer who wanted educational and prison reform as well as women's suffrage. She was also in favor of lynching her black neighbors who wanted equal rights, seeing lynching as a way to free white women from "the brutal lust of these half-civilized gorillas." The Ku Klux Klan, driven underground in the early 1870s, reformed and rebounded in the 1920s.[12]

Meanwhile, in the West, immigrants and Indians were also falling victim to a legal system that established castes. In Texas, officials were hardening racial categories through immigration law that classified migrants across the Mexican border by race. In Arizona, a state law that singled out "treason against the state" as punishable by death was clearly aimed at Apaches and Navahos who might take up arms to fight the legal system ensnaring them. That legal system was laid bare in Oklahoma, where from 1890 to 1920, corrupt legislators arranged its affairs to steal valuable land from Indians, and even honest brokers wrote laws that made it almost impossible for Indians, as well as black immigrants, to hold on to property. The Osage had managed to reserve mineral rights below their land, which should have made them rich when oil turned up there. Instead it put their lives in jeopardy. Criminals married women for access to their land and then murdered them to inherit it, and then officials overlooked the murders.[13]

Violent men turned on Mexican Americans, too. The arrival of the railroad and immigration to the region along the Rio Grande Valley near the Mexican border made that area, which had continued to be largely Mexican, economically attractive. Land prices went up along with taxes, and Mexican ranchers lost their land to Anglos. In just two Texas counties between 1900 and 1910, more than 187,000 acres of land moved from Tejano to Anglo control, and the former owners ended up working for the new ones.[14]

Meanwhile, the 1910 Mexican Revolution inspired some Tejanos to consider a revolt closer to home. These men, named *sediciosos*—the seditious ones—raided Anglo ranches and murdered ranchers known to abuse their Mexican American workers. In response, the Texas Rangers reorganized to protect Anglos in the region. They soon turned to vigilantism against Tejanos, especially after 1917, when U.S. officials intercepted a diplomatic message from the German Foreign Office to the German ambassador to Mexico proposing a German-Mexican alliance in World War I in exchange for handing the American West to Mexico after victory. In 1918, a Tejano Texas legislator demanded an inquiry into the behavior of the Rangers, but the 1919 hearings simply turned into a defense of them. Soon the West had "Juan Crow" laws.[15]

World War I created an economic boom in the country, and the need for labor in the war industries brought black workers from agricultural regions to cities. There, urban violence supplanted rural violence. The 1917 massacre in East St. Louis, Illinois, in which at least forty blacks were murdered, was a prelude to the terrible years after the war. The summer of 1919 was known as the Red Summer, partly because of fears that communism was creeping into America as black citizens demanded equal rights, and partly because of the carnage in more than thirty towns and cities consumed by race riots that took hundreds of lives. Located primarily in the South and West, the rioters echoed the idea that black equality meant communism. As President Woodrow Wilson put it: "The American Negro returning from abroad would be our greatest medium in conveying bolshevism to America."[16]

It was not just people of color who were purged from society, but also any worker or intellectual perceived as seeking to redistribute wealth. When an anarchist assassinated President McKinley in 1901, the event ignited the fear of organized workers that had haunted Americans since the Paris Commune of 1871. Northern states took a lesson from the new Mississippi constitution and placed similar restrictions on voting to suppress the power of organized workers. The 1917 Bolshevik Revolution in Russia and a subsequent series of bombings in America made leaders believe a coup was under way. To crack down on the political left, Wilson's Department of Justice under Attorney General A. Mitchell Palmer launched raids on suspected labor activists in late 1919, on the second anniversary of the Russian Revolution. Officers rounded up suspects without warrants, beating some of them badly, and threw at least ten thousand people into jail, often without access to lawyers. In the end, the Palmer Raids uncovered no plot and no bombs, though it did lead to the deportation of more than five hundred immigrants (as well as to the creation of the American Civil Liberties Union).

★

By the turn of the twentieth century, with people of color and workers back in their place, southerners and westerners began to sign on to government activism. As soon as he was in office, Roosevelt undertook a major infrastructure project for the West, a measure backed by the Trans-Mississippi Commercial Congress and one he later called one of the most important in American history. The Reclamation Act was an attempt to make arid land profitable for farmers. It set aside the money from land sales in the West and Southwest to pay for irrigation projects in those regions. This was a massive undertaking, one that

Roosevelt believed would finally put farmers onto the dry prairies. It was, its proponents declared, a policy to guarantee that the remaining public lands in the West "shall be held and administered as a trust for the benefit of the whole people of the United States, and no grants of title to any of the public land shall ever hereafter be made to any but actual settlers and home builders on the land."[17]

The Reclamation Act was popularly known as the Newlands Act, not because it would create newly arable lands but because its chief sponsor was none other than Nevada's Francis G. Newlands, who had entered the House of Representatives in 1893 just after the representatives of the six recently admitted western states. Southerners and westerners discovered that they shared common ground, objecting both to Republican racial policies and to fiscal policies that favored the Northeast. In the 1890s, westerners of both parties joined with southern Democrats to demand silver coinage, which would boost the western economy, where the silver mines were located, and spark inflation, which would help the struggling South. In its initial incarnation, the cooperation of South and West worked against the East and its attempt to advance democracy. The Trans-Mississippi Commercial Congress, which advocated silver coinage, quite deliberately emphasized that it was nonpartisan.[18]

That legacy of regional cooperation across party lines carried over into support for Rooseveltian progressivism. Indeed, Newlands himself ran for the Senate in 1902, and since state legislators still chose a state's U.S. senators, William Sharon's nephew went out and recruited legislators to vote for Newlands, whose marriage to Sharon's daughter had made him a cousin. It worked. Newlands went to the Senate, where he continued to try to attract major government spending to the South and West. His second effort was a proposal to pour massive sums of money into managing the regions' rivers. The West liked this idea because its leaders maintained that good water management would make the region prosper. The South liked it because the South was periodically paralyzed by floods. The idea was especially popular with Louisiana and other states on the Mississippi River. When it did not pass under Roosevelt, the Democratic Party put support for the plan into its 1908 platform, and again in 1912, when Democratic presidential candidate Wilson promised to back such a measure. Indeed, there was so much accord between westerners of both parties that in 1912 there was talk of creating a new, western political party.[19]

The willingness of southern and western leaders to jump aboard the progressive train depended on its exclusion of certain Americans. While he had spent his adult life in the West, Newlands had been born in Mississippi and was an avowed white supremacist. In 1909, in opposition to Japanese immigration, he wrote that the United States should stop allowing foreign countries to determine who was allowed to emigrate. America should simply shut off all immigration. The "race question" was the most important one facing the nation, he noted. He went on to say that the West, with its wide acreage, would attract immigrants, and it was well established that white people could not assimilate other races, which he classified as "black," "yellow" and "brown." While he worried most about Asian immigration, he noted that the domestic race problem needed a solution. It would be a kindness, he thought, to "recognize that the blacks are a race of children, requiring guidance, industrial training, and the development of self-control," and to limit "the political rights heretofore, perhaps mistakenly, granted them." In 1912, he submitted a platform to Democratic leaders that called for repeal of the Fifteenth Amendment guaranteeing black male suffrage and prohibited immigration by "other than those of the white race," while it also broke up monopolies and developed the West. In this, he argued that he was following the lead of Roosevelt himself.[20]

The election of Wilson in 1912 strengthened the ties between the South and the West. Wilson was a southerner who had lived close to the South Carolina State House from 1872 to 1876, the heart of the Reconstruction struggle, and had gone to school with Thomas Dixon. When Dixon worked with film director D. W. Griffith, the Kentucky-born son of a Confederate colonel, to turn *The Clansman* into the groundbreaking film *Birth of a Nation*, Wilson permitted Dixon to show it at the White House (although Wilson later denied that he had ever endorsed the film in the words so often attributed to him).[21]

The first thing Wilson did as president was to call Congress into emergency session and demand that it reduce tariff rates and replace the lost revenue with an income tax. Westerners had never liked tariffs, and having reductions handed to them by a Democrat encouraged them to swing to that party. Eastern Republicans turned against Wilson instantly over the tariff issue, and would fight his administration tooth and nail from then on. But western Republicans weren't so sure. In the election of 1914, when eastern voters gave a number of seats to Republicans, westerners did not follow suit. In that election, the mountain states continued to deliver for the Democrats, and they would do so right up to the election of Franklin Delano Roosevelt in 1932.[22]

This South-West alliance helped to stop anti-lynching legislation. In 1918, Missouri Republican Leonidas C. Dyer introduced an anti-lynching bill (HR 11279), which passed the House on January 26, 1922, after white mobs destroyed the wealthy black Greenwood neighborhood in Tulsa, Oklahoma, in spring 1921 and murdered as many as three hundred people. The bill ran into trouble in the Senate, and not because of Democrats alone. In 1923–1924, progressive Republican William Borah of Idaho, chairman of a Senate Judiciary subcommittee in charge of the bill, argued against its passage, saying it was an unconstitutional extension of federal power against states' rights. Joining Borah in his opposition were Tennessee Democrat John K. Shields and North Carolina Democrat Lee Slater Overman, who was famous for his attacks on organized labor. The bill died in the Senate under a Democratic filibuster.[23]

Western Republicans continued to have sympathy for Democrats on financial and racial policies both. In 1928, after Republican President Calvin Coolidge had repeatedly vetoed legislation designed to help farmers, some western Republican leaders turned away from their party's nominee and supported Al Smith, the Democratic presidential candidate. By 1929, the coalition of southern Democrats and western Republicans held the balance of power in Congress. Eastern Republicans, who wanted higher tariffs, were so frustrated by the apostacy of their western colleagues that the chairman of the Republican senatorial campaign committee, New Hampshire's Senator George Moses, complained to New England businessmen that the western Republican progressive senators were "sons of the wild jackass." Westerners were incensed at this slur, which tied the old Democratic symbol of the donkey to the western pack animal. Moses refused to back down. And then another eastern Republican, Joseph R. Grundy, from the tariff-loving state of Pennsylvania, told a group of businessmen that they should ignore the demands of western Republicans in "backward and pauper states."[24]

"Thank God for Grundy and Moses," New York Governor Franklin Delano Roosevelt told an audience before the 1930 midterm elections. Running for president in 1932, FDR set out to win the West for the Democrats by promising business regulation and help for struggling farmers. The Depression that had hit in 1929 under Republican president Herbert Hoover had exacerbated the differences between eastern industrialists, on the one hand, and southern Democrats and western Republicans, on the other. As one Republican candidate for the Senate put it, eastern representatives "have no more conception of what an Illinois farm is like than the man in the moon, let alone a North Dakota wheat farm or an Idaho ranch." When Congress tried to combat the Depression by raising tariffs with the Smoot-Hawley Act in June 1930, western Republicans (not including Smoot, a Utah Republican) opposed the bill. By the time of the Republican National Convention of 1928, the only progressive who had not switched to the Democrats was William Borah, whom acerbic cultural critic H. L. Mencken called an "old moo-cow." The rest "had gone over to the New Deal in a body, bellowing 'Glory, glory, hallelujah!' "[25]

When FDR won the 1932 election, he set out to bring a "New Deal" to the American people. Although his vision of placing the power of the federal government behind poor Americans was enough to swing black voters to the Democratic Party, it preserved enough of American racial lines to avoid alienating poor whites. To people of color, the New Deal looked pretty much like the old deal. Because the South's and the West's political leaders tended to stay in power for a long time, they got seniority under FDR, who, even as popular as he was, still needed their support to get New Deal legislation through Congress. They carried the biases of their southern coalition into the new programs, keeping racial discrimination intact. Reimbursements to farmers for taking land out of production went to white farmers, not black; those payments were handed directly to store owners or landowners for payment on bills. Wage supports were adjusted so that white employers could continue to underpay black workers in the South, and where wage minimums were enforced, white employers usually just fired black workers. Low-income housing was segregated, and mortgage programs discriminated according to race. Social Security deliberately excluded domestic workers and farm workers, both fields in which black workers predominated. So America had yet another rebirth of democracy—and a reaffirmation of the original paradox.[26]

★

The resurrection of antebellum southern ideology through the rise of the western individualist rewrote American history. In 1906, after Dixon had helped the ideas contained in *Why the Solid South* to gain popular currency, the former steel baron James Ford Rhodes of Cleveland, Ohio, undertook to write the history of Reconstruction as part of his seven-volume history of the United States. Rhodes had been a Democrat until 1896, when he switched to supporting McKinley (in deference to his brother-in-law Mark Hanna), and then to Theodore Roosevelt in 1904. Rhodes depicted Reconstruction as a misguided attempt to give African American men voting rights that they were entirely unequipped to exercise. He laid that mistake at the feet of those he called "radicals," led—according to him—by

Pennsylvania congressman Thaddeus Stevens. Once in possession of the ballot, black men turned southern governments into an orgy of corruption. Entirely ignoring the widespread racial violence of the postwar years, Rhodes argued that if only the radicals had permitted Lincoln's version of Reconstruction to take hold, a version that would have limited voting to white men and a few educated black men, all the troubles of the era could have been avoided. He pinpointed a date for the ending of Reconstruction: April 1877, when the Hayes administration returned all the southern states to "home rule."[27]

Politician, historian, and former slave John R. Lynch, among others, attacked Rhodes's "history" as "warped," biased," and of "very little if any value for historical purposes," but it was Rhodes's version of history that took over the academy. Rhodes's volume on Reconstruction was finished in time to be available to a professor of political theory at Columbia University, William Archibald Dunning. A key historian during the Progressive Era, Dunning would turn Rhodes's version of Reconstruction into a school of history. He believed that blacks and whites could not coexist, and that once slavery was gone, "its place must be taken by some set of conditions which, if more humane and beneficent in accidents, must in essence express the same fact of racial inequality."[28]

In his scholarly study of Reconstruction, Dunning did Rhodes one better: he blamed the northern armies for the poverty and violence in the South after the war, and he maintained that everything would have been fine if only southerners—"black as well as white"—"could have resumed at once the familiar methods of production." Dunning's version of the postwar years, published in 1907 as *Reconstruction: Political and Economic, 1865–1977*, echoed entirely the southern Democrats' version of the immediate postwar era: southern white men were hardworking individuals who just wanted to make a living, and were prevented from doing so by Republican radicals determined to lord it over the South and by lazy ex-slaves.[29]

Dunning's students followed in his footsteps in the 1920s and 1930s, producing a large body of similar work that dominated scholarship on the era. It was not much of a leap from Dunning's work to declaring that perhaps slavery wasn't such a bad thing. That was the direction taken by Dunning's student U. B. Phillips, another progressive. Phillips argued that the slave system was economically inefficient, that for the most part masters were kind and benevolent, and that masters and slaves were locked into an unequal relationship from which both of them benefited, the slaves by being tutored in the ways of civilization.[30]

Perhaps the most famous adherent of the "Dunning School" was not a Dunning student at all, but rather an Indiana journalist and historian. In 1929, Claude G. Bowers produced *The Tragic Era*, which claimed that Andrew Johnson was one of the nation's best presidents, that "the Southern people literally were put to the torture", and that brutal, hate-filled Republicans had attempted "revolution." "The Constitution was treated as a doormat on which politicians and Army officers wiped their feet after wading in the muck," Bowers wrote. He continued: "The story of this Revolution is one of desperate enterprises, by daring and unscrupulous men, some of whom had a genius of a high order. In these no Americans can take pride. The evil that they did lives after them."[31]

Bowers's condemnation of the Republican effort to promote democracy fell into the lines the scholar Dunning had set, but Bowers had a more public agenda. He was a journalist before he was a historian, and a Democrat all along. He wrote *The Tragic Era* out of concern that southerners might slip to the Republicans after the 1928 landslide election for Hoover. "I have written a book which will be the most powerful single factor in bringing the South back into line," he wrote to a fellow Democrat shortly before the book appeared, "the story of this period during which the Republican party solidified its power by bayonets, and corruption is the most tremendous indictment of that party ever penned in history."[32]

The Tragic Era remains one of the best-selling books about Reconstruction, selling through its first printing of 100,000 copies and going through twelve more hardcover editions and many paperback editions across the decades. The mainstream press reviewed it favorably, and Democratic politicians thought enough of it that they tried to tap Bowers to nominate FDR at the 1932 Democratic National Convention. Bowers's employer, William Randolph Hearst, backed the more conservative John Nance Garner for the presidency, however, and made the disappointed Bowers decline. FDR nonetheless appointed Bowers ambassador to Spain in 1933, and then ambassador to Chile until he retired in 1953. Anyone who disagreed with the way he did history in *The Tragic Era*, Bowers said, could "go to hell in an elevator."[33]

Bowers was not the only one putting a genteel sheen on the individualist image. In 1930, the year after Bowers wrote *The Tragic Era*, a group of southern writers produced a manifesto called *I'll Take My Stand: The South and the Agrarian Tradition*. Pushing back against the popular culture of the 1920s that made fun of backward southerners, writers Allen Tate and Robert Penn Warren (who would later become the first poet laureate of the United States) and ten of their friends celebrated what they called the values of the Old South. The Southern Agrarians, as they were known, blamed modernity, urbanization, and industrialization for destroying the best of American traditions in the name of progress, and they championed what they called an "agrarian" way of life, one steeped in independence, which they believed would answer the South's economic, political, and racial problems.

The Southern Agrarians included some of the South's best-known white literary figures, but it was a housewife from Atlanta who truly popularized their version of Reconstruction. Margaret Mitchell had grown up enamored of Thomas Dixon's books—as a child she organized plays based on them, and she once wrote him a fan letter. When an ankle injury immobilized her, she wrote her own bestseller, *Gone with the Wind*. Published in 1936, this story differed from Dixon's in that its main character, Scarlett O'Hara, was one woman alone, fighting her own war against the government, her society, the economy, and her environment. At a time when white southerners who had depended on New Deal programs to survive were just starting to feel like they could make it on their own again, she gave them a vision of survival through dogged, western-style independence. The book was a runaway bestseller, and as late as 2008 remained one of Americans' favorite books, coming in just behind the Bible.[34]

That individualist vision of America was wildly popular during the Depression. In 1932, the first of another set of books also became a bestseller. That series, too, remains hugely popular, although it often flies under the radar because it is classified as a children's series. The first in the series was *Little House in the Big Woods*, by Laura Ingalls Wilder, who had traveled west from Wisconsin in a covered wagon, grown up on the frontier, lived in South Dakota, and settled in Missouri in the Ozarks. Wilder loathed the New Deal, and her portrait of her upbringing was the western individualist mythology personified. In her stories, Pa was the rock of the family, protecting them from Indians and providing for his wife and four girls with the deer he shot, the muskrat he trapped, and the fields he planted. Men had to look out for themselves, he told Laura, because they were "free and independent."[35]

In fact, Pa had never been able to support his family; he had relied on income from the work of Laura, her sisters, and her mother. To hear Wilder tell it, the family had scrimped and saved to send her blind sister Mary to college; the reality was that the state of South Dakota had paid for six years of tuition and room and board for Mary, and the family had scrimped and saved for the money to buy her clothes and her train ticket. Nonetheless, that image of an independent man caring for his loving wife and daughters struck a chord in the Depression, and the Little House books instantly became—and remain—some of the most influential American literary works of all time.

By 1939, Hollywood was capitalizing on the image of bootstrapped self-reliance. In that one year, it produced five films featuring an individual winning victory over a corrupt and distant government: *Mr. Smith Goes to Washington, Geronimo, The Wizard of Oz, Gone with the Wind,* and *Stagecoach,* and one, *The Women,* in which a wife and mother triumphs over independent women. In all of these classic films, the lines between good and evil were crystal clear.

In each of the first five films, a westerner or southerner faces a catastrophe caused or exacerbated by the government and, after great tribulation, triumphs. In *Gone with the Wind,* Scarlett O'Hara ekes out survival despite the Civil War and its devastating aftermath—and the helplessness of the slaves around her. Dorothy has quite a similar story in *The Wizard of Oz,* although since the book on which it was based was a parable, the troubles the Kansas farm girl encounters are less historically specific than Scarlett's, and the government in her film is the ineffectual "wizard," who simply pretends to give Dorothy and her companions the brains, heart, and courage they already possess.

The others followed the individualist suit. In *Mr. Smith Goes to Washington,* Jimmy Stewart's character is from an unnamed western state—in the screenplay he was from either Wyoming or Montana—sent forth to combat a corrupt Congress (embodied by a machine politician portrayed by actor Claude Rains). In *Geronimo,* the Apache leader (played by Victor Daniels, also known as Chief Thundercloud) carries all the usual stereotypes of a sneaking, vicious Indian, but in fact he is incited to violence by a government Indian agent, who wants to make money from continuing conflict. There is also in that film a gratuitous conversation with a man emigrating to California from the South because, he said, the government there would not let a man be free and independent. Finally, in *The Women,* based on a play by Clare Boothe (later Clare Boothe Luce, the wife of *Time* publisher Henry Luce, and known for her right-wing politics), a loving wife and mother overcomes a grasping shop girl and society matrons in a battle for her husband and home.

John Ford's *Stagecoach*, starring John Wayne in his first feature film, best depicted the cultural maturity of the western individual. The history of late nineteenth-century America is encapsulated in a stagecoach headed west across Apache territory in 1880. The passengers in the coach include a banker, a prostitute, a doctor, the wife of a cavalry officer, a gambler, and a whiskey salesman. Along the way, they pick up the Ringo Kid, played by Wayne, a fugitive who has vowed to kill the man who murdered his father and brother. *Stagecoach* gave viewers the classic western tropes: Indians threaten the lives of the white people on the coach; a Mexican cook helps them; the white female characters are a wife and a prostitute; the cavalry—the government—is always a little too late.

Stagecoach turned society's expectations upside down. The respected banker was, in fact, absconding with his customers' money. The doctor was an alcoholic who promptly confiscated alcohol from the whiskey salesman. The officer's wife was haughty and difficult. The heroes on the stagecoach were Dallas, the prostitute, who overlooks the other passengers' snubs and helps them out; the gambler, who turns out to be a southern gentleman who honors the memory of his commander; and the Ringo Kid. In the end, he and Dallas ride off into the sunset to make a loving home together on their own ranch, out of reach of the government's clutches.

The Ringo Kid role established John Wayne as the prototype of the Western hero—rugged, self-reliant, and suspicious of anyone with authority. He is the outsider, forced into criminality by a system that does not recognize the justice of his crusade. He is the man who, despite the price on his head, saves the rest of the passengers after the government has left them in mortal danger. He is the one who understands that in America, a man does not conform to the expectations of eastern society but insists on living independently on his own land, taking care of his wife and family. During the Depression, when for many the walls seemed to be closing in, John Wayne's cowboy turned the American paradox into the American dream.

CHAPTER 7

The Rise of the New West

Just as it achieved stability through American culture, the individualist ideal collapsed. When the United States declared war on Japan, Germany, and Italy in December 1941, Americans from all backgrounds threw themselves into the effort to defend their nation. In the four years of the war, more than 16 million American men and women served in combat around the globe. Tens of millions more worked in fields and factories to feed and supply the troops, the allies, and the folks at home. Everyone stinted and scraped to save resources for the war effort. When the nation emerged from the carnage triumphant, Americans celebrated their communal effort. They rejoiced at the beginning of what Henry Luce, the publisher of *Time Magazine*, called the "American Century," in which the nation would lead a new birth of democracy and freedom around the world. At home, though, those ideals would throw a monkey wrench into the individualist status quo because, just as they had after a similar national effort in the Civil War, people of color and women wanted the equality their country claimed to stand for. And, just as former slave owners had done after that previous crisis, businessmen set out to destroy that democratic consensus.

In the years from the Depression through World War II, FDR had created an activist federal system, one that promoted equality of opportunity from the ground up. New Deal policies provided jobs for more than 8.5 million people, built more than 650,000 miles of highways, constructed or repaired more than 120,000 bridges, put up more than 125,000 buildings, and brought electricity to the 90 percent of rural Americans who lived in places private power companies considered unprofitable. The government regulated the stock market to stop the risky practices that had led to the Great Crash, and stabilized the financial system with the Glass-Steagall Act, which separated investment and savings banks, and with federal insurance for bank deposits. New Deal policies also gave Americans unemployment and old age insurance—Social Security—and helped poor people buy food. Crucially, they also gave workers real bargaining power in their negotiations with employers.

Then, on December 7, 1941, Japanese airplanes dropped bombs on the U.S. naval fleet anchored in Hawaii, sinking eighteen ships, killing 2,403 Americans, and thrusting the country into a world war. As the government poured $296 billion (more than $4 trillion in today's dollars) into contracts, supplies, and support during the war years, deficit spending jump-started the sluggish economy. Suddenly there were lots of well-paid jobs, and administration officials pressured industrialists to work with unions. Wages and wealth distribution became more equal than ever before, and the nation entered into a period that economists have called the Great Compression.[1]

The story of the war was the unassuming valor of ordinary Americans willing to sacrifice their lives to protect democracy. Journalists like Pulitzer Prize winner Ernie Pyle covered the war from their point of view. Movies celebrated them, and General Dwight Eisenhower, Commander of the Allied Forces, gave "GI Joe" credit for winning the war. The need for all hands on deck broke down the nation's racial, ethnic, and gender boundaries. Men were equally subject to the draft, and by 1945, roughly a million African Americans, 500,000 Latinos, and 1.5 million Italian Americans had served in uniform. Around a million Polish Americans, horrified by Hitler's treatment of their homeland, served alongside roughly 550,000 Jews, 33,000 Japanese Americans, 30,000 Arab Americans, and 20,000 Chinese Americans. Native Americans served at a higher percentage than any other ethnic group—roughly 25,000 people, one-third of all able-bodied men from ages eighteen to fifty joined the service, including the soldiers who developed the famous "code talk," based on tribal languages, which Axis spies never cracked. About 350,000 American women also served in the U.S. military, working as cryptographers, recruiters, radio operators, supply managers, mail sorters, secretaries, and nurses.[2]

As men drained to the battlefields, women also entered factories and fields, while black families traveled from the rural South to northern and western cities to work in the wartime industries. Still short of workers, the United States reversed its Depression-era policy of expelling Mexicans and, beginning with the harvest season of 1942, started the Bracero Program to bring in seasonal migrant workers. It also tapped the Japanese Americans who had been interned in camps after Pearl Harbor, turning about ten thousand of them out to work in the fields.[3]

Multicultural support for the war did not translate to equality, though. Black servicemen were segregated, paid less than their white comrades and received inferior food and equipment. Back home, as people mixed and mingled, race riots broke out. In June 1943, Los Angeles exploded when servicemen attacked young Latino men who flouted fabric rationing and wore voluminous "zoot suits." Rioters claimed the zoot suiters were unpatriotic gangsters, and attacks on Latinos, as well as African Americans, spread across the country. Days later, Detroit erupted when managers at the Packard Motor Car Company followed FDR's prohibition on racial discrimination in wartime industries and promoted three black men to work next to white men on the assembly lines. Over the course of three days, riots killed thirty-four people and wounded more than five hundred others. Recognizing the discrepancy between the ideal of American democracy and its practice, Germany dropped leaflets on black American troops, reminding them that the United States oppressed them and urging them to surrender and spend the rest of the war "well-treated as a prisoner-of-war in a German camp," as one put it, "leading a healthy and pleasant life among your pals."[4]

Black soldiers were not deluded into laying down their arms, but people of color did become more determined than ever to be treated as equals in the nation for which they were risking their lives. Either led or aided by lawyer Thurgood Marshall, who would later become the first African American on the Supreme Court, and other attorneys, they used the courts to challenge Juan and Jim Crow. In the immediate aftermath of the war, Mexican Americans challenged school segregation in California and won, forcing California Governor Earl Warren to change the laws. Then in 1948, in *Shelly v. Kraemer*, the Supreme Court declared that racial housing restrictions violated the equal protection clause in the Fourteenth Amendment.

The California Supreme Court used the same reasoning to decide *Perez v. Sharp*, declaring that the state could not prohibit interracial marriage. This ruling undercut the marriage laws that were the basis for racial discrimination across the western states. They also set the stage for *Brown v. Board of Education*, the sweeping court decision that would change American history.[5]

Asian Americans, too, successfully challenged laws based on the 1882 Chinese Exclusion Act. Americans began to distinguish Filipino, South

Asian, and Chinese allies from Japanese enemies, and in 1943, Congress finally overturned the nation's sixty-year-old anti-Chinese policy.[6]

Hitler's race-based fascism had been inspired in part by America's own legal system, and as the military fought fascism, schools and churches across the country challenged racial hierarchies at home. Democracy, they emphasized, depended on tolerance of racial, ethnic, and religious differences. Rallies championed diversity, and government-sponsored films warned Americans not to succumb to fascist propaganda. Posters trumpeted slogans such as "Catholics-Protestants-Jews . . . Working Side By Side . . . in War and Peace!" and reminded Americans not to "infect" their children "with racial and religious hate." Everyone got involved. Frank Sinatra made a short film in which he told a gang of boys that America was great because "it's made up of a hundred different kind[s] of people, and a hundred different ways of talking, and a hundred different ways of going to church. . . . But they're all American ways."[7]

With the Allied victory, everyone seemed willing to defend American diversity. In 1946, President Harry Truman, who had taken over the office when FDR died a few months before the end of the war, declared Sunday, May 19 to be "I Am an American Day," to honor newly naturalized citizens. The nation's strength, he said, came "from the fact that its citizens, young and old, native-born and foreign-born, work together as one people." In 1947, Superman fought a Ku Klux Klan–like gang trying to keep foreign-born players off high school sports teams, and in 1949, comic book artist Wayne Boring portrayed him on a poster urging a group of American schoolchildren to defend their classmates from "UN-AMERICAN" attacks on their race, religion, or ethnicity.[8]

As the victorious nation redefined itself, scholars concluded that the principles of the Enlightenment and the environment of North America had combined to create a new kind of society, one that had enabled the country to escape both fascism and communism. Americans were moderate, generally thought alike, and sought commonsense answers to society's problems. This seemed to explain the overwhelming popularity of the New Deal, the rising standard of living, and the decisive role the U.S. military had played in defeating the fascists. Here was proof that democracy was the best system of government ever devised.

In the 1950s, politicians and commentators agreed that those commonsense American ideas had produced a "liberal consensus," shared by most Democrats and Republicans alike. The government should regulate business, provide for basic social welfare, and promote infrastructure: the New Deal had finally achieved the government that best reflected democratic values. In this worldview, Americans stood firmly between leftist revolution on one side and right-wing reaction on the other. "Liberalism," the influential literary critic Lionel Trilling wrote, "is not only the dominant but even the sole intellectual tradition . . . there are no conservative or reactionary ideas in circulation."[9]

It sometimes seemed that the only place to find those ideas was in entertainment. Popular radio comedian Fred Allen's show included a caricature, Senator Beauregard Claghorn, a southern blowhard who pontificated, harrumphed, and took his reflexive hatred of the North to ridiculous extremes. A buffoon who represented the past, the Claghorn character was such a success that he starred in his own Hollywood film and later became the basis for the Loony Tunes character Foghorn Leghorn. In the 1950s, the liberal consensus ruled the roost.[10]

★

The dominance of the liberal consensus infuriated old-school Hoover Republicans, libertarians, and fundamentalist Christians who hated the New Deal's secular reforms. Led by Republican Senator Robert Taft of Ohio, the son of former president William Howard Taft, these men insisted that any government intervention in the economy was socialism. It would erase individualism and destroy America. Firmly convinced they alone were defending the Constitution, they wanted to return America to the world of the 1920s, when businessmen ran the country and Protestant Christianity held sway. At first, they thought they would regain power after the war ended, and then they would demand an end to the New Deal. But they quickly discovered that they were a minority even within the Republican Party.[11]

Recognizing that they had little chance of recovering popular support, they abandoned reasoned argument and instead turned to the use of narrative to regain control. They hammered on the idea that the New Deal liberal consensus was destroying America by making it communist. As soon as the war was over, Republicans in Congress, with Taft as their leader, first cut back on the rights of workers by prohibiting unions from donating to national political campaigns, among other things, then launched investigations into whether communists had infiltrated Hollywood and were spreading their dogma through films. The investigators didn't turn up anything, but the anticommunist impulse got new teeth as eastern European countries—Albania, Poland, Bulgaria, Romania, Czechoslovakia, East Germany, and Hungary—fell under the control of the communist government of the Soviet Union in the late 1940s. Then, in 1949, the Communist Party took over China. When communist forces pushed into South Korea in 1950, Taft Republicans insisted that Democrats must be secretly conspiring to spread communism across the world.[12]

This was not true, of course, but it made for good headlines. On February 9, 1950, Wisconsin Senator Joseph McCarthy stood in front of a Republican women's club in Wheeling, West Virginia, gathered to celebrate Lincoln's birthday, and claimed there were 205 members of the Communist Party working in the State Department. Worse, Truman's Secretary of State, Dean Acheson, knew it. McCarthy didn't have time to list the names, he said, but assured his audience that there were "traitors in the government."[13]

McCarthy's shocking announcement rocketed the previously undistinguished senator to instant fame. Keenly aware of the power of publicity, he upped the ante. The day after his Wheeling speech, McCarthy telegraphed President Truman, charging him with protecting communists in the government and suggesting that the Democratic Party was "the bedfellow of international communism." Government officials demanded that the senator produce evidence. The *Washington Post* condemned McCarthy's "sewer politics," and the *New York Times* denounced his hit-and-run attacks and slurs against the State Department. But Taft Republicans jumped on board, fully expecting that McCarthy's attacks would destroy the New Deal's popularity and put pro-business politicians back into power. They were wrong. In the 1950 midterm elections, voters left the Democrats in charge of Congress.[14]

In 1951, William F. Buckley Jr., a devout Catholic fresh out of Yale, the son of an oilman, suggested a new approach to destroying the liberal consensus. In *God and Man at Yale: The Superstitions of "Academic Freedom,"* Buckley suggested that the whole idea that people would make good decisions through argument based on evidence—the Enlightenment idea that had shaped America since its founding—was wrong. Had that been true, Americans would not have kept supporting the government activism launched by the New Deal. Americans' faith in reasoned debate was a worse "superstition," he said, than the superstitions the Enlightenment had set out to replace.[15]

Rather than continuing to try to change people's beliefs through evidence-based arguments, he said, those opposed to the New Deal should stand firm on an "orthodoxy" of religion and individualism and refuse to accept any questioning of those two fundamental principles. Buckley's book showed how this should be done. Rather than making a reasoned argument that fairly presented others' positions, it misrepresented the views of the professors with whom Buckley disagreed, claimed that the wealthy white Yale-educated Buckley was a member of a persecuted minority, and smeared supporters of the liberal consensus as the tools of socialists and atheists.[16]

Published by a small, right-wing press, Buckley's book garnered little attention, and the election of General Dwight D. Eisenhower to the presidency the next year reinforced the dominance of the liberal consensus. Eisenhower tried to quiet the Taft Republicans by supporting the addition of the words "under God" to the Pledge of Allegiance and saying little about McCarthy, but it didn't work. Taft's men hated Eisenhower for taking the 1952 Republican nomination from their beloved senator, and Taft's death the following year hardened their enmity. When the new president embraced the premises of the New Deal with a program he called the Middle Way, they were apoplectic. It had been bad enough when Democrats used the government to promote the general welfare, but when a Republican president signed on, too, they concluded that socialists had taken over the Republican Party as well as the Democrats. Pat Manion, a well-connected radio broadcaster who believed Eisenhower had fallen under the sway of "a vicious internationalist cabal," railed against wealthy "left-wing" figures who had "fallen under the direction of Internationalists, One-Worlders, Socialists, and Communists." Their money was being used to "socialize" the United States.[17]

In January 1953, immediately after Eisenhower took office, McCarthy ramped up his accusations that communists had subverted the government. From a subcommittee of the Senate Foreign Relations Committee, he started investigating the State Department. He made accusations with no evidence, and bullied and badgered witnesses. The nation's ten top daily papers and all the major news magazines noted that McCarthy never produced any evidence for his extraordinary charges, but the Hearst and McCormick newspaper chains, which had supported Taft, loved McCarthy—some of their reporters even dug up witnesses for him. In 1954, McCarthy took on the United States Army, accusing it of coddling communists. Up to 20 million people watched the televised hearings. Seeing him bully and bluster in person was quite different from reading his accusations in print, and many were horrified. When he tried to shore up his crumbling case by accusing a young member of the opposing counsel's team of having communist sympathies, the opposing counsel, Joseph Nye

Welch, responded in a way that summed up the national mood: "Have you no sense of decency, sir, at long last? Have you left no sense of decency?"[18]

McCarthy's popularity plummeted, the Senate condemned him in December 1954, and he died two years later of complications related to alcoholism. But McCarthy had shown the Taft wing of the Republican Party how to advance their agenda by exploiting the media. He yelled, made crazy accusations, badgered, and hectored in what was essentially performance art that advanced a simple, almost mythical narrative—a new version of *Mr. Smith Goes to Washington*, in which an outsider takes on a corrupt government. He alone was defending America by protecting individualism from an all-pervasive government of godless communists. While most Americans found his antics despicable—*Washington Post* cartoonist Herb Block coined the term "McCarthyism" to describe a political smear campaign and witch hunt—Taft Republicans had found a game plan.

Just after the Army McCarthy hearings, Buckley and his brother-in-law L. Brent Bozell expanded this narrative in a book defending the disgraced senator. *McCarthy and His Enemies* argued that McCarthy's ends had justified his crude means, because America was under siege not necessarily by actual communists, but by those who were not sufficiently opposed to communism: "the Liberals," a name they capitalized to make this general leaning sound like a political cabal. The term swept in almost everyone in America, for Buckley and Bozell made no distinction between Soviet-style communism and the widely popular liberal consensus. They praised McCarthy for challenging the orthodoxy of the New Deal and called for a movement that would purge the country of Liberals and create a new orthodoxy of strict Christianity and individualism. They called themselves Conservatives, though their determination to overthrow a popular, stable system of government was, in fact, quite radical. To distinguish their political movement from traditional conservative principles, adherents began to refer to their project as "Movement Conservatism."[19]

The following year, Buckley launched a new magazine to advance the new movement. Bankrolled primarily by a South Carolina mill owner who hated labor unions and desegregation, by a Los Angeles oil baron, and by his wealthy father, Buckley promised that *National Review* would tell the "violated businessman's side of the story." In his initial issue, he insisted that a cabal had taken over both political parties under "such fatuous slogans as 'national unity,' 'middle-of-the-road,' 'progressivism,' and 'bipartisanship.'" Despite the fact that the American economy was the strongest it had ever been, he insisted that politicians who believed in the liberal consensus were destroying both individualism and material progress by strengthening labor unions, which, he said, had "doctrinaire socialist objectives."[20]

Buckley's views were a far cry from traditional conservatism, which called for stability, gradual change, and common-sense-based legislation. His worldview was based on an ideology that looked much like that of James Henry Hammond and his fellow slaveholders a century earlier. Buckley insisted that the government must be limited solely to protecting life, liberty, and property. Only if individuals were allowed to organize their lives as they saw fit would they be able to advance the cause of freedom and spread prosperity spread across the nation. This was precisely the argument slaveholding Democrats had made in the 1850s, and, in much the same way, it would permit the rise of oligarchy.

Buckley's vision was quite explicitly elitist and had little hope of attracting the support of ordinary Americans who had fought for their country and who now looked around at their rising standard of living—thanks to the GI Bill, unions, the minimum wage, and Social Security—and could see no reason to complain. In 1956, Eisenhower backed the largest public works program in America's history, the Federal-Aid Highway Act, which provided $25 billion to construct 41,000 miles of the nation's first interstate highways. The new interstates pumped up the economy by providing construction jobs and tying together the states, but also by creating a market for new hotels, diners, and gas stations, as people who could now afford the decade's candy-colored chrome cars loaded up the family and hit the road to see their country.[21]

Between 1945 and 1960, the gross national product—a leading indicator of economic well-being—jumped 250 percent, from $200 billion to $500 billion, expanding the middle class and creating a strong market for unskilled labor. Because wage laws and taxes kept money from moving upward, incomes across the economic spectrum doubled between 1945 and 1970. While Americans in rural areas and inner cities did not fare as well as those in more affluent areas, the overall sense of the 1950s was one of comfort, prosperity, and stability after the dislocation of the Depression and World War II: single-family homes, steady jobs, education, community, leisure time, sock hops, and innocence. Voters finally felt secure after the deprivation of the 1930s and the devastation of the war. They had little interest in the idea that government policies providing their security must be overturned.[22]

★

On its merits, Buckley's narrative was not going to attract ordinary American voters. The liberal consensus was vulnerable, though, on the same grounds the post–Civil War consensus had been: race and gender. Since the Founding, Americans had been steeped in the argument that equality for white men depended on inequality for people of color and women. Now, as marginalized Americans demanded full inclusion in the national fabric and the government took on issues of racial and gender equality to try to level the playing field, Buckley and his fellow travelers turned to the American paradox, embracing its corollary and claiming that equality would undercut liberty.

In this, they were aided by a major geographic shift that took place during World War II: the country's population had moved westward. Concerned that eastern cities could be vulnerable to bombing, government officials located war industries in the wide expanses of the West. The West had a milder climate that made life easy for workers, and land there was cheap, as developers and businessmen worked to attract government contracts by offering to lease land for nominal rates. During the war, Congress appropriated more than $70 billion for investment in the West, almost half of it for California. This money built 344 new plants for war industries—steel mills, aircraft industries, shipyards—and developed research centers to study topics from ocean currents to physics. By 1943, 280,000 people worked in California's shipyards, and almost 250,000 more worked in the state's new aircraft industry. By 1944, Los Angeles rivaled Detroit as the nation's leading manufacturing center.[23]

The demographic shift west continued with the Cold War. In all past wars, the nation had abruptly turned from military production to a peacetime economy, but after World War II, the global tension between capitalism and communism continued to bolster the new war industries. Between 1950 and 1959, defense took up 62 percent of the federal budget as it expanded 246 percent, up to $228 billion annually, and much of that money moved west.

California alone received more than twice as much annual defense spending as any other state; in the 1950s the Department of Defense poured more than $50 billion into it. Los Angeles boomed as people moved there to work in defense industries, with the city's population rising from 1.5 million in 1940 to more than 6 million by 1960. In 1957, professional baseball took note of the growing western population and approved the Dodgers' move from Brooklyn to Los Angeles and the Giants' move from New York City to San Francisco, exporting one of baseball's key eastern rivalries to the rising West.[24]

Eisenhower, and after him Democratic president John F. Kennedy, expressed concern about the rising power of what Ike called "the military-industrial complex," which by 1961 employed more than 3.5 million Americans directly and many more indirectly. In turn, Americans in the West who depended on that industry began to rail against the "eastern establishment," claiming that it had been corrupted by the "liberal elite" and had gone soft on communism.[25]

That anticommunism dovetailed nicely with the arguments of Movement Conservatives. It grew in the West at the same time that party leaders in Washington were calling for the government to make equality a reality in the American century. Truman and Eisenhower backed desegregation both because it was morally right and because they recognized that communist regimes used the Jim and Juan Crow laws to undermine American influence by calling attention to the hypocrisy of American talk about freedom. In 1948, Truman desegregated the military, and in 1953, as soon as he took office, Eisenhower both desegregated schools and hospitals on military bases and pressured private businesses to desegregate or lose government contracts. He also appointed former Republican California governor Earl Warren chief justice of the Supreme Court. This was a crucial appointment in an era when the Supreme Court was dominated by Democrats, whose party tended to oppose black rights, just as the NAACP and other civil rights organizations were pressing legal cases against segregation. In May 1954, the complicated dance between Thurgood Marshall and Earl Warren led to the unanimous landmark *Brown v. Board of Education* decision, which outlawed the "separate but equal" doctrine that had segregated schools since the Civil War.[26]

While some white southerners accepted or even welcomed the expansion of equality, others worked to restore white control. In August 1955, two white men murdered fourteen-year-old Emmett Till in Mississippi for allegedly whistling at a white woman. The murder, and the subsequent acquittal of the two men, helped spark an organized popular civil rights movement in the African American community. Racial and gendered tension in Montgomery, Alabama, had been rising as black women called out the rape and sexual assault that characterized a society in which white men could not be challenged. And in December 1955, activist Rosa Parks refused to give up her seat on a bus in Montgomery, Alabama to a white man. The year-long Montgomery bus boycott that followed led to the desegregation of the bus system and the increasing prominence of one of the boycott's leaders, the Reverend Martin Luther King Jr.[27]

In 1956, ninety-nine congressmen, led by South Carolina's Strom Thurmond (who, it was discovered many years later, had fathered a biracial daughter with his family's maid), took a stand against government-enforced desegregation. Their "Declaration of Constitutional Principles," which was quickly dubbed the "Southern Manifesto," maintained that desegregation was unconstitutional. Under pressure from these reactionaries, the Governor of Arkansas, Orval Faubus, mobilized the Arkansas National Guard to prevent nine African American students from enrolling in Little Rock's Central High School in 1957. Eisenhower responded by nationalizing the Arkansas National Guard and dispatching the 101st Airborne to protect the "Little Rock Nine." For the first time since Reconstruction, a president had sent federal troops to the South to protect equality for black Americans, and, just as they had done after the Civil War, state politicians began to talk about states' rights.[28]

Buckley's *National Review* gave these segregationists cover by providing an intellectual defense of segregation. Buckley hired James Kilpatrick, a southern newspaper editor, to assure readers that desegregation did not promote American values, as Eisenhower said, but undermined them. The white community had an established right "to peace and tranquillity; the right to freedom from tumult and lawlessness," Kilpatrick insisted in the *National Review*, although, in fact, it was white Americans who were attacking their black neighbors. In another editorial, entitled "Why the South Must Prevail," Buckley made the same argument James Henry Hammond had used in 1858, explaining that a minority could override the wishes of the majority if the majority was wrong. Buckley dismissed the idea of universal suffrage as "demagogy" and declared that whites were entitled to dominate black people because they were "the advanced race."[29]

This was an idea new westerners could get behind. The westward movement had been overwhelmingly white, and the transplants had mixed uneasily with members of the region's minority groups and African American newcomers, when they mixed with them at all. The western postwar boom depended on government spending, which undergirded everything. Paychecks funded by tax dollars paid for the homes, clothing, food, and services the workers needed such as teachers, dentists, doctors, and accountants. But the region's entrepreneurs believed that they were true western individualists, making it on their own, and they resented the regulations and taxation they thought were stealing their profits.[30]

Westerners and southerners agreed that desegregation, which gave black Americans benefits paid for by tax dollars, offered prime evidence of a communist conspiracy. In 1958, Robert Welch, the chairman of the National Association of Manufacturers and the Foundation for Economic Education—a libertarian organization dedicated to ending government regulation and taxation—started the John Birch Society, a secret organization with the goal of stopping the creep of communism under the Eisenhower administration. Backed by powerful industrialists who loathed government regulations—including Fred Koch of Wichita's Koch Engineering and Koch Oil Corporation—Welch attracted supporters by explaining that the civil rights movement roiling the country was really communism: "The trouble in our southern states has been fomented by the Communists . . . to stir up such bitterness between whites and blacks in the South that small flames of civil disorder would inevitably result. They could then fan and coalesce these little flames into one great conflagration of civil war. . . . The whole slogan of 'civil rights,' as used to make trouble in the South today, is an exact parallel to the slogan of 'agrarian reform' which they used in China."[31]

In 1962, when President Kennedy and his attorney general, Robert Kennedy, used the government to desegregate the University of Mississippi in the face of massive white resistance that left two dead and more than three hundred injured, opposition bumper stickers referred to the communist takeover of Cuba: "The Castro Brothers Have

Moved into the White House." In that year, the John Birch Society pulled in more than $1 million (Eisenhower had spent $2.5 million on his entire 1952 campaign). Labeling all opponents—including former president Eisenhower—as communists, Birchers forced Republican politicians to tolerate them out of fear they would be the next victims of such attacks. Between 1964 and 1968, white southerners opposed to integration opened more than 160 all-white private academies for their children, with state legislatures getting around the prohibition on using tax dollars for segregated schools by offering tuition grants or state tax credits.[32]

The rhetoric of Buckley's Movement Conservatives on race mirrored the warning posed by the Democrats during the Reconstruction years: a behemoth federal government was using tax dollars to help redistribute wealth to undeserving black people. And, just as during Reconstruction, the American cowboy was the face of opposition, the self-made man.

In the mid-1950s, the new television sets in all those new homes were tuned in to *Gunsmoke, Rawhide, Bonanza, Wagon Train*, and *The Lone Ranger* to see hardworking white men fighting off evil, seemingly without help from the government. In 1959, there were twenty-six westerns on TV, and in a single week in March 1959 eight of the top shows were westerns. At its peak, *Bonanza*, which had broken ground by being filmed in color, reached 480 million viewers in 97 countries. The shows all embraced the myth of the American West, where cowboys worked hard, stood for what was right, and protected their women from bad men and Indians. The cowboys were white, the storylines simple, and the land unpeopled by anyone of color or women except as they fit into the larger tale of the individualist's fight against evil.[33]

This mythology bolstered the career of Barry Goldwater, who presented himself to voters as a westerner of the old school. In reality, Goldwater had grown up the son of a wealthy man in Phoenix, with a household that had a nurse, chauffeur, and a live-in maid. He had dropped out of the University of Arizona because he didn't like it, and had married an heiress. And while he boasted of how his grandparents had come to Arizona when "there was no federal welfare system, no federally mandated employment insurance, no federal agency to monitor the purity of the air, the food we ate, or the water we drank," and that "everything that was done, we did it ourselves," the Goldwater family's money had come to them the same way it came to other western entrepreneurs: from U.S. government investment. After 1905, federal subsidies for the Roosevelt Dam provided paychecks for workers who spent their earnings at the Goldwater family's department stores. Then more money came in during World War I, and in the 1920s, federal water reclamation projects made up 15 percent of Arizona's economy. Then the New Deal pumped more money into the West. Hoover Dam and the fifty other federal agencies operating in Arizona brought $342 million into the state, while the federal government took less than $16 million out in taxes.[34]

Goldwater nonetheless maintained that his family's fortune came from hard work, and he resented the laws that he claimed gave too much power to workers, sucked tax dollars, and would inevitably lead to riots, bloodshed, and class warfare. He stood with Joe McCarthy to oppose the Democrats' policies, and opposed both the *Brown v. Board* decision and Eisenhower's desegregation of Little Rock Central High School. When Eisenhower proposed federal expenditures of $71.8 billion in his 1958 budget, Goldwater turned on him, accusing a president of his own party of embracing "the siren song of socialism." Republicans lost heavily in the 1958 elections, but Arizona voters swept Goldwater back into office with 56 percent of the vote. *Time* magazine heralded "the tall, bronzed, lean-jawed, silver-haired man of 49," whose grandfather "packed in behind a mule to found the mercantile business which now does $6,000,000 a year in five department stores."[35]

Movement Conservatives had taken a drubbing from Eisenhower, but now they had a personable, handsome westerner to carry their standard. They hoped to convince him to run for president in 1960, and to launch his candidacy they got L. Brent Bozell to ghostwrite a manifesto declaring their principles. The slim book, entitled *Conscience of a Conservative*, hit bookstores in spring 1960.[36]

Bozell started from the same point James Henry Hammond had in South Carolina a century earlier, and for much the same reasons. He insisted that the Constitution strictly limited the functions of government, and that any restrictions on property holders were an infringement on liberty. In the name of that constitutional liberty, Bozell called for the dismantling of the activist state the New Deal had created, insisting that the government had no business in "social welfare programs, education, public power, agriculture, public housing, [or] urban renewal." Leaders must refuse to pass any laws—even if popular or deemed necessary—unless the Constitution explicitly enumerated that power. The Founding Fathers had not set up a democracy, he said, precisely because they had feared "the tyranny of the masses," who would want to redistribute wealth. Instead, they had gathered control of the government into the hands of intelligent elites. In an unmistakable echo of the mudsill theory, Bozell claimed, "Our country's past progress has been the result, not of the mass mind applying average intelligence to the problems of the day, but of the brilliance and dedication of wise individuals who apply their wisdom to advance the freedom and the material well-being of all of our people."[37]

This platform attracted those who still believed they had risen of their own accord, but most Americans rejected it, recognizing that they would not be where they were now without the government stabilizing the economy and promoting opportunity. *Conscience of a Conservative* nonetheless offered two crucial things that appealed to many voters in the South and West. It maintained that the civil rights legislation of the past decade—including *Brown v. Board*—was unconstitutional. And it insisted that the government was spending too little on the military to force back international communism. Voters now had an intellectual justification for both segregation and the increased military spending that fueled their regional economies.

In 1960, the Republican National Committee passed over Goldwater and gave the presidential nomination to Eisenhower's vice president, Richard Nixon. Nixon lost to Kennedy, who continued to expand equality of opportunity. He used the government to promote black equality and also began to work to promote women's rights. In 1961, he established a government commission on the status of women, chaired by former First Lady Eleanor Roosevelt. The commission endorsed equal pay for women, called for an end to sex discrimination in hiring, and advocated paid maternity leave and universal child care. The concept of women as equal to men horrified traditionalists, especially fundamentalists, who insisted that God had made the family the model for society, with women subordinate to men and some men subordinate to others. Overturning that system undercut God's law. Two years later, in 1963, they found evidence of their fears when in her book *The Feminine Mystique* young housewife Betty Friedan skewered the comfortable suburban home life to which most Americans aspired as a "concentration camp" that stifled women as individuals.[38]

Concluding that the nation was falling to communism as their ideas continued to be sidelined, Movement Conservative leaders resolved to not to give up, but to "reverse the whole trend of American intellectual history from the days of Lincoln to those of Franklin Roosevelt and Dwight Eisenhower," as the *National Review* put it. They promised to turn the clock back to the days of the 1850s. To do that, it was imperative to secure the 1964 Republican nomination for Goldwater, and when the party's front-runner, Nelson Rockefeller, the governor of New York, spectacularly self-destructed over an extramarital affair, they got their chance. They nominated Goldwater on a platform that looked much like *Conscience of a Conservative*. It lamented America's "moral decline and drift" and called for individualism, small government, states' rights, low taxes, and the strongest military in the world. Goldwater explicitly addressed criticisms that what he stood for was a radical rejection of what most Americans believed to be the true course for American democracy. In his acceptance speech, he delivered the line that would become famous: "Extremism in the defense of liberty is no vice. And . . . moderation in the pursuit of justice is no virtue."[39]

White delegates to the convention heckled and threatened black attendees. Baseball legend Jackie Robinson—until then a keen Republican—left the Cow Palace shaken. "A new breed of Republicans has taken over the GOP. It is a new breed which is seeking to sell to Americans a doctrine which is as old as mankind—the doctrine of racial division, the doctrine of racial prejudice, the doctrine of white supremacy," Robinson said. He added that he now knew "how it felt to be a Jew in Hitler's Germany."[40]

Goldwater won only 38.5 percent of the vote and carried only six states in 1964. He carried his own western state of Arizona—candidates almost always carry their home states—and he also carried five states of the Deep South: South Carolina, Georgia, Alabama, Mississippi, and Louisiana. The Old South and the New West had come together to stand against the liberal consensus. Dixiecrat South Carolinian Strom Thurmond switched from the Democratic Party to the Republican Party and publicly supported Goldwater. Thanks to Movement Conservative ideology, southern Democrats had begun to shift to the Republican Party. Thanks to the American West, the ideology of the Confederacy had regained a foothold in national politics.[41]

★

Immediately after the 1964 election, most observers thought Goldwater's movement was cooked. Instead, the 1964 Republican campaign marked the start of the process of creating a coherent narrative that could attract voters by selling them on the corollary to the American paradox. Over the next fifteen years, Movement Conservatives would argue that the claims of minorities and women for access to opportunity were destroying individualism and the way of life it represented. That narrative would enable them to move from the political margins to the White House.

Goldwater's candidacy began the process of turning this ideology, one that had been articulated by elite men, into a simple narrative that would appeal to voters. Ever since FDR had turned to a "brain trust" of college professors to construct the New Deal, presidents had relied on experts to formulate policies that would benefit the country. Eisenhower so valued expertise that he had accepted the presidency of Columbia University after the war and continued his practice of consulting a wide range of experts after he moved into the White House. He warned that simple solutions were misleading. The modern world was complex, and inaccurate "stridency" coming from people like Joe McCarthy threatened to undermine democracy by inducing voters to place too much power in the hands of charismatic leaders.[42]

In 1964, Goldwater supporter Phyllis Schlafly turned the idea that the complexities of the postwar world needed expertise on its head. Her book *A Choice Not an Echo* argued that an "Eastern Establishment" was deliberately complicating postwar foreign policy. "Secret kingmakers" supported weak New Deal Republicans in their soft diplomacy so they could continue to profit from America's rising foreign affairs budgets. Communism versus capitalism was a black-and-white issue, she insisted. Eggheads complained that Goldwater "had one-sentence solutions" for complicated problems, but simple solutions were the right ones. His straightforward answers proved that he was a true man of the people, not co-opted by the cabal. Schlafly dismissed evidence from the new pollster George Gallup showing that Americans opposed Goldwater's extremism as part of the cabal's "propaganda machine," which spewed out misinformation in order to guarantee that they stayed in power.[43]

Ronald Reagan, an actor who had turned his movie career into politics by hosting General Electric's weekly television show promoting "free enterprise," seized on this idea in his televised speech just before the 1964 election, entitled "A Time for Choosing." He denigrated "a little intellectual elite in a far-distant capitol" that thought it could "plan our lives for us better than we can plan them ourselves." The problem with society was the "liberals": anyone, whether Republican or Democrat, who believed in active government. Reagan told folksy stories of individuals hurt by government action and dismissed the idea that anyone was helped by it. And he ignored the utter dependence of his region on government contracts. Like Goldwater, Reagan said, he had "faith that you and I have the ability and the dignity and the right to make our own decisions and determine our own destiny."

The tactics of the Goldwater campaign reinforced the idea that it was a grassroots movement. Big political donors tended to support moderates, so the Goldwater team instead used direct-mail lists and sympathetic fringe media to reach people who donated money and in the end gave more than 27 million votes for a candidate pundits thought was a joke. After the election, Movement Conservatives brought their supporters together into national organizations that offered a straitlaced alternative to the rest of the era's young people, who were listening to Bo Diddley and James Brown and The Beatles and tuning in to the idea that the world did not have to be divided by color or nations.[44]

Goldwater's crash-and-burn in 1964 meant that Lyndon Johnson had a supermajority of Congress to support what he dubbed a "War on Poverty." In 1965, Democratic-led coalitions passed federal aid to education, housing legislation, anti-poverty laws, rural development aid, and Medicare/Medicaid. Crucially, Republicans joined Democrats to pass the Voting Rights Act, designed to protect minority voting, especially in the South, where black voters had been kept from the polls for almost a century. They also revised the nation's 1924 immigration law, which had established national quotas that benefited European immigrants, and instead promoted immigration based on job skills and family connections.

Still, many Americans were no longer willing to wait for political leaders to accord them the equality that was their birthright. When young female civil rights workers found themselves excluded from positions of power and expected to defer to men, they launched their own liberation movement. By the mid-1960s, the women's movement was in full swing, and in 1966, women who had participated in the successors to Kennedy's commission on the status of women organized the National Organization for Women. Betty Friedan wrote the organization's statement of purpose, declaring that NOW aimed to "bring women into full participation in the mainstream of American society now, exercising all the privileges and responsibilities thereof in truly equal partnership with men." To call attention to derogatory gender norms, a group of feminists threw girdles, makeup, mops, and bras into a trash can at the 1968 taping of the Miss America pageant and demanded that women be respected as human beings rather than as sex objects.

Minorities also asserted their right to equality. Latinos in the West had successfully integrated schools after World War II. Led by a Texas doctor named Hector Garcia, the American GI Forum had organized voter registration drives in the Latino community and called attention to discrimination against Mexican Americans. In the mid-1960s, activists Dolores Huerta and Cesar Chavez organized a strike of farm workers in order to call attention to the ways in which landowners were flouting labor laws and sexually assaulting their workers. They inspired younger Mexican Americans not simply by their victories but also by their deliberate use of Mexican and Mexican American symbolism and ethnic pride. Younger activists embraced the ethnic identity of Chicanos: an indigenous people—la Raza—whose lands had been taken from them after the Treaty of Guadalupe Hidalgo. In 1968, thousands of Chicano high school students in Los Angeles walked out of schools in "blowouts," demanding better education and more attention to their own part in the history of the American West.

Then, just as Congress tried to expand democracy to minorities in the South with the passage of the Voting Rights Act, black northerners began to riot. Voting rights helped to enfranchise southern African

Americans but did little to help the worsening conditions for black Americans in the North, where manufacturing had declined as industries moved to the West, leaving inner-city minorities underemployed. At the same time, middle-class white families had moved out of the cities to the new suburbs, leaving the cities strapped for tax dollars. Jobless African Americans were stuck in crumbling neighborhoods. In August 1965, a six-day riot in the Watts neighborhood of Los Angeles after a white police officer's arrest of a young black man exacerbated racial tensions left thirty-four people dead, injured more than a thousand, and more than $40 million in property destroyed.[45]

The confluence of a slate of new government measures that would help minority communities with a guarantee that minority voting would now be protected was an almost exact replay of Reconstruction. White tax dollars would be "redistributed" to African Americans, Mexican Americans, and feminists through government programs and the bureaucrats necessary to administer those programs. Yet, just as those programs went into effect, the Watts riots forced the government to call out four thousand federal troops. Those riots, along with Chicanos going on strike and women allegedly burning their bras, convinced many white Americans that their black and brown neighbors, along with feminists, were not only undeserving and ungrateful but also trying to overturn American society. In the 1966 midterms, Republicans won forty-seven seats in the House and three in the Senate, enabling them to slow down what *U.S. News and World Report* called "the big bash." Notably, Reagan won the governorship of California, promising "to send the welfare bums back to work" and also to "clean up the mess at Berkeley," where students were protesting the Vietnam War.

The 1968 Republican nomination for president came down to a contest between Reagan, the darling of Movement Conservatives, and Richard Nixon, whom Republicans in general perceived as the establishment candidate. To bring Movement Conservatives to his standard, Nixon went after the southern states Goldwater had won in 1964. He courted Strom Thurmond with the promise that he would not use the federal government to pursue desegregation. This was the point at which the Republican Party made the decision to abandon its attempts to attract black voters and instead to focus on attracting whites opposed to desegregation, a process that came to be known as the "southern strategy."

With the nomination safely in hand, Nixon then had the problem of winning the election. He loathed television—he had lost badly in a television debate with JFK in 1960, which helped to sink his candidacy that year—but his handlers convinced him to use it to repackage himself. A young advertising executive named Harry Treleaven believed that television could turn politicians from the dull gray men they had always been into celebrities, actors with a narrative that far outweighed any of their policy positions. As a Nixon media advisor put it: "Voters are basically lazy. . . . Reason requires a high degree of discipline, of concentration; impression is easier. . . . The emotions are more easily roused, closer to the surface, more malleable."[46]

Nixon's campaign hired a young television producer named Roger Ailes to stage "town halls" in which the candidate answered questions from hand-picked "regular" people. No press was allowed, and Ailes arranged the questions, the set, the camera angles, the cheering crowds, and even the shading of Nixon's makeup. The campaign carefully packaged advertising, too, presenting the choice between Nixon and his Democratic opponent, Hubert Humphrey, as one between "peace and progress for all the people in the world," on the one hand, and "war and chaos," on the other. To develop the "us versus them" style of the campaign, Nixon turned to former Goldwater advisor Patrick Buchanan, who caricatured Nixon's opponents as enemies of the nation, and Nixon's supporters as good Americans.[47]

Nixon won the election, though a majority of Americans had voted for someone other than him—either Humphrey or segregationist George Wallace. Nonetheless, a key Republican strategist, Kevin Phillips, identified Nixon's election as the moment that marked the end of the New Deal era and "the beginning of a new era in American politics." The lesson of Nixon's victory, according to Phillips, was that the Republican Party could dominate politics for a generation by focusing on white voters in the "emerging Southern, Western, and New York Irish majority." He dedicated his 1970 book outlining this strategy, *The Emerging Republican Majority*, to Nixon in honor of his work as one of the two principal architects of an apparently permanent GOP majority.[48]

That permanent majority felt far off from the White House, where Nixon was keenly aware of how tenuous his popularity was. Indeed, it fell quickly: he had won election with vague promises to find "peace with honor" in Vietnam after his people had deliberately scuttled LBJ's peace talks to help Nixon's campaign, but once in office, Nixon and his advisor Henry Kissinger faced public outcry when they dramatically escalated the war rather than ending it. To defend his policies, Nixon insisted that a "silent majority" supported him against "a vocal minority" that was trying to impose their views over "reason and the will of the majority."[49]

Whether a minority or not, those who were asserting their rights were vocal. In the West, the Chicano high school "blowouts" sparked college students to protest the Vietnam War, which was dispropor-tionately affecting minority youths who could not get the deferments available to wealthy white boys. In August 1970, more than twenty thousand Los Angeles Chicanos turned out, and when police tried to stop them, four people were killed, including Ruben Salazar, a prominent journalist. Antiwar protests by young Chicanos turned into more general protests of social injustice, and in 1971, marches reached a peak, with thirty thousand participants. Disgusted with both Republicans and Democrats, Chicanos in early 1970 organized politi-cally for their own interests as La Raza Unida.[50]

Chicanos were not the only ones demanding that the nation rec-ognize their equality and address past wrongs. In November 1969, Native American activists occupied Alcatraz Island off San Francisco, which government officials had labeled surplus federal land after the prison there closed. The occupiers claimed the island "by right of discovery," and demanded changes in federal policy toward Indians. The occupation stretched on until June 1971, and in the following year activists would march on Washington and occupy the Interior Department building to call attention to broken treaties.

And then there were the feminists. Some deemed them such a threat to American society that in 1967 men determined to stop the church from embracing rights for people of color and women launched a takeover of the Southern Baptists, the nation's largest Protestant denomination, to turn the religion away from the new ways and back to fundamentalism. These fundamentalists purged moderates, insisted on a literal interpretation of the Bible, barred women from positions of authority, and in 1998 oversaw an addition to the Baptist Faith and Message advising wives to "submit . . . graciously" to their husbands.[51]

In January 1970, *Time* magazine assured readers that many "Middle Americans" opposed liberals, radicals, and antiwar protesters. They believed "angry minorities" got government programs while their taxes went up and up to pay for those programs. These Middle Americans resented blacks, intellectuals, professionals, and women who worked outside the home. They saw themselves as traditionalists, holding tight to an American culture under siege. They had supported Goldwater, and believed that the media lied to them.[52]

The Kent State shootings in May 1970, when the Ohio National Guard opened fire on college students, killing four and wounding nine others, committed Nixon fully to the notion of holding power by inflaming Middle Americans against "the media, the left, [and] the liberal academic community." Vice President Spiro Agnew deliberately exacerbated this division before the midterms that year, riling audiences with attacks on "avowed anarchists and communists," "thieves, traitors and perverts," and "radical liberals." Nixon's people were aiming to break the liberal consensus and swing working-class white men to the Republican Party. Agnew later explained that he was working for "positive polarization": positive in the idea that it would bring voters to Nixon. "Dividing the American people has been my main contribution to the national political scene since assuming the office of vice president," he admitted, adding, "I not only plead guilty to this charge, but I am somewhat flattered by it." Pat Buchanan wrote a memo to Nixon urging him to manipulate the media, and warning: "We are in a contest over the soul of the country now and the decision will not be some middle compromise. . . . [I]t will be their kind of society or ours."[53]

In 1971, television producer Norman Lear skewered this division in his hugely popular sitcom series *All in the Family*, which explored the cultural divide at play in America. Set in Queens, New York, the show featured Archie Bunker, a working-class white man who dominated his stay-at-home wife, Edith, and was constantly at odds with his feminist daughter and his hippie son-in-law, who supported civil rights and opposed the Vietnam War. The show's opening song, "Those Were the Days," sung together by Archie and Edith, lamented the loss of the past and encapsulated the show's ethos: "Guys like us we had it made. . . . And you knew who you were then, girls were girls and men were men. Mister we could use a man like Herbert Hoover again. Didn't need no welfare state, everybody pulled his weight." Archie was more bluster than bully, often deferring to his sweet, naive wife and ultimately—despite himself—embracing civil rights, tolerating homosexuality, and backing away from his previous religious bigotry.

Some of the viewers cheering Archie on were not celebrating his evolving views. *All in the Family* ran during the crucial years from 1971 to 1979, the period when the adherents of Movement Conservatism came increasingly to believe that there was a "liberal" conspiracy against America. In 1971, business lawyer Lewis Powell warned the director of the U.S. Chamber of Commerce that socialism was destroying the American system of free enterprise. He urged the director to start a crusade to dominate media, education, politics, and the courts. Nixon appointed Powell to the Supreme Court later that year, and his plan, which only came to light after his confirmation, worked. The board of the Chamber of Commerce pulled together business executives to launch such a crusade, and by 1980, firms had funded lobbyists, political action committees, and think tanks like the Heritage Foundation. In 1973, Movement Conservative activists organized the American Legislative Exchange Council to draft state legislation that promoted their values, and then to work with lawmakers to get it enacted.[54]

Nixon initially tried to steer a middle course between traditional Republicans and the party's growing Movement Conservative faction, but his own political crisis helped boost the latter's narrative. Worried about his chances for reelection in 1972, Nixon and his handlers decided to break off Catholics and southern voters from the Democratic Party by politicizing the issue of abortion. Until the 1970s, abortion had been seen largely as a civil rights issue, with NOW organizer Betty Friedan noting in 1969 that "there is no freedom, no equality, no full human dignity and personhood possible for women until we assert and demand the control over our own bodies." In 1971, even the Southern Baptist Convention supported abortion rights, taking the position that life began at birth, and a Republican campaign document from 1972 revealed data showing that "a sizeable majority of Americans, including Roman Catholics, now favoring liberal abortion laws." More Republicans than Democrats supported abortion rights, a reality reflected in the fact that the 1973 *Roe v. Wade* Supreme Court decision legalizing abortion was written by Justice Harry Blackmun, who, like the chief justice during the case, Warren Burger, was a staunch Republican.[55]

Working on Nixon's behalf, in 1971, Pat Buchanan set out to attract Democrats to the Republican Party over the issue of abortion, which he called "a rising issue and a gut issue with Catholics," who tended to vote Democratic. Obligingly, Nixon parted with his former policy to declare he had a moral objection to abortion. Quickly the abortion issue came to stand for women's rights in general. In early 1972, in her first commentary on the abortion issue, Phyllis Schlafly focused not on morality but on women's rights, arguing that "women's lib is a total assault on the role of the American woman as wife and mother and on the family as a basic unit of society. . . . Women's libbers are promoting free sex instead of the 'slavery' of marriage. They are promoting Federal 'day-care' centers for babies instead of homes. They are promoting abortions instead of families." In 1972, Buchanan planned to attack Democratic presidential candidate George McGovern—whose position on abortion was actually quite similar to Nixon's—with "the extremist, radical labels; the . . . pro-abortion positions; the radical chic." Another strategist predicted that by doing so they would pick up southern segregationists, "conservative Catholics, senior citizens, and other traditionalists." In 1974, the television show *Little House on the Prairie*, based on Laura Ingalls Wilder's books, began its nine-year run, with its portrayal of western women as wives and mothers cared for by menfolk. Prairie dresses, the female version of cowboy garb, became fashionable. The year after it ended, in 1984, a sociologist studying attitudes toward abortion noted that "pro-life" activists felt that selfish "pro-choice" women undermined the value of motherhood.[56]

Movement Conservatives supported private organizations that defended individualism, religion, and a traditional family structure and that viewed postwar liberalism as a plot to make America socialist. So pervasive was their narrative that when Nixon's paranoia about enemies led him to bug the headquarters of the Democratic National Committee in Washington's Watergate Hotel, supporters believed him when he claimed that he had to resign not because he had committed a crime but because the "liberal" press made it impossible for him to do his job.[57]

With the increasing prevalence of the Movement Conservative narrative—a vision of heroic individuals standing against collectivism—American popular culture swung away from inclusion and toward western individualism even as most Americans still embraced the liberal consensus. Western clothing and culture moved from the ranch into the mainstream. While blue jeans signaled that film star James Dean was an outsider in the 1950s, by the 1970s, everyone wore them. Seventy-five million pairs of Levis were sold in 1975, and they were worn to symbolize dislike of the government both by those who op-posed civil rights legislation and by those who opposed the Vietnam War. Those anti-government types flew Confederate flags, which had fallen into disuse during the Depression and World War II, but started making a dramatic comeback in the 1950s. Southern rockers began to use Confederate iconography, even the Allman Brothers Band and Lynyrd Skynyrd, who campaigned for Democratic presidential candidate Jimmy Carter in 1976. Lots of Americans were willing to wear clothes identified with dislike of the government, some because that government appeared to be wasting tax dollars on undeserving minorities, others because it backed an unjust and unwinnable war in Southeast Asia. These themes came together in the blockbuster 1977 film *Star Wars*, which was the classic western story mythologized into space, with Luke Skywalker and the Resistance taking on the Empire by rejecting expertise and relying on "the Force."[58]

This cultural trend played into Movement Conservatives' political fortunes. In the 1970s, Americans faced riots; the kidnapping of heiress Patty Hearst by a leftist "army" that wanted to end racism, sexism, capitalism, and ageism; inflation; the oil crisis; the taking of fifty-two hostages in Iran when Islamic fundamentalists ousted the American-backed Shah; and the Russian invasion of Afghanistan, a land off-limits to both East and West since the "Great Game" of the nineteenth century. These were complicated problems all, with many moving pieces. But Movement Conservatives continued to blame everything on the growing liberal government, which, they said, had ballooned under Jimmy Carter, whom they also blamed for the gas shortage and the Iran hostage situation (although he had no control over either).

They had a simple solution: the government must get out of the way of individualism. It must slash taxes and regulation, restore tradi-tional values, and build up the military, just as Goldwater had called for in *Conscience of a Conservative*. To this plan they now added the authority of economics professor Milton Friedman, who explained that if the government stopped worrying about protecting workers and consumers (the demand side of the economy) and instead cut taxes and permitted money to accumulate at the top of the economy (the supply side), wealthy people would invest in new businesses, more people would find work, production would go up, and revenue would increase. Tax cuts would pay for themselves. The booming economy would spread prosperity to everyone. Friedman summed up his theory in an article for the *New York Times Magazine*: "The Social Responsibility of Business is to Increase Its Profits."[59]

This argument, which echoed precisely what the southern slaveholders had claimed, gained the most traction in the West, where blaming eastern liberals for the nation's problems became an article of faith. Evangelical religion had grown in the South and West as desegregation and the women's movement had gained momentum. In the early 1970s, a secretive Christian organization known as The Family began to sponsor prayer meetings in businesses, colleges, and the government. By the mid-1970s, they were effectively mobilizing white evangelicals as a voting bloc. Southern and western televangelists like Billy Graham, Oral Roberts, Jimmy Swaggart, Jim and Tammy Faye Bakker, Jerry Falwell, and Pat Robertson promised a return to a traditional culture in which the values of the modern world would be rejected. In 1976, direct marketer Richard Viguerie persuaded Falwell to form the Moral Majority to get Christians to support Movement Conservative politicians, and by 1979, about 10 percent of all television programming was religious, with televangelists attacking communism, feminism, abortion, homosexuality, and the "humanism" coming from godless eastern "liberals." They preached the prosperity gospel, which said that people would become rich if only they believed.[60]

The rise of the religious right worked in tandem with a western revolt against taxes. Rising prices pushed middle-class Americans into higher tax brackets, and they blamed minorities and eastern liberals for taking their money. In 1976, Reagan began to develop the image of the "welfare queen," a woman from the South Side of Chicago (which implied that she was black without saying so) who lived on tax dollars.

At a campaign rally in 1976, challenging President Gerald Ford for the Republican presidential nomination, Reagan told an audience, "She has 80 names, 30 addresses, 12 Social Security cards and is collecting veteran's benefits on four non-existing deceased husbands. . . . She's got Medicaid, getting food stamps, and she is collecting welfare under each of her names." In 1978, California voters amended the state constitution by approving Proposition 13, which limited property taxes to 1 percent of the cash value of the property and required a two-thirds majority of the state legislature to increase the state's taxes.[61]

In the 1980 presidential election, Reagan brought the South and the West together to take over national politics as he rode the Movement Conservative narrative into the White House. Wearing a jaunty white cowboy hat, he launched his presidential campaign in Philadelphia, Mississippi, just miles from where three civil rights workers had been murdered in 1964, and promised that he would not take tax exemptions away from segregated private schools. He blamed taxes and federal bureaucracy for stifling the American dream. "I believe in states' rights," he told the crowd. "I believe in people doing as much as they can for themselves." When he won the election, he was the first to deliver his inaugural address not from the East Front of the Capitol but from the West Front. The move was practical—there was more room for spectators—but it reflected the rising power of the West in the nation. "Government is not the solution to our problem," he announced to the nation. "Government is the problem."[62]

CHAPTER 8

Oligarchy Rides Again

When Reagan tapped the thirty-five-year-old Michigan Congressman David Stockman to be his Budget Director, Stockman, who had grown up on *Conscience of a Conservative*, set out to bring Goldwater's dream to life. As soon as he took office in 1981, Reagan proposed cutting $47 billion from the previous year's budget. To do that, Stockman slashed funding for food stamps, education, job training, and unemployment insurance. Then the administration turned to tax cuts. When computer simulations at the Office of Management and Budget showed that the proposed tax cuts would not increase revenues but instead would decrease them and explode the deficit, Stockman simply reprogrammed the computers. "None of us really understands what's going on with all these numbers," he rationalized. "The whole thing is premised on faith . . . on a belief about how the world works."[1]

That faith was the one shared by William F. Buckley Jr. and Barry Goldwater—and by James Henry Hammond, William Sharon, Herbert Hoover, and Robert Taft: if the government simply turned rich men loose to work their magic, they would create ever-expanding prosperity and everyone would get richer. "A rising tide lifts all boats," as they said, and the election of Reagan was the latest step in a long-standing campaign to destroy the liberal consensus and replace it with the kind of unfettered capitalism that had preceded it.

And so, with Reagan in office, these true believers set their sights on destroying the activist state that had been in place since the 1930s and freeing up businessmen to develop the economy. That required taking over the Republican Party entirely, much as elites had taken over the Democratic Party in the 1850s. First they developed policies to protect their interests, and then they purged from party leadership anyone who did not share their convictions.

"When I took the oath of office," Reagan said, "I pledged loyalty to only one special interest group—'We the people.'" Congress cut $35 billion from social welfare spending in the next year's budget and passed a sweeping tax cut that cut 23 percent off individual tax rates, slashed capital gains and estate taxes, and cut top income rates from 70 percent to 50 percent. Stockman explained to a journalist that supply-side economics was really just a new way to package the old idea of cutting taxes for the rich and letting the beneficial effects "trickle down" to everyone else. Reagan signed the bills at his sprawling 688-acre California ranch in August 1981.[2]

Tax cuts became Republican orthodoxy. After a deep recession at the beginning of Reagan's term, the economy began to recover in 1983. It did so for a number of reasons. Oil prices dropped dramatically, and the Federal Reserve Board slashed interest rates. Perhaps more important, Congress had poured money into the military, increasing its budget by $17 billion in 1982—40 percent in real spending—at the same time it was slashing taxes. Congress also deregulated savings and loan banks, enabling them to pump $160 billion more into the economy. Although the deficit spending and speculation that fueled the boom would have to be repaid, administration supporters insisted that the extraordinary economic growth proved that supply-side economics worked. When Democrats tried to raise taxes to plug the holes in the budget, wage workers joined the "anti-tax" movement. An up-and-coming economist for the U.S. Chamber of Commerce named Grover Norquist warned politicians that voters didn't want to be taxed to pay down deficits; they preferred the Republicans' promise that tax cuts would pay for spending by increasing growth.[3]

In 1986, a second major tax cut revealed the ideological underpinnings of the Republican tax policies. By increasing deductions, that law relieved about 6 million lower-income Americans from paying income taxes. But on the other end of the scale, it cut the capital gains tax, cut the marginal tax rate for the highest tax bracket from 50 percent to 28 percent, and raised it for the bottom bracket from 11 percent to 15 percent. It also cut the corporate tax rate from 48 percent to 34 percent. When Democratic Senator George Mitchell of Maine objected that the bill gave 16 percent of the tax relief in it to the richest 0.5 percent of Americans, while most Americans would get only a 6.4 percent share of that relief, Oregon Senator Bob Packwood, Republican chairman of the Senate Finance Committee, insisted that anyone who wanted higher tax brackets for the wealthy were simply trying to run "social welfare schemes." The bill's deductions for poor families infuriated Phyllis Schlafly, who protested that such a benefit was "just an idea of liberal bureaucrats who want to redistribute the wealth." She dismissed the idea that the tax break was pro-family: anything "anti-growth" was "anti-family" by definition.[4]

Like Buckley and Bozell, Reagan firmly believed that his economic ideology reflected God's plan, and it had global implications. In 1983, he outlined a foreign policy initiative, which became known as the "Reagan Doctrine," calling for rolling back communism by supporting local insurrections that fought against communist governments in third-world countries—a policy that led to the United States backing "freedom fighters" in Nicaragua, Angola, and Afghanistan. He explained that the fight against what he believed was collectivism at home was just one theater in an epic struggle. Speaking to the National Association of Evangelicals in Orlando, Florida, Reagan explained that America was engaged in a great battle between "right and wrong and good and evil." On one hand were secularism and bureaucracy that crushed the individual; on the other were individualism, morality, and God. Modern-day America had sacrificed morality for bureaucracy, he warned, and to save the nation it was imperative to return religion to public life. To illustrate his point, Reagan focused on abortion and what he insisted was creeping infanticide: Americans who believed in big government were literally killing babies.[5]

To protect the tax cuts that lay at the heart of his vision, Reagan and his team supported Norquist's plan to organize business leaders, evangelicals, and social conservatives into a political juggernaut. The group Americans for Tax Reform used money from business interests to push the religious themes of Reagan's economic ideology, harnessing the electoral power of poorer Americans in favor of policies backed by big business. And what businessmen wanted was tax cuts. "Traditional Republican business groups can provide the resources," Norquist explained, "but these groups can provide the votes."[6]

Norquist's coalition proved an uneasy one at first, but by 1988 evangelicals had become politically powerful enough to push one of their own ministers, Southern Baptist leader Pat Robertson, for the Republican presidential nomination. When Robertson lost to Reagan's vice president, traditional Republican George H. W. Bush, Norquist's friend Ralph Reed helped to turn Robertson's following into a permanent political pressure group: the Christian Coalition. This group organized evangelicals behind Movement Conservative policies, arguing that traditional family values depended on an individualist economic system. It also encouraged evangelicals to run for state and local offices, attacking regulation and taxes while they spread their religious policies at every level.

This combination enabled the Movement Conservative wing of the party to overpower traditional Republicans. To protect the 1986 tax law, Norquist had developed a litmus test for candidates for office, a pledge for them to sign promising they would oppose any increase in tax rates or elimination of tax deductions. His anti-tax stance was influential enough that in 1988, 101 House Republicans and 2 House Democrats signed it. Furthermore, during the 1988 campaign, Bush had had to court conservatives with the promise "Read my lips: no new taxes."

Once elected, however, Bush had to reckon with four unfortunate financial legacies from the Reagan administration: the federal debt had tripled from $994 billion to $2.8 trillion; interest payments alone cost $200 billion a year; the budget was still way out of balance; and deregulation had precipitated the collapse of savings and loan banks that would cost $132 billion to bail out. In 1990, facing a $171 billion deficit for the next fiscal year, Bush hammered out a deal with Democrats that would slash funding for social programs while also raising $134 billion in taxes. Led by Georgia Republican Newt Gingrich, Movement Conservatives signed onto the bill in private, but in public they attacked the deal, claiming it would destroy growth, work against the interests of ordinary Americans, and betray Reagan's legacy.[7]

Gingrich and Norquist intended to purge the Republican Party of all liberals and to ride their own ideology to power. "You are killing us," Bush told Gingrich as he went after the tax deal, "you are just killing us." But that was the point. Gingrich intended to kill off those he called RINOs—Republicans in Name Only. This undercut Bush's chances for reelection, and although polls suggested that most Americans weren't terribly concerned about taxes, Gingrich and Norquist made tax cuts the centerpiece of Republican platforms. "We worked from the assumption that our economic policies worked and theirs didn't," Norquist explained. "We ran on this message . . . and we won."

When voters elected Democrat Bill Clinton in 1992, Republicans in Congress held the line: not a single Republican supported Clinton's first annual budget, even though the administration had stripped it of major programs it had promised voters. The budget raised taxes: it set a 36 percent tax bracket for incomes over $115,000, and a 39.6 percent bracket for incomes over a quarter of a million dollars.[8]

Norquist and Gingrich went into the 1994 midterm elections swinging. Backed by the Republican National Committee, which poured $15 million into House races, they offered voters a "Contract with America." It promised that, if given control of Congress, Republicans on their first day would audit Congress, cut one-third of the House committees and their staff, and ram through a requirement that any future tax increase would require a three-fifths majority to pass. In the next ninety-nine days, they would push the Movement Conservative platform as far as they could. Their message worked. Voters gave control of the House to the Republicans for the first time since 1954, and Republicans picked up eight Senate seats as well. The election results made Republicans giddy. "Speaker Gingrich," read a T-shirt selling in Washington, D. C.: "Deal with it."[9]

Now in control of Congress, Gingrich's Republicans set the terms of political debate. Rush Limbaugh, a talk-show host who had been so instrumental in pushing the Contract with America that Gingrich's revolutionaries named him an honorary member of the incoming class of representatives, explained the agenda. Republicans must, he said, "begin an emergency dismantling of the welfare system, which is shredding the social fabric," bankrupting the country, and "gutting the work ethic, educational performance, and moral discipline of the poor." They must further cut capital gains taxes to drive economic growth upward; it would create hundreds of thousands of jobs and produce billions in federal revenue, he insisted. In April 1995, an internal memo identified tax cuts as the central principle of Republicanism, and Norquist explained why: "All reductions in federal spending weaken the left in America. . . . Defunding the government is defunding the left." His plan, he said, was to "run up 100 yards and blow [up] the train tracks." "Mr. Norquist has become one of the main power brokers in the new Republican majority," noted the *Wall Street Journal*. "His rise helps explain both the power of Newt Gingrich and the ideological makeover of Republicans." When President Clinton refused to sign a budget that slashed funding for Medicare, public health, the environment, and education, Gingrich and his colleagues shut down the federal government for twenty-eight days, from November 1995 to January 1996, to pressure him to get their way.[10]

Eventually, the Republicans had to back down in the face of popular anger and reopen the government, and the Contract with America was all but forgotten by March 1996. But Gingrich's conservatives had permanently changed the government. Not only had they put tax cuts at the center of Republican policy, they had also reoriented the mechanics of lawmaking. After decades of Democratic power in Congress, lobbyists had close ties to Democratic power brokers. Under Gingrich, Republican leaders had warned lobbyists that they must favor Republicans with contributions and hiring. This "K-Street Project," as it was called, established a revolving door between lobbyists and Republican officials. At the same time, Gingrich's cuts to House staff meant that bewildered representatives turned to lobbyists to explain issues and write bills.

As Stockman's numbers had shown before they reprogrammed the computers, however, supply-side economics—"voodoo economics," as George H. W. Bush, a traditional Republican, had called it—did not, in fact, create widespread prosperity. As had been the case a century and a half before, the program of keeping capitalists free from regulations and taxes moved wealth upward. Beginning in 1981, tax cuts, the destruction of social welfare spending, and hostility to unions reversed the Great Compression of the liberal consensus and replaced it with what economists call the Great Divergence. Most people got poorer, while a few got very rich indeed. By 2015, the top 1 percent of American families took home more than 20 percent of income. Wealth distribution was ten times worse than that: the families in the top 1 percent owned as much wealth as the families in the bottom 90 percent.

While it hollowed out the American middle class and consigned workers generally to falling increasingly behind, this stratification of wealth disproportionately hit minorities and women. The median white household in 2011 had a yearly income of $50,400 and owned $111,146 in wealth. This stood in dramatic contrast to the median Latino household's yearly income of $36,840 and ownership of $8,348 in wealth. Even worse, the median black household had an income of $32,028 and owned only $7,113 in wealth. On the Pine Ridge Reservation of Lakotas, the poorest area in the nation, the statistics were even more sobering. Its forty thousand residents had an average income of between $2,600 and $3,500 a year.[11]

Movement Conservatives had taken over the Republican Party with the intention of destroying the liberal consensus. Wealth was moving upward, and women and minorities were headed toward positions of subordination. America was on its way to becoming an oligarchy.

★

From their beginning in the 1950s, Movement Conservative leaders had recognized that they could not win over voters with policy, for the activist state they opposed was quite popular. So they shaped their message around vignettes that made a compelling story. In the 1980s, as it became clear to most voters that they were falling behind under the Republican program, leaders stayed in power by deliberately crafting a narrative that harked back to western individualism. The hardworking individual—the cowboy—was endangered by a behemoth state. To protect him, they invoked the corollary to the American paradox, arguing that equality for women and people of color would destroy the freedom that lay at the heart of democracy. Then they sought to spread that narrative as widely as they could. The story they told of an America under siege by "takers" was not based in fact. Rather, it followed a formula that rewrote history in order to divide voters and win election by turning their supporters against minorities and women. In this narrative, the popular policies of the liberal consensus were just what the Reconstruction years had been in this telling: a redistribution of wealth from hardworking white men to the undeserving. To sell to voters a program that hurt most of them, the new Republicans deliberately shaped popular culture to bolster their ideology.

Reagan was always a master of the telling anecdote, from his welfare queen image to his insistence that creeping infanticide was the obvious product of the spread of godless communism into America, and he had drawn those vignettes into a compelling story of the little guy under siege by a government that was replacing liberty with communism. But as Movement Conservatives took over the Republican Party, other politicians developed this story, drawing on that fundamental American idea that admitting people of color and women to positions of equality with white men would, by definition, destroy American freedom. To make their case, they reached back to the history of the Reconstruction Era, when southern Democrats insisted that government policies to enforce racial equality destroyed white freedom by sucking tax dollars out of hardworking white men to fund the bureaucracy charged with enforcing civil rights. And of course they embraced the idea of the American cowboy, who had taken on a mythical role during Reconstruction as the quintessential American who worked hard, took care of his womenfolk, and wanted nothing from the government but to be left alone. So invested had Americans become in the image of the heroic westerner that when an academic historian proved definitively that Davy Crockett had surrendered at the Alamo rather than fighting until the bitter end, he received hate mail.[12]

When the theme of the lone hero taking on an oppressive government entered the entertainment industry, it reached a much wider swath of ordinary Americans, most of them men. In summer 1984, director John Milius brought to the nation's movie theaters what was, at the time, the most violent film ever made. *Red Dawn* was the story of high school football players in Colorado, the Wolverines, fighting off a communist invasion after the local mayor and his son sold out the town to the invaders. Reagan's first Secretary of State, Al Haig, had been an advisor on the film, and it so inspired a generation of young men with its nationalism and heroism that when Captain Geoffrey McMurray picked the code name of the operation to capture Saddam Hussein in 2003, he named it Operation Red Dawn. "I think all of us in the military have seen *Red Dawn*," McMurray said.[13]

Recognizing how effective popular media could be in building support for their ideas, Movement Conservative Republicans launched a campaign against the "fairness doctrine." Since the 1920s, the government had required public broadcast media stations to present information honestly, balancing different points of view. That arguments should be based on facts put the ideology of Movement Conservatives at a disadvantage. Adherents insisted that the fairness doctrine biased the media against them. The media was, they said, liberal. Under pressure, and with Reagan's appointees voting, in 1987 the FCC caved and ended the policy.

Released from the constraints of the fairness doctrine, the media, rather than presenting informed debate and encouraging listeners to weigh evidence, could simply push ideology. And it did. Within a year talk radio had become a national phenomenon. Hosts like Rush Limbaugh warned that socialism was creeping through America, and he identified the enemy: black people, feminazis, "Liberals."

Their message worked. In summer 1988, when George Bush was running 18 points behind the Democratic nominee for president, Massachusetts governor Michael Dukakis, Bush's campaign manager, Lee Atwater, picked up the central image of Movement Conservatism pushed by talk radio. Atwater made the point that special interests, especially black Americans aided by liberals like Governor Dukakis, were literally killing America. With the help of Roger Ailes, who had promoted Nixon in 1968, Bush's team produced the infamous "Willie

Horton" ad. Packaged as if it were a news story, the ad showed a mug shot of a black murderer who raped a white middle-class woman and stabbed her boyfriend while on a weekend parole from prison. The reality was that Horton had been paroled under a law signed by Dukakis's Republican predecessor in the Massachusetts governorship, and that the federal parole program under Reagan and Bush was even more lenient than that of Massachusetts. The reality didn't matter. Ailes and Atwater had encapsulated in thirty seconds the idea that Democrats were socialists working for black criminals. The "Willie Horton" ad reversed Bush's abysmal poll numbers. (At the end of his life, Atwater apologized for the "naked cruelty" of his actions, and noted that "In part because of our successful manipulation of his campaign themes, George Bush won handily.")[14]

The image of the western individualist offered status to white men, as it set them above people of color and above women, who in the western vision could be either wives and mothers, dependent on their men, or sex objects. By 1984, most Americans had come to believe that women who wanted equality were, in fact, demanding handouts, and opposed them. When Democratic 1984 presidential candidate Walter Mondale tapped prominent New York Representative Geraldine Ferraro to be his running mate, 60 percent of Americans believed he was simply catering to women who wanted special-interest legislation. As the postwar economy faltered, young white men whose easy future was no longer ensured used their dominance over women to cling to the idea they were special. On the one hand, white supremacists emphasized Christianity, individualism, and their masculine protection of dependent women. On the other, in Lakewood, California, in 1993, a gang of teenage boys who called themselves the Spur Posse boasted they were the stars, the studs, the athletes—"a step above everyone else." They divided their female classmates into "the girls that, you know, that you have respect for and that you'll romance," and "these other girls, you know, you're going to drive over there, you already know what's going to happen, you know, it's no romance, you know, it's just—wham." When their casual rape of girls in the latter category came to light, their religious parents blamed not their sons but the girls, who were blowing things out of proportion; the liberals, who had brought sex into the schools; and the media, who called attention to the situation.[15]

Beginning in the 1990s, western men marginalized in the new economy increasingly took their cue from *Red Dawn* and vowed to stand against the government that talk radio hosts told them was socialistic or communistic. Western individualism dovetailed with evangelical Christianity. Francis Schaeffer's 1981 bestseller *A Christian Manifesto* argued that America had initially been a Christian nation but was corrupted by secularism. More and more evangelical families, particularly in the western states, took their children out of public schools to homeschool them without the corrupting influence of government and its secular principles.

These two themes ran together, and in August 1992, they came to a violent conclusion at Ruby Ridge, Idaho, when government forces tried to arrest Randy Weaver, a former factory worker who had moved his family to northern Idaho to escape what he saw as the corruption of American society. Weaver had failed to show up for trial on a firearms charge, and when federal marshals tried to arrest him, a firefight left Weaver's fourteen-year-old son and a deputy marshal dead. In the aftermath of the shooting, federal and local officers laid an eleven-day siege to the Weavers' cabin, and a sniper wounded Weaver and killed his wife, Vicki.

Far-right activists and neo-Nazis from a nearby Aryan Nations compound swarmed to Ruby Ridge to protest the government's attack on what they saw as a man protecting his family, a modern Jesse James. Negotiators eventually brought Weaver out, but the standoff at Ruby Ridge convinced western men they had to arm themselves to fight off the government. In February of the next year, during the Democratic Bill Clinton administration, the same theme played out in Waco, Texas, when officers stormed the compound of a religious cult whose former members reported that their leader, David Koresh, was stockpiling weapons. A gun battle and a fire that ended the fifty-one-day siege on April 19, 1993, left seventy-six people dead.[16]

While a Republican investigation cited "overwhelming evidence" that exonerated the government of wrongdoing, talk radio hosts nonetheless railed against the administration, especially Attorney General Janet Reno, for the events at Waco. Rush Limbaugh stoked his listeners' anger with reports of the "Waco invasion" and talked of the government's "murder" of citizens, making much of the idea that a group of Christians had been killed by a female government official who was single and—as opponents made much of—unfeminine (reactionary rocker Ted Nugent featured an obscene caricature of her for years in his stage version of "Kiss My Glock"). Horrified by the government's attempt to break into the cult's compound, Alex Jones, who would go on to become an important conspiracy theorist and founder of *InfoWars*, dropped out of community college to start a talk show on which he warned that Reno had "murdered" the people at Waco and that the government was about to impose martial law. The modern militia movement took off.[17]

The combination of political rhetoric and violence inspired a former Army gunner, Timothy McVeigh, to bring the war home to the government. "Taxes are a joke," he wrote to a newspaper in 1992. "More taxes are always the answer to government mismanagement. . . . Is a Civil War Imminent? Do we have to shed blood to reform the current system? I hope it doesn't come to that. But it might." On April 19, 1995, a date chosen to honor the Waco standoff, McVeigh set off a bomb at the Alfred P. Murrah Federal Building in Oklahoma City. The blast killed 168 people, including 19 children younger than six, and wounded more than 800. When the police captured McVeigh, he was wearing a T-shirt with a picture of Abraham Lincoln and the words "Sic Semper Tyrannis."[18]

Far from backing off their extremism, Republicans turned up the heat. In 1990, under Newt Gingrich, a Republican training group had distributed a guide for the new Republican members of Congress urging them to refer to their opponents with words like "decay," "failure," sick," "pathetic," "liberal," and "traitors." The document was entitled "Language: A Key Mechanism of Control." Then, in 1993, Clinton began his term by raising taxes, and Republicans howled that he was ruining the economy to funnel money to special interests. When the economy instead boomed, Republicans were determined to destroy him and the activist government he championed. In 1992, Roger Ailes began to produce a television show hosted by Rush Limbaugh to spread the word to new audiences. In October 1996, an ideological media network became a reality when Australian-born media mogul Rupert Murdoch established the Fox News Channel (FNC)—with Roger Ailes as its CEO.[19]

From the beginning, FNC blurred the line between reality and image. "Fox News" was simply the name of the channel, and while it did have some news shows, most of its political material was not news, with reporting and fact checking, but rather "entertainment." The sets used by Fox personalities like Bill O'Reilly and Sean Hannity looked like news sets, and they commented on news events, but they were simply offering commentary on American society, a commentary that countered the "liberal" media. Fox could call itself "fair and balanced" because it offered the ideological opposite to what other news shows, which relied on fact-based arguments, produced.

FNC presented a mythologized America to those left behind under Republican policies. It was based on the narrative that Americans were white and rural—although by 1990 more than three-quarters of Americans lived in a city of more than 100,000 people—and wanted simply to take care of themselves. They hated taxes and an intrusive government, and would do just fine if they could get the socialistic, anti-Christian Democrats to leave them alone. It was a message built on image alone: FNC personalities whipped up anger over perceived slights inflicted by minorities and women against white Christians, or over conspiracy theories. The optics of FNC reinforced the image of western individualist men running society while women were wives or sex objects. Most FNC personalities were older men, while the network's women were young, beautiful, and deferential.[20]

Murdoch offered $10 per subscriber to each cable company that carried the new channel, and it soon became a major political player. By the time of the 2000 election, 17.3 percent of Americans were watching the Fox News Channel, and of its viewers who voted, 3 to 8 percent of them moved into the Republican column. FNC insisted that all other news stations were biased, and offered as proof that other stations did not entertain their point of view. As they tried to avoid charges that they were not presenting the news fairly, other major media outlets, especially those that operated on the broadband network and thus had to be licensed by the FCC, began to air the ideological positions of FNC. As the Powell Memo had urged twenty years earlier, Movement Conservatives had finally managed to take over the political conversation, and they continued to move it rightward. A vice president of the Mackinac Center for Public Policy, a think tank, explained that there was a window of ideas the public would accept. To move that set of ideas rightward, believers had to promote fringe ideas aggressively until they became acceptable. FNC moved the Overton Window to the right with a constant stream of media chatter about creeping socialism and the assault by minorities and women on American freedom.[21]

★

If Movement Conservatives were right that women and minorities were dangerous to democracy, it was imperative to remove them from positions of influence in the government, the same way elite slaveholders had sought to take the government out of the hands of their opponents a century and a half earlier. This led its adherents to purge the system of anyone they considered a "liberal"—Democrats, of course, but also any RINOs, Republican who believed that the government had any role to play in society other than funding the military and protecting business and religion.

Democrats were obvious targets. Clinton had won as a "New Democrat," the leader of a movement that accepted many of the deregulatory and austerity policies of the Republican Party while also maintaining the principle that the government had a role to play in the economy, social welfare, and infrastructure, and should fund that activism with taxes. Movement Conservatives incorrectly predicted that the economy would crash under Clinton, and the danger that Clinton's policies would succeed made them apoplectic. From the beginning of his term in 1993 they searched for a scandal that would destroy his presidency. At last, in 1998, a special prosecutor charged with investigating Clinton's investment in a land deal in Arkansas turned up the fact that the president had engaged in an extramarital affair with a White House intern. When Clinton lied about that affair under oath, House Speaker Gingrich (who was himself having an affair with a staffer, Callista Bisek) launched impeachment proceedings. While they argued that impeaching the president for lying about an extramarital affair was a "character issue" rather than a constitutional one, it was clear they sought to cripple the presidency of a man Arkansas Republican activist James D. Johnson called a "queer-mongering, whore-hopping adulterer; a baby-killing, draft-dodging, dope-tolerating, lying, two-faced, treasonable activist."[22]

The impeachment was intended to kill off liberal power altogether, but it backfired. Clinton's popularity only rose—his approval rating was at 70 percent at the end of the impeachment process—and in the 1998 midterm elections, Democrats actually picked up House seats and held even in the Senate, an outcome unheard of for an administration in its sixth year (the last time it had happened was 1822). To Movement Conservatives, this was unthinkable. Clinton was such an obvious affront to the American system, it was clear that the voting process itself had to be fixed.

They began to purge the system of voters they perceived as illegitimate because they tended to support liberal candidates. Party operatives had talked of cutting down black voting under a "ballot integrity" initiative in 1986, and they bitterly opposed a 1993 Democratic expansion of voter registration at certain state offices, known as the "motor-voter law," which a *New York Times* writer noted they saw "as special efforts to enroll core Democratic constituencies in welfare and jobless-benefits offices." On the heels of that law, key Republican operative Ed Rollins boasted that he had spent hundreds of thousands of dollars suppressing the black vote to elect a Republican governor in New Jersey. In 1994, losing candidates were charging that Democrats won elections with "voter fraud"; one of the leading voices charging such irregularities had used Rollins as a campaign consultant. In 1996, House and Senate Republicans each launched year-long investigations into what they insisted were problematic elections, one in Louisiana and one in California. Keeping the cases in front of the media for a year helped to convince Americans that voter fraud was a serious issue and that Democrats were winning elections thanks to illegal, usually immigrant, voters.[23]

Although repeated investigations proved that voter fraud was a myth, the House began to talk of passing a voter ID law to ensure that everyone who voted was a U.S. citizen. The Florida legislature took the lead, passing a law to clean up voting after the 1997 Miami mayoral race proved to be a fraudulent mess. While the corrupt mayoral election reflected a local struggle between two Cuban Americans—one a Republican and the other an Independent—the Florida law quickly became a purge of black voters, people presumed to vote Democratic. Observers estimated that up to 100,000 legitimate voters were removed from the system.[24]

This purge paid off in the election of 2000, when George W. Bush of Texas, the son of President George H. W. Bush, ran against Clinton's vice president, Al Gore Jr., who chose conservative Democrat Joe Lieberman for his vice president to appeal to middle-of-the-road voters influenced by Movement Conservatives. Gore won the popular vote by more than half a million votes but was four votes short of a win in the Electoral College. Florida, where Bush's brother Jeb was governor and which had implemented the 1998 voter purge, would decide the election. A series of events, including a confusing ballot that siphoned off about 10,000 votes meant for Gore to far-right Republican Pat Buchanan, and a riot of Republican operatives—including Lee Atwater's former partner Roger Stone—at the headquarters of the Miami-Dade County polling headquarters, resulted in the Supreme Court stepping in to decide the winner. After widespread reports of irregularities, an investigation by the United States Commission on Civil Rights revealed "an extraordinarily high and inexcusable level of disenfranchisement," primarily of Democratic African American voters. To elect your party's candidate, Stone later told a reporter, "it's attack, attack, attack."[25]

Republicans continued to harp on the idea of voter fraud until it became an article of faith that their opponents could win an election only by leveraging the votes of illegitimate voters. In 2013, in the landmark *Shelby County v. Holder* decision, the Republican Supreme Court gutted the 1965 Voting Rights Act by declaring unconstitutional its rule that states could not change voting laws without prior clearance from the Department of Justice. Immediately, Republican state officials began to introduce voter ID laws and bills restricting voter registration.[26]

Another way to manipulate the makeup of the government was through the process of redistricting congressional units, in such a way that they dramatically favored Republicans, a process called "gerrymandering," after Elbridge Gerry, an early governor of Massachusetts who signed off on such a scheme (even though he didn't like it). Both parties had always engaged in such machinations, but after Democrat Barack Obama won the presidency in 2008, some Republicans hatched a plan to hamstring his ability to accomplish anything: they would make sure he had a hostile Congress. Party operatives raised money from corporate donors to guarantee that state legislatures were Republican in 2010. REDMAP, as they called it (short for Redistricting Majority Project), had huge political implications, because it meant that Republicans would redistrict their states after the 2010 census, a redistricting that would last for a decade. It worked. After the 2010 election, Republicans controlled the key states of Florida, Wisconsin, North Carolina, Ohio, and Michigan, as well as other, smaller states, and they redrew congressional maps using precise computer models. In the 2012 election, Democrats won the White House decisively, the Senate easily, and a majority of 1.4 million votes for House candidates. And yet Republicans came away with a thirty-three-seat majority in the House of Representatives.[27]

This system placed the power of the government in the hands of a Republican Party that had been taken over by Movement Conservatives and was no longer responsible to a majority of voters, let alone to a majority of Americans. They controlled government simply by refusing to compromise on their principles, enacting policies designed to destroy the liberal consensus, and refusing to consider any measures advanced by their opponents. Thanks to gerrymandering, they didn't have to. Grover Norquist said triumphantly: "We don't need a president to tell us in what direction to go. We know what direction to go. We just need a president to sign this stuff. . . . Pick a Republican with enough working digits to handle a pen to become president of the United States."[28]

In the long term, Republicans could cement their power through the courts. Reagan's attorney general, Edwin Meese, had deliberately politicized the Department of Justice in an attempt, as he said, to "institutionalize the Reagan revolution so it can't be set aside no matter what happens in future elections." Reagan appointed more judges than any other president in history, including three Supreme Court justices and one chief justice. The rightward swing of the court continued thanks to the elevation of George W. Bush, who appointed two Supreme Court justices, including a chief justice. To stop Obama from changing this trend, Senate Majority leader Mitch McConnell of Kentucky held up Obama's judicial appointments, and finally took the unprecedented step of refusing even to consider the president's moderate nominee to replace one of Reagan's Supreme Court appointees.[29]

★

By 2016, Republican leaders sounded eerily like antebellum slaveholders in their defense of a system in which wealthy elites ruled over the masses. Presidential candidate Mitt Romney and his running mate, future Speaker of the House Paul Ryan of Wisconsin, talked vaguely in 2012 about "makers and takers," but some Republicans were more explicit. Journalist and pundit Josh Barro tweeted in December 2013, "Elites are usually elite for good reason, and tend to have better judgment than the average person."[30]

The flip side of this message was that takers belonged at the bottom of society and should have no say in government. In 2012, Romney claimed that 47 percent of the American people felt they were "entitled to health care, to food, to housing, to you name it," and told supporters that those people would only vote for Democrats who would give them stuff. Former Republican senator Rick Santorum put it more starkly: "I don't want to make black people's lives better by giving them someone else's money." Republicans had poured vitriol on women and minorities since Reagan invented the welfare queen in the 1970s, but in March 2016, *National Review*'s Kevin Williamson turned on poor white people. It was not the dramatic tilting of the economic scales toward the rich after 1980 that had hurt people dependent on welfare, he wrote; rather, "they failed themselves." In 2009, entrepreneur Peter Thiel came out and said it. He longed for a return to the 1920s, he wrote in an article for a libertarian journal, because since then, "the vast increase in welfare beneficiaries and the extension of the franchise to women—two constituencies that are notoriously tough for libertarians—have rendered the notion of 'capitalist democracy' into an oxymoron."[31]

Republicans wrapped their actions in a cloak of paternalism, but in 2016, Republican presidential candidate Donald Trump, a former reality-show television host who read audiences remarkably well, revealed the core of their ideology. He played to the fears Republicans had stoked for a generation, declared that he alone could save America from the dangerous forces arrayed against it, and actively cultivated the support of white supremacist groups. He announced his candidacy by calling Mexican immigrants murderers and rapists, and openly denigrated women. A leaked videotape in which Trump boasted of sexual assault revealed his conviction that women were objects for the use of wealthy men, and the willingness of Republican leaders to overlook that language as "locker room talk" indicated that many of them shared Trump's worldview.[32]

Trump warned supporters that he alone stood between them and a dystopian nightmare. His message was not a winner: like George W. Bush, he lost the popular vote to his Democratic rival—Hillary Clinton won by 2.78 million votes, a 2.1 percent margin—but Trump won in the Electoral College. His inaugural address portrayed "Mothers and children trapped in poverty in our inner cities; rusted-out factories scattered like tombstones across the landscape of our nation; an education system, flush with cash, but which leaves our young and beautiful students deprived of knowledge; and the crime and gangs and drugs that have stolen too many lives and robbed our country of so much unrealized potential." This vision of America was one of, as he put it, "American carnage." As he continued to attack minorities and women, his aides frequently and deliberately chose to disseminate photographs of government meetings dominated by older white men. The message was clear.[33]

Trump's administration put into place the policies Movement Conservatives had advocated since the 1950s. With the help of true believers in Congress, he set out to destroy the policies that had been in place since the 1930s and which were designed to put the American government at the service of democracy. He began with a massive tax cut that dropped the corporate tax rate from 35 percent to 21 percent, dropped income tax levels, and virtually eliminated the estate tax. The bill delivered eye-popping profits to corporate executives, while wages actually fell. When the Congressional Budget Office finally scored the law, it projected that the cuts would add $1.9 trillion to the national debt in the decade after 2018. To pay for those deficits, the president and congressional Republicans called for cuts to social programs and federal workers' pay.[34]

The Trump administration slashed regulations and gutted the Affordable Care Act passed by the Democrats under the Obama administration, a popular healthcare reform that nonetheless had stood as Movement Conservatives' prime example of the misuse of government to create a form of socialism in America. Trump simply refused to fill vacancies in government positions, cutting agencies' operations by starving them to death. Those he had filled, he tended to sabotage. He put in charge of government departments officials whose only qualification was great wealth, and they proceeded to use those departments for their own profit or for those of their friends. Stephen Moore, a nominee for the Federal Reserve Board of Governors, who withdrew amid criticism of his public comments about women and his disproven claims about economics, said that "capitalism is a lot more important than democracy."[35]

In that, most of all, the Trump administration reflected the ideology of oligarchy. Government was not designed to promote equality of opportunity by guaranteeing equality before the laws. Rather, such meddling interfered with the ability of a few to arrange society as they saw fit; they, and they alone, truly understood what was best for everyone. In that understanding, President Trump showed an affinity with other autocratic leaders: Russia's Vladimir Putin, Turkey's Recep Tayyip Erdogan, Saudi crown prince Mohammed bin Salman, and North Korea's Kim Jong Un. Like them, he brooked no challenge to his authority, concentrated wealth among his friends, and tried to silence opposition by calling the press "the enemy of the people." In the lead-up to the 2018 midterms, Trump warned supporters that if his opponents won, they would "overturn everything that we've done and they'll do it quickly and violently." He added, "You're one election away from losing everything you've got."[36]

On a Saturday night in July a Georgia Representative stood before the crowd at a town hall in Athens to give a similar warning. "As you all know," James Jackson said, ' "there exists . . . a political organization banded together by . . . one common tie—*hostility to you and to your property*." Politicians, college professors, writers, poets, ministers, elites, and congressmen all were determined to dominate and destroy both the property and the culture of beleaguered southerners. They had illegally taken over the political system to destroy "*the equal rights of every citizen of every State.*" This political cloud "is black and ominous, and threatens to discharge its flood of fury—its storm of hail and lightening [*sic*] upon you at any moment." It had to be stopped, he said, "or your peace is at an end—your property destroyed—your land now blooming like a garden, left desolate as a desert." The government's role was to protect life, liberty, and property, and the minute that protection for private property fell into doubt because of regulations or restrictions, allegiance to that government should end.[37]

Jackson was speaking in 1860, warning his listeners what would happen if "black Republicans" reined in the institution of human slavery and gave rights to African Americans. The politician he stood against was Abraham Lincoln. When Lincoln won in 1860, men like Jackson would make good their threats to take their cause to the battlefields, unwilling to continue in a Union that yoked them to "Socialists, Communists and Abolitionists."[38]

Three years later, in the midst of the carnage that would take more than 600,000 lives, Lincoln would attempt to destroy the oligarchic principles of the Confederacy once and for all. He rededicated the nation to the principles of the Declaration of Independence, and called for Americans to "highly resolve that these dead shall not have died in vain—that this nation, under God, shall have a new birth of freedom— and that government of the people, by the people, and for the people, shall not perish from the earth."

CONCLUSION

What Then Is This American?

A nd so we have come full circle. By 2018, the nation that had begun four hundred years before in the dream of a land of possibilities was defined by its president as a land of carnage, a nightmare. This image enabled the Movement Conservatives who had taken over the Republican Party to enact their vision, slashing regulation and taxes on the wealthy, establishing government policies to benefit party leaders and people with money, and arranging public policy to remand the vast majority of Americans to positions from which they could never rise. The world of 2018 looked a lot like that of 1860.

America was born in idealism and the profound principle that all human beings had a right to self-determination. It grew up, though, in an environment that limited that right to white men of property. The struggle between those two concepts determined the early years of the American republic. In 1860, when the conflict between the concept of democracy and the hierarchical ideology of the slaveholders became irreconcilable, Americans set out to reclaim the government from an oligarchy and rededicate it to the proposition that all men are created equal. While they won, they never erased the slaveholders' ideology entirely.

The new American West was fertile ground for preserving and propagating a vision of society based on hierarchies. Mythology tells us that the theme of the American West was freedom, but the opposite was true. Like the antebellum South, society in the West was hierarchical according to race, class, and gender. When Americans moved there after the Civil War, they kept alive the same vision of the world that had inspired Confederates. Just as the South was a cultural and political force that came to dominate American society in the early nineteenth century, the West was a cultural and political force that came to dominate American society in the late twentieth century.

In both of those eras, rich men attempted to garner power through words and images that convinced American voters that extending the right of self-determination to people of color, women, and poor Americans would destroy it for white men. That argument is based on the American paradox, and it is a reflection of American history, not of logic. American democracy was built on the principle of human self-determination for all. Its extension will not destroy democracy; it will preserve it by drawing the fangs of the paradox that has been used by oligarchs twice in order to rise to power.

The conflict between a hierarchical society and one based on equality is rooted deeply in European-American society, and it is a battle America has fought since its founding. When a group of slaveholders embraced the idea that they, and they alone, should control the nation's political and economic system, thus threatening democracy in the 1860s, Americans fought back and rededicated the country to equality. A quirk of geography and timing meant they failed to make their principles stick. The idea of the American paradox moved west, where its adherents over time reasserted control over American culture. From Reconstruction through World War II, Americans recreated a hierarchical society. The fight against fascism—the modern form of hierarchical society—once again challenged that paradox. The ensuing drive for universal equality, though, enabled oligarchs to mobilize their corollary to the American paradox, gaining power by convincing voters that equality for people of color and women destroyed liberty. Now, for the second time, we are called to defend the principle of democracy.

Crucially, this time all Americans have a say in the outcome. In the 1870s, as voters reestablished the Founders' paradox, half of the country's population was still written entirely out of the political equation, and thus was politically silenced. Women did not become part of the electorate until 1920. Until 1980, though, they were still not an independent voice; they tended to vote like their male relatives. In 1980, with the second rise of American oligarchy, that pattern changed. Women began to break against the individualism Reagan and his supporters embraced and voted for Jimmy Carter by 8 points more than men did. That gender gap has grown since, until by 2018 it was 23 points. A majority of women reject the construction of a society in which a few elite white men control the destinies of the rest of the country.[1]

In the 2018 midterm elections, female candidates began to articulate a new vision of the country to replace the old American paradox. They emphasized community and fairness over individualism and the race, class, and gender roles individualism has always implied. Women and voters of color are helping to redefine the image of an American for the twenty-first century, as they did, briefly, after the Civil War and after World War II.

In 1612, as English colonists were starving in Virginia, Shakespeare's Miranda exclaimed in wonder at the possibilities of a brave new world of people who created a society untrammeled by traditional hierarchies. One hundred and seventy-five years later, America's Founders put that idea into practice in what George Washington called a "Great Experiment": a government based on the idea that human beings had the right to determine their own fate. Could such a government endure?

Our country's peculiar history has kept the question open.

NOTES

INTRODUCTION

1   On the ways in which systems shape emerging societies, see Perry Miller, *The New England Mind: The Seventeenth Century* (New York: Macmillan, 1939), and John Tutino, *Making a New World: Founding Capitalism in the Bajio and Spanish North America* (Durham, NC: Duke University Press, 2011). On this American paradox, see Edmund S. Morgan, *American Slavery, American Freedom: The Ordeal of Colonial Virginia* (New York: W.W. Norton & Company, 1975).

2   My understanding of these stages is based on Eric Hoffer, *The True Believer: Thoughts on the Nature of Mass Movements* (1951; rpt., New York: Harper, 2010).

3   Abraham Lincoln, Speech at Chicago, Illinois, July 10, 1858, in *The Collected Works of Abraham Lincoln*, ed. Roy P. Basler (New Brunswick, NJ: Rutgers University Press, 1953), 2: 484-502.

4   Josh Bivens, "The Top 1 Percent's Share of Income from Wealth Has Been Rising for Decades," Economic Policy Institute, April 23, 2014.

5   Peter Thiel, "The Education of a Libertarian," *Cato Unbound*, April 13, 2009.

6   David Corn, "Romney Tells Millionaire Donors What He REALLY Thinks of Obama Voters," *Mother Jones*, September 17, 2012. Kevin D. Williamson, "Chaos in the Family, Chaos in the State: The White Working Class's Dysfunction," *National Review*, March 17, 2016. Mark Berman, "Cliven Bundy wonders if black people were 'better off as slaves,'" *Washington Post*, April 24, 2014.

7   Derrick Johnson, "Trump Is Undoing the Diversity of the Federal Bench," *Washington Post*, January 22, 2019. Robbie Gramer and Jefcoate O'Donnell, "White and Male: Trump's Ambassadors Don't Look Like the Rest of America," *Foreign Policy*, September 17, 2018.

CHAPTER 1

1 Bill Bryson, *Shakespeare: The World as Stage* (2007; rpt., New York: Atlas Books, 2016), pp. 71–76. Stephen Greenblatt, *Will in the World: How Shakespeare Became Shakespeare* (New York: W. W. Norton, 2004), pp. 291–293.

2 Bryson, *Shakespeare*, pp. 22–24, 45–52.

3 Roger Schlesinger, *In the Wake of Columbus: The Impact of the New World on Europe, 1492–1650* (Chichester, UK: Wiley-Blackwell, 2006), pp. 51–80. Lisa Jardine, *Worldly Goods: A New History of the Renaissance* (New York: W. W. Norton, 1998).

4 *The Tempest*, 1.2.565. Greenblatt, *Will*, 370–381. There is no record that *The Tempest* was performed at the Globe. The King's Men played it first at Blackfriars in 1611, but *A Winter's Tale* played there several days later and then moved to the Globe, the summer venue of Shakespeare's troupe. By 1613, *The Tempest* was very well known, and thus must have played outside the exclusive Blackfriars, likely at the large Globe in summer 1612, before the venue burned the following year. (Thanks to Dr. Peter Josephson for his explanations of Shakespearean performance history.)

5 *The Tempest*, 5.1.186–187.

6 James L. Huston, *The British Gentry, the Southern Planter, and the Northern Family Farmer* (Baton Rouge: Louisiana State University Press, 2015), pp. 4–10. Susan Dwyer Amussen, *An Ordered Society: Gender and Class in Early Modern England* (Oxford: Basil Blackwell, 1988).

7 Perry Miller, *The New England Mind: The Seventeenth Century* (New York: Macmillan, 1939), pp. 398–413.

8 Schlesinger, *Europe in the Wake of Columbus*, pp. 81–105. Carl Van Doren, *Benjamin Franklin* (1938: rpt., New York: Penguin Books, 1991), pp. 73–80, 129–197. Bernard Bailyn, *The Ideological Origins of the American Revolution* (Cambridge, MA: Harvard University Press, 1967), pp. 26–28.

9 James T. Kloppenberg, *Toward Democracy: The Struggle for Self-Rule in European and American Thought* (New York: Oxford University Press, 2016), pp. 61–93.

10 Bailyn, *Origins*, pp. 34–54.

11 Bailyn, *Origins*, pp. 55–93.

12 John Adams to Thomas Jefferson, December 25, 1813, National Archives, Founders Online.

13 Jeffrey L. Pasley, *The Tyranny of Printers: Newspaper Politics in the Early American Republic* (Charlottesville: University Press of Virginia, 2001), pp. 33–40. Pauline Maier, *From Resistance to Revolution: Colonial Radicals and the Development of American Opposition to Britain, 1765–1776* (New York: Alfred A. Knopf, 1972), p. 91. John Adams, September 3, 1769, in *Diary and*

Autobiography of John Adams, ed. L. H. Butterfield, series 1 of the Adams Papers (Cambridge, MA: Belknap Press of Harvard University Press, 1961), I:343, quoted in Robert G. Parkinson, *The Common Cause: Creating Race and Nation in the American Revolution* (Chapel Hill: University of North Carolina Press, 2016), p. 16.

14 Alan Heimert, *Religion and the American Mind: From the Great Awakening to the Revolution* (Cambridge, MA: Harvard University Press, 1966). Catherine A. Brekus, *Sarah Osborn's World: The Rise of Evangelical Christianity in Early America* (New Haven: Yale University Press, 2013.

15 The argument in this section is based on Edmund S. Morgan, *American Slavery, American Freedom: The Ordeal of Colonial Virginia* (New York: W. W. Norton, 1975).

16 Schlesinger, *Wake of Columbus*, pp. 51–80. On the history of racist thought in America, see Winthrop D. Jordan, *White over Black: American Attitudes Toward the Negro, 1550–1812* (Chapel Hill: University of North Carolina Press, 1968), and Ibram X. Kendi, *Stamped from the Beginning: The Definitive History of Racist Ideas in America* (New York: Nation Books, 2016).

17 MaryLynn Salmon, *Women and the Law of Property in Early America* (Chapel Hill: University of North Carolina Press, 1986). Carol Berkin, *First Generations: Women in Colonial America* (New York: Hill and Wang, 1996).

18 Michael Guasco, *Slaves and Englishmen: Human Bondage in the Early Modern Atlantic World* (Philadelphia: University of Pennsylvania Press, 2014), pp. 25–33.

19 C. S. Everett, " 'They Shalbe Slaves for Their Lives': Indian Slavery in Colonial Virginia," in *Indian Slavery in Colonial America*, ed. Alan Gallay (Lincoln: University of Nebraska Press, 2009), pp. 67–108.

20 Alan Gallay, "Indian Slavery in Historical Context," in *Indian Slavery in Colonial America*, ed. Alan Gallay (Lincoln: University of Nebraska Press, 2009), pp. 1–32. Guasco, *Slaves and Englishmen*, pp. 199–209.

21 Ira Berlin, *Many Thousands Gone: The First Two Centuries of Slavery in North America* (Cambridge, MA: Harvard University Press, 1998), pp. 29. *An Enquiry into the Causes of the Encrease and Miseries of the Poor of England* (London, 1738), pp. 6–9. Lawrence Braddon, *A Proposal for Reliving, Reforming and Employing All the Poor of Great Britain* (London, 1721), dedication. See also Morgan, *American Slavery*, pp. 320–327.

22 Berlin, *Many Thousands Gone*, pp. 32–46. Guasco, *Slaves and Englishmen*, pp. 196–226.

23 Morgan, *American Slavery*, pp. 215–234.

24 Morgan, *American Slavery*, pp. 235–249.

25 Guasco, *Slaves and Englishmen*, pp. 33–40. *Bread for the Poor* (London, 1698), p. 4. Morgan, *American Slavery*, pp. 320–327.

26 Brent Tarter, "Bacon's Rebellion, the Grievances of the People, and the Political Culture of Seventeenth-Century Virginia," *Virginia Magazine of History and Biography* 119 (2011): 2–41. Morgan, *American Slavery*, pp. 250–270.

27 James D. Rice, *Tales from a Revolution: Bacon's Rebellion and the Transformation of Early America* (New York: Oxford University Press, 2012), pp. 190–201.

28 Morgan, *American Slavery*, pp. 332.

29 Morgan, *American Slavery*, pp. 331–337.

30 Morgan, *American Slavery*, pp. 312–313, 332–333.

31 Morgan, *American Slavery*, pp. 331–336.

32 Morgan, *American Slavery*, pp. 321, 327–331; "An Act Concerning Servants and Slaves," passed by the Virginia General Assembly, October 1705, https://www.encyclopediavirginia.org/_An_act_concerning_Servants_and_Slaves7_1705.

33 Morgan, *American Slavery*, pp. 338–362.

34 Morgan, *American Slavery*, pp. 363–387.

35 Parkinson, *Common Cause*, pp. 185–263.

CHAPTER 2

1 J. Hector St. John de Crèvecoeur, *Letters from an American Farmer* (New York: Fox, Duffield, 1904), Letter III, "What Is an American."

2 Thomas Jefferson, *Notes on the State of Virginia* (Philadelphia: Prichard and Hall, 1787), p. 175.

3 Laurel Thatcher Ulrich, *A Midwife's Tale: The Life of Martha Ballard, Based on Her Diary, 1785–1812* (New York: Alfred A. Knopf, 1991), pp. 72–101. Carol Berkin, *Revolutionary Mothers: Women in the Struggle for America's Independence* (New York: Alfred A. Knopf, 2005), pp. 148–161. Linda Kerber, "The Republican Mother: Women and the Enlightenment—An American Perspective," *American Quarterly* 28 (Summer 1976): 187–205. Linda K. Kerber, *Women of the Republic: Intellect and Ideology in Revolutionary America* (Chapel Hill: University of North Carolina Press, 1980).

4 Alan Taylor, *The Civil War of 1812: American Citizens, British Subjects, Irish Rebels, and Indian Allies* (New York: Alfred A. Knopf, 2010), pp. 15–28.

5 William R. Taylor, *Cavalier and Yankee: The Old South and American National Character* (New York: George Braziller, 1961), pp. 18–22. Tricia Cusack, *Riverscapes and National Identities* (Syracuse, NY: Syracuse University Press, 2010), pp. 24–26. Elizabeth McKinsey, *Niagara Falls: Icon of the American Sublime* (Cambridge: Cambridge University Press, 1985), pp. 31–125.

6 Mark Cheathem, *Andrew Jackson, Southerner* (Baton Rouge: Louisiana State University Press, 2013), esp. pp. 90–98. On "monied men of the commercial cities" as the "nucleus of the aristocratic party," see *Democratic Review*, October

1837, p. 96. Andrew Jackson, "Veto Message Regarding the Bank of the United States, July 10, 1832," The Avalon Project, http://avalon.law.yale.edu/19th_century/ajveto01.asp. "The Moral of the Crisis," *Democratic Review*, October 1837, p. 111.

7   "Introduction," *Democratic Review*, October 1837, pp. 2, 14–15. "On the Elevation of the Laboring Portion of the Community," Democratic Review, June 1840: 529–540. *Democratic Review*, Introduction, October 1837, pp. 7–11. Walt Whitman, "I Hear America Singing," in Leaves of Grass (Boston: Small, Maynard & Company, 1897), p. 17. Edward Widmer, *Young America: The Flowering of Democracy in New York City* (New York: Oxford University Press, 1999), pp. 27–92.

8   Joshua D. Rothman, *Flush Times and Fever Dreams: A Story of Capitalism and Slavery in the Age of Jackson* (Athens: University of Georgia Press, 2012). Sven Beckert, *Empire of Cotton: A Global History* (New York: Vintage Books, 2014), pp. 104–108.

9   Matthew Karp, *This Vast Southern Empire: Slaveholders at the Helm of American Foreign Policy* (Cambridge, MA: Harvard University Press, 2016), pp. 82–124. John L. O'Sullivan, "Annexation," *Democratic Review*, July 1845, pp. 5-10.

10   W. Kirkland, "The West, the Poor Man's Paradise," *Democratic Review*, August 1844, 182–191. "True Theory and Philosophy of Our System of Government," *Democratic Review*, September 1844, pp. 219-232, 320. "The Texas Question: A Letter From Alexander H. Everett," *Democratic Review*, September 1844, pp. 250-270. "Our Indian Policy," *Democratic Review*, February 1844, pp. 169-185. "The Texas Question," *Democratic Review*, April 1844, pp. 423–430.

11   Jeremy Atack and Fred Bateman, *To Their Own Soil: Agriculture in the Antebellum North* (Ames: Iowa State University Press, 1987), pp. 3-4.

12   John Tutino, *Making a New World: Founding Capitalism in the Bajío and Spanish North America* (Durham, NC: Duke University Press, 2011).

13   Thomas Jefferson to John Holmes, April 22, 1820, in *Thomas Jefferson: Writings*, ed. Merrill D. Peterson (New York: Library of America, 1984), pp. 1433–1435.

14   Manisha Sinha, *The Counterrevolution of Slavery: Politics and Ideology in Antebellum South Carolina* (Chapel Hill: University of North Carolina Press, 2000), pp. 14–19.

15   Taylor, *Cavalier and Yankee*, pp. 177–201. John Pendleton Kennedy, *Swallow Barn; or A Sojourn in the Old Dominion* (Philadelphia: Carey & Lea, 1832). Bertram Wyatt-Brown, *Southern Honor: Ethics and Behavior in the Old South* (New York: Oxford University Press, 1982), pp. 327–493.

16 Mitchell Snay, *The Gospel of Disunion: Religion and Separatism in the Antebellum South* (Chapel Hill: University of North Carolina Press, 1993), pp. 54–75. Drew Gilpin Faust, *James Henry Hammond and the Old South: A Design for Mastery* (Baton Rouge: Louisiana State University Press, 1982), pp. 37–104.

17 Susanna Delfino and Michele Gillespie, eds., *Neither Lady Nor Slave: Working Women of the Old South* (Chapel Hill: University of North Carolina Press, 2002), pp. 75–154. Taylor, *Cavalier and Yankee*, pp. 173–174. [Nathaniel Beverly Tucker], *George Balcombe: A Novel* (New York: Harper & Brothers, 1936), 1:98–100, 273–282; 2:51–54. Faust, *Hammond*, pp. 312–313. Wyatt-Brown, *Southern Honor*, pp. 199–324. [Tucker], *Balcombe*, 1:22–24.

18 Stephanie McCurry, *Masters of Small Worlds: Yeoman Households, Gender Relations, and the Political Culture of the Antebellum South Carolina Low Country* (New York: Oxford University Press, 1995). Carl R. Osthaus, "The Work Ethic of the Plan Folk: Labor and Religion in the Old South," *Journal of Southern History* 70 (November 2004): 745–782, quotations from pp. 767–768, 780, 770. See also *The American Cotton Planter*, February 1853, p. 83, and Keri Leigh Merritt, *Masterless Men: Poor Whites and Slavery in the Antebellum South* (Cambridge: Cambridge University Press, 2017), p. 287.

19 J. G. Randall, *The Civil War and Reconstruction*, 2nd ed. (Boston: D. C. Heath, 1953), pp. 6–13. Manly Wade Wellman, *Giant in Gray: A Biography of Wade Hampton of South Carolina* (New York: Charles Scribner's Sons, 1949), pp. 180–183. Elizabeth W. Allston Pringle, *Chronicles of Chicora Wood* (New York: Charles Scribner's Sons, 1922), pp. 22, 80–81, 124, 230.

20 *The American Cotton Planter*, January 1853, pp. 8–13.

21 Matthew Karp, *This Vast Southern Empire: Slaveholders at the Helm of American Foreign Policy* (Cambridge, MA: Harvard University Press, 2016), esp. pp. 132–149. Merritt, *Masterless Men*, pp. 274–285.

22 Faust, *Hammond*, pp. 241–245. James Henry Hammond, *Secret and Sacred: The Diaries of James Henry Hammond, a Southern Slaveholder*, ed. Carol Bleser (New York: Oxford University Press, 1988), pp. 169–176.

23 James Henry Hammond, "Speech on the Admission of Kansas . . . March 4, 1858," in *Selections from the Letters and Speeches of the Hon. James H. Hammond* (New York: John F. Trow, 1866), pp. 301–357. See also Michael E. Woods, "Mudsills vs. Chivalry," *Muster*, December 21, 2018, at https://www.journalofthecivilwarera.org/2018/12/mudsills-vs-chivalry/.

24 Hinton Rowan Helper, *The Impending Crisis of the South: How to Meet It* (New York: Burdick Brothers, 1857), pp. 144–145. Randall, *Civil War*, pp. 60–62.

25 On the Democratic Party's split between Young America adherents and the Slave Power, see Yonathan Eyal, *The Young America Movement and the Transformation*

of the Democratic Party, 1828–1861 (Cambridge, MA: Harvard University Press, 2007).

26 *New York Times*, May 23, 1856, p. 1. Rachel A. Shelden, *Washington Brotherhood: Politics, Social Life, and the Coming of the Civil War* (Chapel Hill: University of North Carolina Press, 2013), pp. 120–166. Joanne B. Freeman, *The Field of Blood: Violence in Congress and the Road to Civil War* (New York: Farrar, Straus and Giroux, 2018), pp. 217-234. *New York Times*, May 26, 1856, p. 1; and "Correspondence of the Chicago Tribune," noted in *New York Times*, May 26, 1856, p. 1.

27 *Chicago Tribune*, March 5, 1857, p. 1. James Buchanan, Inaugural Address, March 4, 1857, American Presidency Project.

28 *New-York Daily Tribune*, March 10, 1857, p. 4. See also *Chicago Tribune*, March 13, 1857, p. 2; *New York Times*, May 10, 1857, p. 1; *New York Evening Post*, quoted in *Chicago Tribune*, March 13, 1857, p. 2.

29 Jean H. Baker, *James Buchanan* (New York: Times Books, 2004), pp. 85–86. See also *New-York Daily Tribune*, March 7, 1857, p. 4.

30 Helper, *Impending Crisis*, p. 120. David Brown, *Southern Outcast: Hinton Rowan Helper and The Impending Crisis of the South* (Baton Rouge: Louisiana State University Press, 2006), p. 182. Michael Winship, "Uncle Tom's Cabin: History of the Book in the 19th-Century United States," Uncle Tom's Cabin and American Culture: A Multimedia Archive, University of Virginia, http://utc.iath.virginia.edu.

31 Abraham Lincoln, "A House Divided, June 16, 1858, in *The Collected Works of Abraham Lincoln*, ed. Roy P. Basler (New Brunswick, NJ: Rutgers University Press, 1953), 2: 461-469.

32 Abraham Lincoln, "Address Before the Wisconsin State Agricultural Society," September 30, 1859, in Baseler, *Lincoln's Collected Works*, 3: 471–482.

33 Michael F. Holt, *The Election of 1860: A Campaign Fraught with Consequences* (Lawrence: University Press of Kansas, 2017), pp. 27–66, 115–133. Sinha, *Counterrevolution*, pp. 187–207, also pp. 210–219. Merritt, *Masterless Men*, pp. 290- 298. Robert Bunch, quoted in Sinha, *Counterrevolution*, pp. 211.

34 Snay, *Gospel*, pp. 151–180; Alexander Stephens, "Cornerstone Speech," March 21, 1861, in Henry Cleveland, *Alexander H. Stephens. . . Letters and Speeches* (Philadelphia, PA: National Publishing Company, 1866), pp. 717-729.

35 James Buchanan, Fourth Annual Message, December 3, 1860, American Presidency Project.

36 Heather Cox Richardson, *The Greatest Nation of the Earth: Republican Economic Policies During the Civil War* (Cambridge, MA: Harvard University Press, 1997), pp. 31-65.

37 Richardson, *Greatest Nation*, pp. 66-102.

38 Richardson, *Greatest Nation*, pp. 103-138.

39 Richardson, *Greatest Nation*, pp. 103-138.

40 Philadelphia *Daily Evening Bulletin*, March 14, 1862, quoted in Richardson, *Greatest Nation*, p. 116.

41 Richardson, *Greatest Nation*, pp. 139-169.

42 Richardson, *Greatest Nation*, pp. 139-169.

43 Richardson, *Greatest Nation*, pp. 170-208.

44 James G. Blaine, *Twenty Years of Congress* (Norwich, CT: Henry Bill, 1893), 2: 262.

45 Julia Ward Howe, *Reminiscences: 1819-1899* (Boston: Houghton, Mifflin, 1900), p. 373.

46 *New York Times*, July 5, 1870, p. 1.

CHAPTER 3

1 John Filson, *The Discovery, Settlement, and Present State of Kentucke* (London: John Stockdale, 1793).

2 Thomas Jefferson, autobiography manuscript, 1821, page 152, Library of Congress, Manuscript Division, http://www.loc.gov/exhibits/jefferson/jeffwest.html#152.

3 "President Thomas Jefferson's White House History Museum," *White House History* 34 (Fall 2013), https://www.whitehousehistory.org/president-thomas-jeffersons-white-house-museum.

4 Hampton Sides, *Blood and Thunder: An Epic of the American West* (New York: Doubleday, 2006). p. 6.

5 On Alamo history: James E. Crisp, *Sleuthing the Alamo: Davy Crockett's Last Stand and Other Mysteries of the Texas Revolution* (New York: Oxford University Press, 2005), pp. 27–47, 61–65, 79–92. David Crockett, *A Narrative of the Life of David Crockett* (Philadelphia: E. L. Carey and A. Hart, 1834).

6 Crisp, *Sleuthing the Alamo*, pp. 103–195.

7 Charles E. Averill, *Kit Carson, The Prince of the Gold Hunters* (Boston: G. H. Williams, 1849), pp. 44–45.

8 Anne F. Hyde, *Empires, Nations, and Families: A History of the North American West* (Lincoln: University of Nebraska Press, 2011).

9 Pekka Hamalainen, "The Rise and Fall of Plains Indian Horse Cultures," *Journal of American History* 90 (December 2003): 833–862.

10 Sides, *Blood and Thunder*, pp. 247–248, 252–259. Kit Carson, *Kit Carson's Own Story of His Life* (Santa Fe, NM: Sunstone Press, 2006).

11 William D. Carrigan and Clive Webb, "The Lynching of Persons of Mexican Origin or Descent in the United States, 1848 to 1928," *Journal of Social History* 37, no. 2 (Winter 2003): 414, 422. James J. Rawls, "Gold Diggers: Indian

Miners in the California Gold Rush," *California Historical Quarterly* 55 (Spring 1976): 28–45. Pringle Shaw, *Ramblings in California* (Toronto, 1854), p. 17, quoted in Carrigan and Webb, "Lynching," p. 419. See also Susan Lee Johnson, *Roaring Camp: The Social World of the California Gold Rush* (New York: W. W. Norton, 2000), pp. 185–234.

12 *Statutes of California Passed at the First Session of the Legislature, Begun the 15th Day of Dec. 1849, and Ended the 22d Day of April, 1850, at the City of Pueblo de San Jose* (San Jose: J. Winchester, 1850), pp. 39–43, 455, 424. 102.

13 *Statutes of California* (1850), pp. 251, 409–410.

14 *Statutes of California* (1850), pp. 221–222. *People vs. Hall,* in *Statutes of California Passed at the Sixth Session of the Legislature* (Sacramento: B. B. Redding, 1855), p. 194–195.

15 *Statutes of California* (1855), pp. 217–218.

16 Richard White, *"It's Your Misfortune and None of My Own": A New History of the American West* (Norman: University of Oklahoma Press, 1991), p. 238. On the political and economic structure of this region under Mexico, see David J. Weber, *The Mexican Frontier, 1821-1846: The American Southwest Under Mexico* (Albuquerque: University of New Mexico Press, 1982).

17 Pronunciamientos, September 30 and November 23, 1859, in Jerry D. Thompson, ed., *Juan Cortina and the Texas-Mexico Frontier* (El Paso: University of Texas at El Paso Press, 1994), pp. 14–18, 23–28.

18 Citizens of Brownsville and the Rio Grande Frontier to Hon. John B. Floyd, Secretary of War, enclosed in a letter from John Hemphill and Matt. Ward to Hon. John B. Floyd, March 21, 1859, in "Difficulties on Southwestern Frontier," 36th Congress, 1st Session, House Executive Document, 52, pp. 11–12. General D. E. Twiggs to General Scott, San Antonio, March 28, 1859, in "Difficulties," p. 14–15. See also Thompson, *Cortina,* p. 5. Walter Prescott Webb, *The Texas Rangers: A Century of Frontier Defense* (Boston: Houghton Mifflin, 1935), pp. 175–193.

19 James Pierson Beckwourth, *The Life and Adventures of James P. Beckwourth,* ed. T. D. Bonner (1865; rpt., New York: Alfred A. Knopf, 1931), pp. 75–79.

20 Hidetaka Hirota, *Expelling the Poor: Atlantic Seaboard States and the 19th Century* (New York: Oxford University Press, 2017), pp. 16–125.

21 Abraham Lincoln, Fragment on Slavery, [1854], in *Collected Works of Abraham Lincoln,* ed. Roy P. Basler (New Brunswick, NJ: Rutgers University Press, 1953), 2:222–223.

22 Lincoln, Fragment on Slavery.

23 Abraham Lincoln to Joshua Speed, August 24, 1855, at www.abrahamlincolnonline.org.

24   Republican Party Platform, May 17, 1860, American Presidency Project, http://
     www.presidency.ucsb.edu/ws/index.php?pid=29620.

25   Paul Finkelman, "I Could not Afford to Hang Men for Votes—Lincoln the Lawyer,
     Humanitarian Concerns, and the Dakota Pardons," *William Mitchell Law Review*
     39, no. 2 (2013): Article 2.

26   Megan Kate Nelson, " 'The Difficulties and Seductions of the Desert': Landscapes
     of War in 1861 New Mexico," in *The Blue, the Gray, and the Green: Toward an
     Environmental History of the Civil War*, ed. Brian Allen Drake (Athens: University
     of Georgia Press, 2015), pp. 34–51.

27   James H. Carleton to Col. Christopher Carson, Santa Fe, New Mexico, October
     12, 1862, in *The War of the Rebellion: Official Records of the Union and Confederate
     Armies*, (Washington: Government Printing Office, 1886), Series 1, Volume 15,
     p. 579.

28   Carleton to Carson, October 12, 1862. Orson Squire Fowler, *Human Science or
     Phrenology* (1880), pp. 1195–1197.

29   For the story of Carson and Canyon de Chelly, see *War of the Rebellion: Official
     Records*, Series 1, Volume 34, Part 1, pp. 71–80; General Orders No. 3: Synopsis of
     Operations in the Department of New Mexico, May 16–December 28, 1863, *War
     of the Rebellion: Official Records*, Series 1, Volume 26, Part 1, pp. 23–32.

30   Philip Weeks, *Farewell, My Nation: The American Indian and the United
     States in the Nineteenth Century* (Wheeling, IL: Harlan Davidson, 1990),
     pp. 115–116.

31   Lt. James D. Cannon, Testimony, in *War of the Rebellion: Official Records*, Series 1,
     Volume 16, Part 1, pp. 970-971.

CHAPTER 4

 1   Elizabeth W. Allston Pringle, *Chronicles of Chicora Wood* (New York: Charles
     Scribner's Sons, 1922), pp. 240–241.

 2   Edward McPherson, *The Political History of the United States of America, During
     the Period of Reconstruction* (Washington, DC: Philip & Solomons, 1871),
     pp. 29–44.

 3   James West Davidson, William E. Gienapp, et al., *Nation of Nations: A Narrative
     History of the American Republic* (New York: McGraw-Hill, 1990), 2:627–628.
     Heather Cox Richardson, *West from Appomattox: The Reconstruction of America
     After the Civil War* (New Haven, CT: Yale University Press, 2007), pp. 55–57.
     W. A. Carey, "The Federal Union—Now and Hereafter," *De Bow's Review*, June
     1866, p. 588.

 4   Andrew Johnson, Message to Congress, December 4, 1865, in Heather Cox
     Richardson, *The Death of Reconstruction: Race, Labor, and Politics in the*

Post-Civil War North, 1865-1901 (Cambridge, MA: Harvard University Press, 2001), pp. 20-22.

5 Heather Cox Richardson, *To Make Men Free: A History of the Republican Party* (New York: Basic Books, 2014), pp. 60-62.

6 Eric Foner, *Reconstruction: America's Unfinished Revolution, 1863-1877* (New York: Harper & Row, 1988), pp. 457-459. Lou Falkner Williams, *The Great South Carolina Ku Klux Klan Trials, 1871-1872* (Athens: The University of Georgia Press, 1996), pp. 27-112, quotation on p. 92.

7 Mark R. Wilson, *The Business of Civil War: Military Mobilization and the State* (Baltimore: Johns Hopkins University Press, 2006), pp. 5-147.

8 *New York Times*, July 1, 1867, p. 4. Richardson, *To Make Men Free*, pp. 70-75. Richardson, *Death of Reconstruction*, pp. 84-85. Scribner's Monthly, December 1870, pp. 214-215.

9 Richardson, *Death of Reconstruction*, pp. 87-88.

10 Richardson, *Death of Reconstruction*, pp. 85-86.

11 Richardson, *Death of Reconstruction*, pp. 86-89. *New York Times*, April 17, 1871, p. 4.

12 Richardson, *Death of Reconstruction*, pp. 53-57, 89-91. Michael Fitzgerald, *The Union League Movement in the Deep South: Politics and Agricultural Change During Reconstruction* (Baton Rouge: Louisiana State University Press, 1989), pp. 16-23. *Philadelphia Inquirer*, May 23, 1867, p. 4. Thomas Holt, *Black over White: Negro Political Leadership in South Carolina During Reconstruction* (Urbana: University of Illinois Press, 1979), pp. 152-170.

13 Carole K. Rothrock Bleser, *The Promised Land: The History of the South Carolina Land Commission, 1869-1890* (Columbia: University of South Carolina Press, 1969). Richardson, *Death of Reconstruction*, p. 93.

14 *New-York Daily Tribune*, May 1, 1871, 1; Richardson, *Death of Reconstruction*, pp. 94-96.

15 Richardson, *Death of Reconstruction*, p. 97. *New-York Daily Tribune*, May 10, 1871, p. 2; May 11, 1871, p. 4; May 12, 1871, p. 5; May 13, 1871, p. 5; May 15, 1871, p. 1; May 17, 1871, p. 4.

16 Frank Norton, "Our Labor System and the Chinese," *Scribner's Monthly*, May 1871, 62, emphasis in original.

17 David G. Surdam, *Northern Naval Superiority and the Economics of the American Civil War* (Columbia: University of South Carolina Press, 2001), pp. 26-33, 48, 61-71.

18 J. Evetts Haley, *Charles Goodnight: Cowman and Plainsman* (Norman: University of Oklahoma Press, 1928), pp. 103, 125-26, 131, 142; Richardson, *West from Appomattox*, pp. 69-70.

19 John A. Hart et al., *Pioneer Days in the Southwest from 1850 to 1879* (Guthrie, OK: State Capital Co., 1909), p. 13. Haley, *Goodnight*, 121–122. Richardson, *West from Appomattox*, pp. 70–73.

20 On the government in the West, see Richard White, *"It's Your Misfortune and None of My Own": A New History of the American West* (Norman: University of Oklahoma Press, 1991).

21 Richardson, *To Make Men Free*, pp. 84–86.

22 Richardson, *West From Appomattox*, pp. 221–224.

23 Richardson, *To Make Men Free*, pp. 88–90, 96–99.

24 W. Raymond Wood, "Cats! Their Lives and Lore on the Missouri River," Museum of the Fur Trade Quarterly, 47 (Fall 2011): 6–10.

25 Heather Cox Richardson, *Wounded Knee: Party Politics and the Road to an American Massacre* (New York: Basic Books, 2010), pp. 41–46. James C. Olson, *Red Cloud and the Sioux Problem* (Lincoln: University of Nebraska Press, 1965), pp. 68–73.

26 Treaty of Fort Laramie, available at http://www.ourdocuments.gov/doc.php?flash=old&doc=42. W. T. Sherman to John Sherman, June 17, 1868, and September 23, 1868, in Rachel Sherman Thorndike, ed. *The Sherman Letters: Correspondence between General and Senator Sherman from 1838-1891* (New York: Scribner's Sons, 1894), pp. 320–321.

27 Russell R. Elliot, *Servant of Power: A Political Biography of Senator William M. Stewart* (Reno: University of Nevada Press, 1983), 63–64. William Gillette, *The Right to Vote: Politics and the Passage of the Fifteenth Amendment* (Baltimore: Johns Hopkins University Press, 1965), pp. 153–158. Michael S. Green, *Nevada: A History of the Silver State* (Reno: University of Nevada Press, 2015), pp. 95–96.

28 1st Congress, Session 11, Chapter 3, 1790, pp. 103–104.

29 *General Laws . . . of the Territory of Wyoming*, December 10, 1869, p. 371, and preface, p. iv. Virginia Scharff, *Twenty Thousand Roads: Women, Movement, and the West* (Berkeley: University of California Press, 2003), pp. 68–114.

CHAPTER 5

1 Heather Cox Richardson, *West from Appomattox: The Reconstruction of America After the Civil War* (New Haven, CT: Yale University Press, 2007), 195. Andrew Gyory, *Closing the Gate: Race, Politics, and the Chinese Exclusion Act* (Chapel Hill: University of North Carolina Press, 1998).

2 Harry J. Sievers, *Benjamin Harrison: Hoosier Statesman* (New York: University Publishers, 1959), pp. 426–429.

3 Howard Lamar, *Dakota Territory, 1861–1889* (New Haven, CT: Yale University Press, 1856).

4 *New York Times*, February 13, 1888, p. 1; February 24, 1888, p. 3; February 15, 1889, p. 5; February 17, 1889, p. 4; February 25, 1889, p. 1. Frances Chamberlain Holley, *Once Their Home or Our Legacy from the Dahkotahs* (Chicago: Donohue & Henneberry, 1890), p. 393. *Frank Leslie's Illustrated Newspaper*, March 16, 1889.

5 Heather Cox Richardson, *Wounded Knee: Party Politics and the Road to an American Massacre* (New York: Basic Books, 2010), pp. 142–144. Merle Wells, "Idaho's Season of Political Distress: An Unusual Path to Statehood," *Montana: The Magazine of Western History* 37 (Autumn 1987): 58–67.

6 Thomas Adams Upchurch, *Legislating Racism: The Billion Dollar Congress and the Birth of Jim Crow* (Lexington: University Press of Kentucky, 2004), pp. 129–185.

7 Alva Adams, Address, October 19, 1891, in *Report of the Proceedings of the Trans-Mississippi Congress* (Omaha, NE: Bechtold Bros., 1892), pp. 7–10.

8 Speech of Nebraska Governor [John Milton] Thayer, October 19, 1891, in *Report of the Proceedings of the Trans-Mississippi Congress* (Omaha, NE: Bechtold Bros., 1892), pp. 4–7. *Los Angeles Herald*, January 18, 1893, p. 4. Edward Leo Lyman, "Isaac Trumbo and the Politics of Utah Statehood," *Utah Historical Quarterly* 41 (Spring 1973): 128–149. *New York Times*, January 28, 1894, p. 9.

9 David J. Weber, *The Mexican Frontier, 1821-1846: The American Southwest Under Mexico* (Albuquerque: University of New Mexico Press, 1982), pp. 207-218. John Tutino, *Making a New World: Founding Capitalism in the Bajio and Spanish North America* (Durham: Duke University Press, 2011), pp. 451-492. Richard White, *"It's Your Misfortune and None of My Own": A New History of the American West* (Norman: University of Oklahoma Press, 1991), pp. 29-46. Andres Resendez, *The Other Slavery: The Uncovered Story of Indian Enslavement in America* (Boston: Mariner Books, 2016).

10 Michael J. Makley, *The Infamous King of the Comstock: William Sharon and the Gilded Age in the West* (Reno: University of Nevada Press, 2006), pp. 10–26.

11 Makley, *Infamous King*, pp. 25–32.

12 Richard E. Lingenfelter, *The Hardrock Miners: A History of the Mining Labor Movement in the American West, 1863–1893* (Berkeley: University of California Press, 1974), pp. 4–30. Makley, *Infamous King*, pp. 32–35.

13 E. C. "Teddy Blue" Abbott and Helena Huntington Smith, *We Pointed Them North: Recollections of a Cowpuncher* (1939; rpt., Norman: University of Oklahoma Press, 1955), p. 6. J. Evetts Haley, *Charles Goodnight: Cowman and Plainsman* (Norman: University of Oklahoma Press, 1928), pp. 249–250. Gunther Peck,

Reinventing Free Labor: Padrones and Immigrant Workers in the North American West, 1880–1930 (Cambridge: University of Cambridge Press, 2000). Elizabeth Pingree, "Policing Footloose Rebels: Internal Migration in the Early Twentieth-Century Pacific Northwest," paper presented at the Labor and Working Class History Association conference, Durham, North Carolina, June, 2019.

14 Makley, *Infamous King*, pp. 35–83.

15 Makley, *Infamous King*, pp. 84–102.

16 Makley, *Infamous King*, pp. 94–97.

17 Makley, *Infamous King*, pp. 110–136.

18 Kenneth N. Owens, "Pattern and Structure in Western Territorial Politics," *Western Historical Quarterly* 1 (October 1970): 373–392. William D. Rowley, *Reclaiming the Arid West: The Career of Francis G. Newlands* (Bloomington: Indiana University Press, 1996).

19 Populist Party Platform, 1892. White, *It's Your Misfortune*, pp. 373–374.

20 Marilyn S. Johnson, *Violence in the West: The Johnson County Range War and the Ludlow Massacre* (Boston: Bedford/St. Martin's, 2009), pp. 12–14.

21 Johnson, *Violence*, pp. 15–17. Richardson, *West from Appomattox*, pp. 253–254.

22 Richardson, *West from Appomattox*, pp. 252–253.

23 Andrew Carnegie, *The Gospel of Wealth and Other Timely Essays* (New York: The Century Co., 1901), pp. 1–44.

24 Paul Kens, *Justice Stephen Field: Shaping Liberty from the Gold Rush to the Gilded Age* (Lawrence: University Press of Kansas, 1997). Stephen J. Field, *Address at the Centennial Celebration of the Organization of the Federal Judiciary* (Washington, D.C., 1890), pp. 23–24, at The Making of Modern Law. Makley, *Infamous King*, pp. 161–162.

25 "Official Announcement", printed in *Twenty-First Annual Session of the Trans-Mississippi Commercial Congress* (1910), p. 21. Speech of President Thomas, *Report of the Proceedings of the Trans-Mississippi Congress* (Omaha, NE: Bechtold Bros., 1892), pp. 19–22.

26 *Harper's Weekly*, October 22, 1887, p. 759.

27 Wilbur R. Jacobs, *The Historical World of Frederick Jackson Turner* (New Haven, CT: Yale University Press, 1968), pp. 1–4.

28 Theodore Roosevelt, *An Autobiography* (New York: Macmillan, 1913), pp. 132–133.

29 Jacobs, *Historical World of Turner*, pp. 1–4.

30 *New York Times*, January 1, 1898, p. 3; January 2, 1898, p. 3; January 3, 1898, p. 7. Richardson, *West from Appomattox*, p. 313. Theodore Roosevelt, *The Rough Riders* (1899; rpt., New York: Modern Library, 1999), pp. 3–5.

31 Lentz, quoted in Murat Halstead, *Our Country in War and Our Foreign Relations* (n.p.: F. Oldach Sr., 1898), p. 502. Arthur Wallace Dunn, *Gridiron Nights* (New York: Frederick A. Stokes, 1915), p. 72. Richardson, *West from Appomattox*, pp. 318–319.

32 Roosevelt, *Rough Riders*, pp. 7–24; Roosevelt, *Autobiography*, p. 133. *New York Times*, April 28, 1898, p. 1; May 1, 1898, p. 3; June 3, 1898, p. 2. Richardson, *West from Appomattox*, p. 320.

33 Roosevelt, *Rough Riders*, pp. 7–24; Richardson, *West from Appomattox*, pp. 321–322.

34 John Hay to Theodore Roosevelt, quoted in Frank Freidel, *"The Splendid Little War"* (Boston: Little, Brown, 1958), p. 3.

35 Brigadier General Thomas M. Anderson, "Our Rule in the Philippines," *North American Review* 170 (February 1900): 272–284. William R. Segeman, "On the Right Path," *Harper's Weekly*, March 16, 1901, p. 297.

36 John Barrett, "The Problem of the Philippines," *North American Review* 167 (September 1898): 259-267. "William R. Segeman, "On the Right Path," *Harper's Weekly*, March 16, 1901, p. 297. Charles Bonnycastle Robinson, "We Must Stay," *Harper's Weekly*, March 16, 1901, p. 297. Brigidier General Thomas M. Anderson, "Our Rule in the Philippines," *North American Review* 170 (February 1900): 272-284." For a good description of these cases and what they decided, see Christina Duffy Burnett and Burke Marshall, eds., *Foreign in a Domestic Sense: Puerto Rico, American Expansion, and the Constitution* (Durham, NC: Duke University Press, 2001), pp. 389–390.

37 Christina Duffy Burnett, " 'They Say I Am Not an American . . .': The Noncitizen National and the Law of American Empire," Opinio Juris, retrieved May 28, 2018, http://opiniojuris.org/2008/07/01/they-say-i-am-not-an-american-the-noncitizen-national-and-the-law-of-american-empire.

CHAPTER 6

1 Roosevelt to Henry Cabot Lodge, September 23, 1901, in *Selections from the Correspondence of Theodore Roosevelt and Henry Cabot Lodge, 1884–1918* (New York: Charles Scribner's Sons, 1925), 1:506. On Leon Czolgosz and McKinley's assassination, see Eric Rauchway, *Murdering McKinley: The Making of Theodore Roosevelt's America* (New York: Hill and Wang, 2003).

2 Theodore Roosevelt, speech at Springfield, Illinois, in *New York Times*, June 5, 1903, p. 6.

3 Heather Cox Richardson, *To Make Men Free: A History of the Republican Party* (New York: Basic Books, 2014), pp. 152–156.

4 Ellen Fitzpatrick, ed., *Muckraking: Three Landmark Articles* (Boston: Bedford Books, 1994), pp. 1–36.

5   Theodore Roosevelt in Idaho, in *Chicago Daily Tribune*, May 29, 1903, p. 5.

6   Peggy Pascoe, *What Comes Naturally: Miscegenation Law and the Making of Race in America* (New York: Oxford University Press, 2009).

7   Hilary Abner Herbert et al., *Why the Solid South? Or Reconstruction and Its Results* (Baltimore: R. H. Woodward, 1890), pp. 23, 31–36, 430–442.

8   *New York Times*, January 21, 1890, p. 4; November 9, 1898.

9   Winthrop D. Jordan, *White over Black: American Attitudes Toward the Negro, 1550–1812* (Chapel Hill: University of North Carolina Press, 1968), pp. 32–40.

10   Thomas Dixon Jr., *The Leopard's Spots: A Romance of the White Man's Burden, 1865–1900* (New York: Doubleday, Page, 1902), pp. 411–412. John Hope Franklin, " 'Birth of a Nation': Propaganda as History," *Massachusetts Review* 20 (Autumn 1979), pp. 417–434.

11   Julian S. Carr, "Unveiling of Confederate Monument at University. June 2, 1913," Julian Shakespeare Carr Papers #141, Southern Historical Collection, Wilson Library, University of North Carolina at Chapel Hill. Transcribed by Hilary N. Green.

12   Leon F. Litwack, *Trouble in Mind: Black Southerners in an Age of Jim Crow* (New York: Knopf, 1999), p. 213.

13   Julian Lim, *Porous Borders: Multiracial Migrations and the Law in the U.S.-Mexico Borderlands* (Chapel Hill: University of North Carolina Press, 2017). Angie Debo, *And Still the Waters Run: The Betrayal of the Five Civilized Tribes* (Princeton, NJ: Princeton University Press, 1940). Bonnie Lynn-Sherow, *Red Earth: Race and Agriculture in Oklahoma Territory* (Lawrence: University Press of Kansas, 2004). David Grann, *Killers of the Flower Moon: The Osage Murders and the Birth of the FBI* (New York: Doubleday, 2017).

14   Benjamin Heber Johnson, *Revolution in Texas: How a Forgotten Rebellion and Its Bloody Suppression Turned Mexicans into Americans* (New Haven: Yale University Press, 2005).

15   Rebecca Onion, "America's Lost History of Border Violence," *Slate*, May 5, 2016.

16   Cameron McWhirter, *Red Summer: The Summer of 1919 and the Awakening of Black America* (New York: Henry Holt, 2011), p. 56.

17   Roosevelt, quoted in *Chicago Daily Tribune*, May 29, 1903, p. 5. "Objects of the National Irrigation Association, organized June 2, 1899," quoted in Francis Griffith Newlands, *Memorial Addresses Delivered in the Senate of the United States* (Washington, 1920), p. 148. William D. Rowley, *Reclaiming the Arid West: The Career of Francis G. Newlands* (Bloomington: Indiana University Press, 1996), pp. 100–104.

18 *Official Proceedings of the Twenty-First Annual Session of the Trans-Mississippi Commercial Congress* (1910), pp. 112–113.

19 *Atlanta Constitution*, April 8, 1912, p. 1. *Washington Post*, April 8, 1912, p. 5. *Memorial Addresses Delivered in the Senate of the United States, 1918* (Washington, DC, 1920), pp. 75–182. *Atlanta Constitution*, January 8, 1912, p. 1. See also *New York Times*, February 2, 1912, p. 3.

20 Francis G. Newlands, "A Western View of the Race Question," *Annals of the American Academy of Political and Social Science* 34 (July–December 1909): 269–271. *Atlanta Constitution*, June 17, 1912, p. 2. *New York Times*, June 17, 1912, p. 7. *Washington Post*, August 6, 1912, p. 2.

21 Franklin, "'Birth of a Nation,'" 418, 424, p. 434 n. 12.

22 David Sarasohn, "The Election of 1916: Realigning the Rockies," *Western Historical Quarterly* 11 (July 1980): 285–305.

23 *Atlanta Constitution*, May 24, 1922, p. 1. *New York Times*, June 12, 1922.

24 *New York Times*, November 17, 1929, p. XX1. *Chicago Daily Tribune*, August 1, 1930, p. 11. *New York Times*, November 17, 1929, p. XX1. *Boston Globe*, November 9, 1929, p. 1. There was debate at the time about whether he said this or "sons of wild jackasses," but Moses insisted he had said the former (*Chicago Tribune*, November 10, 1929, p. 6). *New York Times*, November 18, 1929, p. 3. *Chicago Daily Tribune*, December 11, 1929, p. 2. *Atlanta Constitution*, December 14, 1929, p. 10.

25 *Chicago Daily Tribune*, December 11, 1929, p. 2. Ruth Hanna McCormick, Senate Candidate from Illinois, quoted in *Chicago Daily Tribune*, January 15, 1930, p. 7. H. L. Mencken, *A Carnival of Buncombe: Writings on Politics*, ed. Malcolm Moos (1956; rpt., Chicago: University of Chicago Press, 1984), p. 334.

26 Harvard Sitkoff, *A New Deal for Blacks: The Emergence of Civil Rights as a National Issue* (New York: Oxford University Press, 1978), pp. 34–59. Steve Valocchi, "The Racial Basis of Capitalism and the State, and the Impact of the New Deal on African Americans," *Social Problems* 41 (August 1994): 352–353. Eric Rauchway, *Winter War: Hoover, Roosevelt, and the First Clash Over the New Deal* (New York: Basic Books, 2018), pp. 105–133.

27 James Ford Rhodes, *History of the United States from the Compromise of 1850 to the McKinley-Bryan Campaign of 1896*, vols. 6 and 7 (New York: The Macmillan Company, 1906 and 1910).

28 John R. Lynch, "Some Historical Errors of James Ford Rhodes," *Journal of Negro History* 2 (October 1917): 345–368. John David Smith and J. Vincent Lowery, eds., *The Dunning School: Historians, Race, and the Meaning of Reconstruction* (Lexington: University Press of Kentucky, 2013), esp. John David Smith,

"Introduction," pp. 1–47, and James S. Humphreys, "William Archibald Dunning: Flawed Colossus of American Letters," pp. 77–105. William A. Dunning, "The Undoing of Reconstruction," *The Atlantic*, October 1901.

29 William A. Dunning, *Reconstruction, Political and Economic, 1865–1877* (New York: Harper & Brothers Publishers, 1907), p. 12.

30 John David Smith, "Ulrich Bonnell Phillips (1877–1934)," *New Georgia Encyclopedia*, http://www.georgiaencyclopedia.org/articles/history-archaeology/ulrich-bonnell-phillips-1877-1934.

31 Claude G. Bowers, *The Tragic Era: The Revolution After Lincoln* (Cambridge, MA: Riverside Press, 1929), pp. v–vii.

32 David E. Kyvig, "History as Present Politics: Claude Bowers' *The Tragic Era*," *Indiana Magazine of History* 73 (March 1977): 17–31.

33 Kyvig, "History as Present Politics," pp. 17–31.

34 "The Bible Is America's Favorite Book Followed by Gone with the Wind," Business Wire, April 8, 2008.

35 Laura Ingalls Wilder, *The Long Winter* (1940; rpt. HarperCollins, 1953).

CHAPTER 7

1 Stephen Daggett, "Cost of Major US Wars," Congressional Research Service, RS22926, July 24, 2008, https://www.history.navy.mil/research/library/online-reading-room/title-list-alphabetically/c/costs-major-us-wars.html. Mark R. Wilson, *Destructive Creation: American Business and the Winning of World War II* (Philadelphia: University of Pennsylvania Press, 2016), pp. 152–189. Claudia Goldin and Robert A. Margo, "The Great Compression: The Wage Structure in the United States at Mid-Century," *Quarterly Journal of Economics* 107 (February 1992): 1–34.

2 On Eisenhower and GI Joe, see *New York Times*, May 9, 1945. Numbers are vague because while the Army kept records about race, ethnic identity was self-reported. For a rough round-up, see "Ethnic Minorities in the US Armed Forces During World War II," *Wikipedia*, retrieved November 12, 2019. Thomas Bruscino, *A Nation Forged in War: How World War II Taught Americans to Get Along* (Knoxville: University of Tennessee Press, 2010), pp. 35-70. Alison R. Bernstein, *Walking in Two Worlds: American Indians and World War Two*, Columbia University dissertation, 1986). Ronald Takaki, *Strangers from a Different Shore: A History of Asian Americans* (Boston: Little, Brown, 1989). Heather Cox Richardson, "Remembering Our First Female Soldiers on Memorial Day," *We're History*, May 25, 2015.

3 Roger Daniels, *Prisoners Without Trials: Japanese Americans in World War II* (New York: Hill and Wang, 1993), pp. 74-77.

4   Eduardo Obregon Pagan, *Murder at the Sleepy Lagoon: Zoot Suits, Race, and Riot in Wartime LA* (Chapel Hill: University of North Carolina Press, 2003). https://medium.com/@HolocaustMuseum/the-nazi-plan-to-divide-and-conquer-the-us-army-296a3c97fb54

5   *Mendez v. Westminster School Dist.*, 64F. Supp. 544 (S.D. Cal. 1946)., *Perez v. Sharp*, 32 Cal.2d 711.

6   Takaki, *Strangers from a Different Shore*, pp. 370–378.

7   James Q. Whitman, *Hitler's American Model: The United States and the Making of Nazi Race Law* (Princeton, NJ: Princeton University Press, 2017), pp. 17–131. Lucas Reilly, "What's the Story Behind This Superman Comic?," *Mental Floss*, January 20, 2017. Wendy L. Wall, *Inventing the "American Way": The Politics of Consensus from the New Deal to the Civil Rights Movement* (New York: Oxford University Press, 2008). Frank Sinatra, *The House I Live In* (short film), 1945, written by Albert Maltz, produced by Frank Ross, posted on YouTube by krt1934 on November 10, 2008, https://youtu.be/vhPwtnGviyg. Superman vs. The Knights of the White Carnation: Complete Radio Show, (1947) available at: https://www.youtube.com/watch?v=Cc72lda7Dm4&t=2s

8   Harry S. Truman, Proclamation 2680, "I Am an American Day," March 12, 1946, American Presidency Project; Reilly, "What's the Story."

9   Alexander Bloom, *Prodigal Sons: The New York Intellectuals and Their World* (New York: Oxford University Press, 1986) p. 178.

10 "Senator Claghorn Southern Rant," YouTube, posted October 9, 2012, by lordoftheexacto, https://youtu.be/N6-JddDUnyY.

11 Darren E. Grem, *The Blessings of Business: How Corporations Shaped Conservative Christianity* (New York: Oxford University Press, 2016), pp. 13–48. Kevin M. Kruse, *One Nation Under God* (New York: Basic Books, 2015), pp. 3–57. Mary C. Brennan, *Turning Right in the Sixties: The Conservative Capture of the GOP* (Chapel Hill: University of North Carolina Press, 1995), pp. 12–13. Kathryn S. Olmstead, *Right Out of California: The 1930s and the Big Business Roots of Modern Conservatism* (New York: New Press, 2015). Heather Cox Richardson, *To Make Men Free: A History of the Republican Party* (New York: Basic Books, 2014), pp. 208–209.

12 Rick Perlstein, *Before the Storm: Barry Goldwater and the Unmaking of the American Consensus* (New York: Hill and Wang, 2001), p. 29. William S. White, *The Taft Story* (New York: Harper & Brothers, 1954), p. 66–79. Richardson, *To Make Men Free*, pp. 217–218.

13 *Chicago Tribune*, February 9, 1950, p. 5.

14 *Chicago Tribune*, February 11, 1950, p. 7, and February 12, 1950, p. 1. *New York Times*, February 12, 1950, p. 5. *Boston Globe*, February 12, 1950, p. C29. *Boston Globe*, February 14, 1950, p. 12. *Washington Post*, February 14, 1950, p. 22.

New York Times, February 22, 1950, p. 28. *Washington Post*, February 18, 1950, p. B13.

15 Wiliam F. Buckley Jr., *God and Man at Yale: The Superstitions of Academic Freedom* (Chicago: Henry Regnery, 1951).

16 On Buckley's rhetorical style, see Michael J. Lee, "WFB: The Gladiatorial Style and the Politics of Provocation," *Rhetoric and Public Affairs* 13 (Summer 2010): 43–76.

17 Kruse, *One Nation*, pp. 57–87. Dwight D. Eisenhower, *Mandate for Change* (New York: Doubleday, 1963), p. 135. Perlstein, *Before the Storm*, pp. 9–11.

18 Robert Griffith, *The Politics of Fear: Joseph R. McCarthy and the Senate*, 2nd ed. (Amherst: University of Massachusetts Press, 1987), pp. 60–65. David M. Oshinsky, *A Conspiracy So Immense: The World of Joe McCarthy* (New York: Free Press, 1983), p. 182. Richardson, *To Make Men Free*, pp. 243–245.

19 William F. Buckley Jr. and L. Brent Bozell, *McCarthy and His Enemies: The Record and Its Meaning* (Chicago: Henry Regnery, 1954), pp. 267–335. William S. White, "What the McCarthy Method Seeks to Establish," *New York Times Book Review*, April 4, 1954. R. Emmett Tyrrell Jr., *After the Hangover: The Conservatives' Road to Recovery* (Nashville, TN: Thomas Nelson, 2010), pp. 127–136. Sidney Blumenthal, "Verities of the Right Have Young Roots," *Washington Post*, September 25, 1985, p. A15.

20 Perlstein, *Before the Storm*, pp. 73. William F. Buckley Jr., "Our Mission Statement," *National Review*, November 19, 1955.

21 Glenn C. Altschuler and Stuart M. Blumin, *The GI Bill: A New Deal for Veterans* (New York: Oxford University Press, 2009), pp. 52–87.

22 Claudia Goldin and Robert A. Margo, "The Great Compression: The Wage Structure in the United States at Mid-Century," *Quarterly Journal of Economics* 107 (February 1992): 1–34. Alan Brinkley and Ellen Fitzpatrick, *America in Modern Times: Since 1890* (New York: McGraw-Hill, 1997), p. 407.

23 Gerald D. Nash, *The American West Transformed* (Bloomington: Indiana University Press, 1985), pp. 17–20. Richard White, *"It's Your Misfortune and None of My Own": A New History of the American West* (Norman: University of Oklahoma Press, 1991), pp, 496–499. Lisa McGirr, *Suburban Warriors: The Origins of the New Right* (Princeton, NJ: Princeton University Press, 2001), pp. 25–26.

24 McGirr, *Suburban Warriors*, pp. 25–26.

25 Olmstead, *Right Out of California*. Dwight D. Eisenhower, Farewell Address, January 17, 1961. Nash, *American West Transformed*, pp. 210–213.

26 Eisenhower, *Mandate for Change*, pp. 234–236.

27 Darryl Mace, *In Remembrance of Emmett Till: Regional Stories and Media Responses to the Black Freedom Struggle* (Lexington: The University Press of Kentucky, 2014). Danielle L. McGuire, *At the Dark End of the Street: Black Women, Rape, and Resistance—A New History of the Civil Rights Movement from Rosa Parks to the Rise of Black Power* (New York: Knopf, 2010), pp. xv-134.

28 David L. Chappell, "Diversity Within a Racial Group: White People in Little Rock, 1957–1959," *Arkansas Historical Quarterly* 54 (Winter 1995): pp. 444–456. Richardson, *To Make Men Free*, pp. 249–251.

29 James Jackson Kilpatrick, "Right and Power in Arkansas," *National Review*, September 28, 1957, pp. 273–275. William F. Buckley Jr., "Why the South Must Prevail," *National Review*, August 24, 1957.

30 McGirr, *Suburban Warriors*, pp. 27–29. Perlstein, *Before the Storm*, pp. 124–125.

31 Perlstein, *Before the Storm*, pp. 114–118. McGirr, *Suburban Warriors*, pp. 76–79.

32 Perlstein, *Before the Storm*, pp. 116-118. John Dickerson, Louise Dufresne, "JFK defends 'extravagant' campaign spending in 1960," *CBS News*, June 11, 2015, at https://www.cbsnews.com/news/jfk-defends-extravagant-campaign-spending-in-1960/. Olati Johnson, "The Story of Bob Jones University v. United States: Race, Religion, and Congress's Extraordinary Acquiescence (2010)" *Columbia Public Law & Legal Theory Working Papers*, Paper 9184, pp. 4-5.

33 Autry Museum of the American West, Los Angeles. "Westerns," *Time*, March 30, 1959, p. 52.

34 Barry M. Goldwater, *With No Apologies: The Personal and Political Memoirs of United States Senator Barry M. Goldwater* (New York: William Morrow, 1979), pp. 15-25. Perlstein, *Before the Storm*, pp. 19-21.

35 Perlstein, *Before the Storm*, pp. 20-42. Goldwater, *No Apologies*, pp. 59-61. Dwight D. Eisenhower, *Waging Peace, 1956–1961* (New York: Doubleday, 1965), pp. 378-381.

36 Perlstein, *Before the Storm*, pp. 33.

37 Barry Goldwater, *Conscience of a Conservative* (1960; rpt., Princeton, NJ: Princeton University Press, 2007).

38 Kimberly Wilmot Voss, "Women Didn't Just March," *We're History*, March 28, 2016. Grem, *Blessings of Business*, pp. 13-25.

39 Frank. S. Meyer, "Principles and Heresies: Hope for the '60s," *National Review*, January 14, 1961, p. 19. Republican Party Platform, July 13, 1964. Brennan, *Turning Right*, pp. 74-81.

40 Leah Wright Rigueur, *The Loneliness of the Black Republican: Pragmatic Politics and the Pursuit of Power* (Princeton, NJ: Princeton University Press, 2015), pp. 57-60. Matthew Delmont, "When Jackie Robinson Confronted a Trump-like Candidate," *The Atlantic*, March 19, 2016.

41 "Statistics: 1964," American Presidency Project, https://www.presidency.ucsb.edu/
    statistics/elections/1964. Kevin Phillips, *The Emerging Republican Majority* (1970;
    rpt., Princeton, NJ: Princeton University Press, 2015), 62–66.

42 Eisenhower to Robert J. Biggs, February 10, 1959, in L. Galambos and Daun Van
    Ee, eds., *The Papers of Dwight David Eisenhower*, vol. 19: *The Presidency: Keeping
    the Peace* (Baltimore: Johns Hopkins University Press, 2001), pp. 1340-1343.

43 Phyllis Schlafly, *A Choice Not an Echo* (Alton, IL: Pere Marquette Press, 1964).

44 Mary C. Brennan, *Turning Right in the Sixties: The Conservative Capture of the
    GOP* (Chapel Hill: University of North Carolina Press, 1995), pp. 71-72. McGirr,
    Suburban Warriors: pp. 113-147.

45 Rigueur, *Loneliness,* pp. 79–80.

46 Joe McGinnis, *The Selling of the President, 1968* (London: Andre Deutsch, 1970),
    pp. 36, 41–45.

47 McGinnis, *Selling,* pp. 62–76, 97–111.

48 Phillips, *Emerging Republican Majority*, pp. 23, 62–66, 374–379.

49 Richard Nixon, "Address to the Nation on the War in Vietnam," November
    3, 1969.

50 Mario T. Garcia, *The Chicano Generation: Testimonios of the Movement*
    (Oakland: University of California Press, 2015), pp. 3–17.

51 Jonathan Merritt, "Southern Baptists Call Off the Culture War," *The Atlantic,* June
    16, 2018; Chris Caldwell, "The 1963/1998 Baptist Faith and Message," https://
    www.utm.edu/staff/caldwell/bfm/1963-1998/index.html.

52 *Time,* January 5, 1970.

53 Spiro Agnew, quoted in Thomas Byrne Edsall with Mary D. Edsall, *Chain
    Reaction: The Impact of Race, Rights, and Taxes on American Politics* (New York:
    W. W. Norton, 1991), p. 85. Patrick J. Buchanan, "Media Memorandum
    for the President," May 21, 1970, President Richard Nixon—Pat Buchanan
    Papers, BACM Research, http://www.paperlessarchives.com/FreeTitles/Nixon-
    BuchananPapers.pdf.

54 Kimberly Phillips-Fein, *Invisible Hands: The Businessmen's Crusade Against
    the New Deal* (New York: W. W. Norton, 2010); Bill Moyers, "How Wall Street
    Occupied America," *The Nation*, November 21, 2011.

55 Southern Baptist Convention, "Resolution on Abortion," 1971, at http://www.sbc.
    net/resolutions/13/resolution-on-abortion; Linda Greenhouse and Reva B. Siegel,
    "Before (and After) Roe v. Wade: New Questions About Backlash," *Yale Law
    Journal* 120 (June 2011): 2028–2059.

56 Greenhouse and Siegel, "Before (and After)." See Peggy O'Donnell, "The
    Settler Fantasies Woven Into the Prairie Dresses," *Jezebel,* January 30, 2019.
    Kristin Luker, *Abortion and the Politics of Motherhood* (Berkeley: University of

California Press, 1984), pp. 192–215. Alan Crawford, *Thunder on the Right: The "New Right" and the Politics of Resentment* (New York: Pantheon, 1980), pp. 144–168.

57 Richard Nixon, *The Memoirs of Richard Nixon* (New York: Grosset & Dunlap, 1978), pp. 1044-1045.

58 Harold Evans, *They Made America: from the Steam Engine to the Search Engine: Two Centuries of Innovators* (Back Bay Books, 2009), p. 113.

59 Milton Friedman, "The Social Responsibility of Business Is to Increase Its Profits," *New York Times Magazine*, September 13, 1970.

60 Allan J. Lichtman, *White Protestant Nation: The Rise of the American Conservative Movement* (New York : Grove Press, 2008), pp. 342-349.

61 Josh Levin, *The Queen: The Forgotten Life Behind an American Myth* (New York: Little, Brown and Company, 2019).

62 Randall Balmer, "The Real Origins of the Religious Right," *Politico*, May 27, 2014. Olatie Johnson, "The Story of *Bob Jones University v. United States*: Race, Religion, and Congress' Extraordinary Acquiescence," Columbia Public Law and Legal Theory Working Paper no. 9184 (2010).

CHAPTER 8

1 William Greider, "The Education of David Stockman," *Atlantic Monthly*, December 1981. Sean Wilentz, *The Age of Reagan: A History, 1974–2008* (New York: HarperCollins, 2008), pp.141–143.

2 Ronald Reagan, "Address Before a Joint Session of the Congress on the Program for Economic Recovery," April 28, 1981. Greider, "Education."

3 Timothy Naftali, *George H. W. Bush* (New York: Times Books, 2007), pp. 73–75. Wilentz, *Age of Reagan*, p. 170. Heather Cox Richardson, *To Make Men Free: A History of the Republican Party* (New York: Basic Books, 2014), pp. 297-298.

4 Wilentz, *Age of Reagan*, pp. 204–205. Jane Mayer, "Ways and Means Panel's Tax-Overhaul Proposal Brings 'Family' Strife to Conservative Coalition," *Wall Street Journal*, November 27, 1985, p. 52. Anne Swardson, "Senate Rejects Proposal for 35% Tax Bracket," *Washington Post*, June 19, 1986, p. A3.

5 NSC-NSDD-75, January 17, 1983, Ronald Reagan Library, https://www. reaganlibrary.gov/sites/default/files/archives/reference/scanned-nsdds/nsdd75.pdf. Ronald Reagan, speech to the National Association of Evangelicals, March 8, 1983.

6 Jane Mayer, "Ways and Means Panel's Tax-Overhaul Proposal Brings 'Family' Strife to Conservative Coalition," *Wall Street Journal*, November 27, 1985, p. 52. Anne Swardson, "Senate Rejects Proposal for 35% Tax Bracket," *Washington Post*, June 19, 1986, p. A3.

7   Timothy Naftali, *George H. W. Bush* (New York: Times Books, 2007), pp. 97, 117. Wilentz, *Age of Reagan*, pp. 306–309.

8   Eric Pianin and David S. Hilzenrath, "House Passes Clinton Budget Plan by 2 Votes," *Washington Post*, August 6, 1993; William J. Eaton, "Clinton Budget Triumphs, 51–50," *Los Angeles Times*, August 7, 1993.

9   Peggy Noonan, "Bliss to Be Alive," *Wall Street Journal*, January 9, 1995, p. A14.

10 Richardson, *To Make Men Free*, pp. 315–316.

11 Laura Sullivan, Tatjana Meschede, Lars Dietrich, Thomas Shapiro, "The Racial Wealth Gap," Institute for Assets & Social Policy, Brandeis University, at http://www.demos.org/sites/default/files/publications/RacialWealthGap_1.pdf.

12 James E. Crisp, *Sleuthing the Alamo: Davy Crockett's Last Stand and Other Mysteries of the Texas Revolution* (New York: Oxford University Press, 2005), p. 139.

13 "Red Dawn Imitated Art," *USA Today*, December 17, 2003.

14 "Atwater Apologies for '88 Remark About Dukakis," *Washington Post*, January 13, 1991.

15 Evelyn A. Schlatter, *Aryan Cowboys: White Supremacists and the Search for a New Frontier, 1970–2000* (University of Texas Press, 2006); George L. Church and Ed Magnuson, "Geraldine Ferraro: A Break with Tradition," *Time*, July 23, 1984; Joan Didion, "Trouble in Lakewood," *The New Yorker*, July 26, 1993.

16 Jason Wilson, "Ruby Ridge, 1992: The Day the American Militia Movement Was Born," *The Guardian*, August 26, 2017.

17 John C. Danforth, "Interim Report to the Deputy Attorney General Concerning the 1993 Confrontation at the Mt. Carmel Complex, Waco, Texas," U.S. Department of Justice, July 31, 2000; Amanda Marcotte, "The Clinton BS Files: Conspiracy Theorists Paint the Branch Davidian Mass Suicide as Murder at the Hands of the Clinton Administration," *Salon*, September 19, 2016; "Alex Jones," Southern Poverty Law Center, https://www.splcenter.org/fighting-hate/extremist-files/individual/alex-jones; Wilson, "Ruby Ridge."

18 Letter from Timothy McVeigh to *Union-Sun and Journal* (Lockport, NY), published February 11, 1992, by CNN.

19 Michael Oreskes, "Political Memo; For G.O.P. Arsenal, 133 Words to Fire," *New York Times*, September 9, 1990.

20 Brian Stelter, "Tucker Carlson Refuses to Apologize for His Misogynistic Remarks," CNN Business, March 11, 2019.

21 Stefano DellaVigna and Ethan Kaplan, "The Fox News Effect: Media Bias and Voting," *Quarterly Journal of Economics* 122 (August 2007): 1187–1234.

22 Wilentz, *Age of Reagan*, pp. 331, 341–346.

23 Martin Tolchin, "G.O.P. Memo Tells of Black Vote Cut," *New York Times*, October 25, 1986, p. 7; "The Measure of Republican 'Integrity,'" *New York Times*, November 1, 1986, p. 30; Michael Wines, "House Passes Voter Bill over G.O.P. Opposition," *New York Times*, February 5, 1993, p. A15. See, for example, Godfrey Sperling, "Why in the World Did Ed Rollins Say This?," *Christian Science Monitor*, November 23, 1993; B. Drummond Ayres Jr., "Feinstein Opponent Hopes to Uncover Ballot Fraud," *New York Times*, November 30, 1994, p. B11; Michael Janofsky, "Loser for Maryland Governor Files Suit to Overturn Election," *New York Times*, December 29, 1994, p. A16; "Challenge in California Senate Race Is Withdrawn," *New York Times*, February 8. 1995, p. B6; Lizette Alvarez, "Doubts Rising on Election in California, Gingrich Says," *New York Times*, September 26, 1997, p. A23.

24 "Debunking the Voter Fraud Myth," Brennan Center for Justice, January 31, 2017, https://www.brennancenter.org/analysis/debunking-voter-fraud-myth; Lizette Alvarez, "G.O.P. Bill Proposes Check on Whether Voter Is a Citizen," *New York Times*, February 27, 1998, p. A22.

25 Beth Reinhard, "Bush Strategist Shares Insight on '00 Recount,:" *The Miami Herald*, May 17, 2008. U.S. Commission on Civil Rights, *Voting Irregularities in Florida During the 2000 Presidential Election*, June 2001, https://www.usccr.gov/pubs/vote2000/report/main.htm, quotation from executive summary.

26 Brennan Center for Justice, "Voting Laws Roundup 2017," May 10, 2017, https://www.brennancenter.org/analysis/voting-laws-roundup-2017.

27 Hedrick Smith, "Gerrymandering May Prove a Pyrrhic Victory for the GOP," *Los Angeles Times*, October 7, 2015.

28 Grover Norquist, quoted in David Frum, "Norquist: Romney Will Do as Told," *Daily Beast*, February 13, 2012.

29 Wilentz, *Age of Reagan*, pp. 187–194.

30 David Corn, "Romney Tells Millionaire Donors What He REALLY Thinks of Obama Voters," *Mother Jones*, September 17, 2012. Lucy Madison, "Santorum Targets Blacks in Entitlement Reform," *CBSNews*, January 3, 2012. Kevin D. Williamson, "Chaos in the Family, Chaos in the State: The White Working Class's Dysfunction," *National Review*, March 17, 2016. Nathan J. Robinson, "We Should Probably Try to be Humane and Care About People," *Current Affairs*, March 26, 2017.

31 Peter Thiel, "The Education of a Libertarian," *Cato Unbound*, April 13, 2009.

32 Molly Ball, "Donald Trump and the Politics of Fear," *The Atlantic*, September 2, 2016.

33 Donald J. Trump, Inaugural Address, January 20, 2017.

34 Jeanne Sahadi, "What's in the GOP's Final Tax Plan," CNN Money, December 22, 2017; Patrick Temple-West and Victoria Guida, " 'Eye-Popping' Payouts for CEOs Follow Trump's Tax Cuts," *Politico*, July 30, 2018; Noah Smith, "Trump's Tax Cut Hasn't Done Anything for Workers," *Bloomberg*, August 3, 2018; Niv Elis, "GOP Tax Law Will Add $1.9 Trillion to Debt: CBO," *The Hill*, April 9, 2018; Frances Coppola, "American Public Sector Workers Will Pay for Trump's Tax Cuts," *Forbes*, August 31, 2018.

35 Tal Axelrod, "Trump's Fed Board Nominee Has a History of 'Radical' Views on Economy, Democracy: CNN," *The Hill*, April 12, 2019.

36 Jill Colvin, "Trump Warns of 'Violence' if Republicans Lose Fall Elections," Associated Press, August 29, 2018.

37 James Jackson, July 7, 1860, reprinted in *Southern Banner* (Athens, Georgia), July 26, 1860, pp. 1–3, Georgia Historic Newspapers, Digital Library of Georgia, www.gahistoricnewspapers.galileo.usg.edu.

38 Manisha Sinha, *The Counterrevolution of Slavery: Politics and Ideology in Antebellum South Carolina* (Chapel Hill: University of North Carolina Press, 2000), p. 191.

CONCLUSION

 1 Janie Velencia, "The 2018 Gender Gap Was Huge," *FiveThirtyEight*, November 9, 2018.

LIST OF FIGURES

INTRODUCTION (page xiii): Movement Conservatives celebrated the image of the American cowboy, who, they insisted, was an individualist who wanted nothing of the government. Tapping into the powerful history of that image, they alleged to stand against communism both overseas and also at home, where they claimed that people of color wanted programs that would redistribute wealth through taxation. (LIFE Magazine, November 1, 1963, Leonard McCombe/The LIFE Premium Collection/Getty Images.)

CHAPTER 1 (page 1): This 1851 painting by Junius Brutus Stearns celebrates the American paradox: President George Washington represents American freedom, and at the same time he is master of his domain and the people of color, children, and poorer white men on it. There are no adult white women in this scene; the viewer can imagine the children's mother inside the plantation house in the background. ("Washington as a Farmer at Mount Vernon," ©Everett Collection Historical/Alamy Stock Photo, PD-US.)

CHAPTER 2 (page 23): In 1860, an artist captured presidential candidate Abraham Lincoln as a larger-than-life hardworking common man, destined to work his way to the White House looming in the background, where he can return the government to the service of men like him. ("The Railsplitter, Abraham Lincoln," Chicago Historical Society.)

CHAPTER 3 (page 52): The cover of an 1874 popular novel captured the link between the movement of Americans to the West and dominance over people of color as trapper Kit Carson's "rescue" of someone off-stage requires knifing two American Indians. ("The Fighting Trapper" or "Kit Carson to the Rescue," The American News Company: New York, 1874, PD-US.)

CHAPTER 4 (page 75): After the Civil War, Americans opposed to the idea of equality for men of color rallied around the image of the cowboy as an independent, hardworking individualist holding the line against rising "socialism" in the East, where they insisted black and immigrant voters were using the government to redistribute wealth through tax dollars. (Buffalo Bill Cody, Sarony, circa 1880, PD-US.)

CHAPTER 5 (page 97): (Left) John Wayne: The rise of the West as a political bloc in the 1890s advanced the old idea that American individualism, personified now by the cowboy, depended on the subordination of women and people of color. (©TCD/Prod.DB/Alamy Stock Photo.)

(Right) *Gone with the Wind*: Western and southern political leaders worked together to secure that subordination, and by 1939 these themes were so well established that the films based on them, *Stagecoach* and *Gone with the Wind*, were immediately iconic. (©Popperfoto/Getty Images.)

CHAPTER 6 (page 124): With power firmly back in their hands, white men were willing to use the government to advance the interests of white men and their families. In 1928, nodding to the interests of southern and westerners who wanted both water power and flood control, Congress launched a giant water reclamation project to dam the Colorado River. President Franklin Delano Roosevelt dedicated Hoover Dam in 1935. (Ansel Adams, Photograph of the Hoover Dam, 1941, U.S. National Archives and Records Administration, PD-US.)

CHAPTER 7 (page 145): (Left) "A company of men has set up its office between the columns (Doric) of an ancient Greek temple of Neptune, built about 700 B.C." (September 22, 1943. Courtesy of the National Archives and Records Administration at College Park, MD.)

(Right) World War II challenged racial and gender hierarchies as women and people of color rushed to defend American democracy against fascism. In the war's aftermath, they demanded both the right to vote and legislation that leveled the national playing field. (U.S. National Archives and Records Administration, PD-US. Group of Women Airforce Pilots and B-17 Flying Fortress, circa 1944, U.S. Air Force photo, PD-US.)

CHAPTER 8 (page 179): The new voices in politics resurrected the corollary to the American paradox, the idea that equality for women and people of color would destroy American freedom. Politicians tapped into the imagery of the cowboy and the ideology it represented. (Ronald Reagan with Cowboy Hat, 1976, U.S. National Archives and Records Administration, PD-US.)

CONCLUSION (page 202): The government commissioned the Statue of Freedom in 1855, putting Secretary of War Jefferson Davis in charge of oversight. He adamantly opposed the inclusion of a liberty cap, the Roman symbol of an emancipated slave. In 1861, Davis left the U.S. government to lead the Confederacy. Two years later, formerly enslaved Americans hoisted to the top of the United States Capitol the Statue of Freedom, a woman, draped in a Native American blanket, carrying a sword, a shield, and laurel wreath for triumph. (Statue of Freedom by Thomas Crawford, Architect of the Capitol, PD-US.)

INDEX

For the benefit of digital users, indexed terms that span two pages (e.g., 52–53) may, on occasion, appear on only one of those pages.